T0300261

Leading Complex Projects

To the artists, writers and musicians (too many to name) who take me on journeys into unknown, but mysteriously inter-connected territories, challenge me, and dump me back at my computer to continue my journey.

To my ever patient and loving partner John McInnes who puts up with me, encourages me and is generally wonderful.

To Jane Helm who worked with me on both sets of interviews (2004–2005 and 2010–2011) and who is both a delightful and talented research assistant.

Leading Complex Projects

KAYE REMINGTON

Routledge
Taylor & Francis Group
LONDON AND NEW YORK

First published 2011 by Gower Publishing

2 Park Square, Milton Park, Abingdon, Oxon OX14 4RN
711 Third Avenue, New York, NY 10017, USA

Routledge is an imprint of the Taylor & Francis Group, an informa business

First issued in paperback 2016

British Library Cataloguing in Publication Data
Remington, Kaye.
Leading complex projects.
  1. Project management. 2. Leadership.
  I. Title
  658.4'04-dc22

  ISBN 978-1-4094-1905-1 (hbk)
  ISBN 978-1-138-27047-3 (pbk)

Library of Congress Cataloging-in-Publication Data
Remington, Kaye.
Leading complex projects / Kaye Remington.
    p. cm.
  Includes bibliographical references and index.
  ISBN 978-1-4094-1905-1 (hardback)
  1. Leadership. 2. Portfolio management. I. Title.
  HD57.7.R46 2011
  658.4'092--dc23

                                                                2011019351

Contents

List of Figures   *vii*

List of Tables   *ix*

Acknowledgements   *xi*

Jane Helm's Impressions   *xiii*

Preface   *xv*

Introduction: Leadership for Complex Projects   1

**SECTION ONE: WHAT GOOD LEADERSHIP DOES
WHEN PROJECTS ARE COMPLEX**   11

Chapter 1   Comprehend Complexity   13

Chapter 2   Communicate, Communicate, Communicate   31

Chapter 3   Cultivate Effective Teams *from Project Teams to
              Executive Board*   81

Chapter 4   Employ Portfolio-programme Thinking   103

Chapter 5   Challenge Through Innovation   121

Chapter 6   Think About Thinking   147

Chapter 7   Consider Culture   165

Chapter 8   Exercise Political Skill   189

Chapter 9   Pilot Projects Through Crises   211

**SECTION TWO: WHAT GOOD LEADERSHIP
NEEDS WHEN PROJECTS ARE COMPLEX**   231

Chapter 10   Governance That Matches the Complexity   233

Chapter 11   Authority Over Key Roles   257

Chapter 12   Partners for Peace   275

**SECTION THREE: HOW GOOD LEADERSHIP
BEHAVES WHEN PROJECTS ARE COMPLEX**   293

Chapter 13   As Humble Iconoclasts   295

Chapter 14   With Charisma, Resilience, Determination and Courage   305

Index   *321*

List of Figures

1.1   A diagrammatic representation of a simple, goal-seeking
        system   16
1.2   Most projects exist on a continuum between control and
        chaos   18
1.3   A decision network for a complex project illustrating
        reinforcing loops that compound the problem due to
        non-linear effects   20
2.1   Simplified map of informal communication pathways in
        project under stress   43
2.2   A socio-gram indicating informal communication
        networks   48
5.1   Model of the interactions during the early phases of a low
        energy car project   125
5.2   Thirty senior project managers rated their skill sets   127
10.1   Project Wickenby governance arrangements   240
12.1   Uncertainty graphed against flexibility needed   284
12.2   Level of flexibility required against trust needed   285
12.3   Questions and steps for partnering   285

List of Tables

2.1   A summary of the relationship between communication
        style and leadership style based on various findings   50

2.2   Essential communication styles associated with
        productivity in conditions of uncertainty   53

2.3   Leaders' communication styles and knowledge sharing
        tendencies   55

2.4   Questions to assist communications planning   62

5.1   Differences between critical thinking and creative or
        innovative thinking   124

7.1   Cultural audit example based on Cooke's (1993)
        Organisation Culture Inventory   172

7.2   Organisational cultural artefacts questionnaire   177

8.1   A quick assessment of the type of political activity
        expected (positive or negative)   198

8.2   Some political management strategies   201

10.1   Exploratory questions to stimulate the conversations
        that governance teams need to conduct to explore
        potential differences and find constructive ways to
        work together   253

11.1   Executive leadership – essential role capabilities   260

11.2   Project leadership – essential role capabilities   263

Acknowledgements

The author would like to thank the project and executive leaders who generously shared their professional knowledge and experience. Participants who were recommended to us had taken key leadership roles in very complex projects. In the process of determining the sample of interviewees many other excellent leaders were referred to us. However, like all projects there were constraints; time to interview and process the data, and our desire to investigate project leadership practice over a broad range of industry sectors. However the following list is not complete. Some interviewees chose to remain completely anonymous. Thank you to everyone who participated. Your contribution has been invaluable. Names are listed in alphabetical order.

Ray Abe, Program Manager Treatment Asset Solutions Division, Sydney Water; Lesley Bentley, Managing Director Living Planit P/L; Commodore Martin Brooker, Program Director New Generation Navy, Royal Australian Navy; Peter Brouggy, National Manager Market Support, Australian Stock Exchange; Stewart Brown, Principal Consultant, Halcrow; Peter Cantwell, Strategic Development Manager, C4 Systems, BAE Systems Australia; Kerry Costello, Special Projects Officer, NSW Health Professionals Registration Boards; Peter Curtis, Architect, Project Manager; Joan Davies, Executive Officer, various Voluntary Organisations; Stephen Dawson, Head of Projects at AMP; Raphael Dua, CEO & Owner, Micro Planning International P/L; Graeme Gherashe, former HR Director, Aviva Life International, Consultant; Tony Grebenshikoff, Director, Strategy & Business Improvement, Naval, Thales Australia; Mark Heath, Managing Director, MBH; Ken Holmes, Environment, Health and Safety Manager, Kraft Foods; Professor Peter Homel, Griffith School of Criminology; Janet Hoy, Project Director; Adjunct Professor Brian Kooyman, Director International Business, Tracey Brunstrom & Hammond Group; Dr. Jenny Leonard, former Project Manager, Lecturer; Mark Lomas, Hong Kong Branch Chairman, APM; Adam Nicholls, Project Manager, ATO; Christine Nixon, Chief Commissioner (Rtd), Victoria Police; Dr David Paul, Organisational Change

Consultant; Brian Phillips, Managing Director, Yellowhouse.net P/L; Dr Julien Pollack, Project Manager; Andrew Pyke, General Manager Security Solutions, Raytheon Australia; Dr Isabel Rimanoczy, Founding Director Minervas; Robert (Bob) Robinson, Project Manager; Charles Rottier, Group Executive Manager, Sustainability, Transfield; Sean Selva, Director Smart Publishing Australia P/L; Miles Shepherd, Consultant Project Manager, past Chair of IPMA and APM, past president of IPMA; Andrew Skeet, Senior Project Manager, Asset Management; Jackie Smith, Executive Leadership Consultant; Ian Sutherland, Senior Associate, Evans & Peck, Dr Rebecca Taylor, Quality, Health & Safety Manager, Kraft Foods; Dr Susan Tiffin, former Director HR, Consultant; Enrique Ugarte, Founder, Chairman, Australian Institute of Business Analysis (AIBA); Paul Vevers, Acting Executive Director, Assets Division, Housing NSW; David West, Senior Technical Director, WSP UK Ltd, Management & Industry; Madelon Willemsen, Curator of Life Sciences, Werribee Open Range Zoo; Ben Wilson; Petra Wyrwa-Weinheim, Director of Project Management EMEA; Dr Bill Young, Project Manager, PM Researcher.

Finally many thanks to Jonathan Norman, Fiona Martin, Matt Irving, Sue White, Claire Bell, David Atkins and the rest of the team at Gower Publishing. It has been a pleasure to work with you all.

Jane Helm's Impressions

As Kaye Remington's researcher, I have been involved in this project since 2005. Since then we have interviewed seventy people who identified aspects of leadership that, in their opinion, assisted in achieving project success. Each senior leader we interviewed was endorsed by one of his or her peers. It became clear that as leaders and human beings, the interviewees were frequently out of the ordinary, and the attributes that emerged from the interviews were encouraging and often inspiring.

There are many excellent leaders who deploy orthodox management tools. But the salient fact about the leaders we interviewed is that they often did the unexpected. Many of the respondents showed an endearing disregard for convention; they respected authority, but were ready to challenge it if they perceived it as inappropriate to meet the needs of the project. One interviewee described the best leaders as: 'rebels and non-conformists'.

All the interviewees had enormous reserves of energy and enthusiasm for what they do. They were different, and enjoyed difference. But beyond this, each interviewee possessed extremely strong relationship skills. Relationships with others were a crucial part of their success. They took the time to identify and map out individual stakeholder issues. They built relationships through communication, and habitually made accurate predictions about what needed to be communicated, and to whom.

Typically, respondents cited that they worked hard to gain the confidence and trust of those who worked for and with them before a working relationship could be established. It became clear that the interviewees were not motivated by a desire for dominance in their relationships. Their approach was inclusive rather than exclusive; they emerged as consultative and collaborative, and tended to use these attributes as tools to deal with ambiguity and complexity. They understood that 'the person who knows the way to go isn't necessarily in a traditional leadership position, but their views have to be embraced and taken for the next step forward. A leader is able to corral that and keep the thing moving in the same direction but with a huge comfort zone around the fact that not everything at their fingertips as to the next move.' They were able to 'show you're willing to learn things you don't understand, but at the same time hold yourself forward as an expert so they also have confidence in your expert ability, and to also be very sensitive to the language of the organisation, the organisational and individual language.'

My impression was that these leaders were successful in a large part because a strong sense of integrity informed their readiness to challenge authority and their relationships with others. Many interviewees communicated a sense of contributing to something they perceived as larger and more important than themselves; transcending internal politics. They valued their own role in a large part because it helped bring about an outcome that they genuinely believed to be valuable and worthwhile:

> *I think part of it is not being ego driven. It's not about me, in a sense. I'm doing a task.*

The successful leaders we interviewed were uniformly able to assess situations, determine solutions to problems, and carry them out quickly and decisively, while taking into consideration the needs of the project, the organisation and the people involved. They observed, listened and reflected before they acted. They revealed themselves to comprehensively understand that effective leadership comes from a place of integrity, and more than anything else relies on open communication, and the ability to earn and sustain trust of other people.

Preface

Too often, we hear of multi-sector complex projects that have stalled in development, blown their budgets, or simply failed to deliver their full potential despite the best efforts of everyone involved. Whether it is in capital acquisition, infrastructure development, ongoing sustainment, logistics, business evolution or even disaster relief, organisations and individuals constantly face the leadership challenges of managing in ever increasing complexity.

Against this backdrop of massive failure, in 2009 the International Centre for Complex Project Management conducted a global round table series titled *The Conspiracy of Optimism – Why Mega Projects Fail*. The two key findings of the report were that complex Project Managers are not necessarily equipped as Program Delivery Leaders, and that current tools are insufficient for managing complex projects. Kaye Remington and Julien Pollack's earlier book *Tools for Complex Projects* goes some way to addressing the latter point and is an important text in the world's first Executive Masters in Complex Project Management. Kaye's latest book addresses the second fundamental issue – that of Delivery Leadership in complex projects.

The challenge lies in navigating the uncertainty and ambiguity inherent in accelerating social, organisational and technological change, and expanding cultural diversity. Project leaders must recognise today's transformational shift from an 'information age' of interrelated systems to a 'knowledge age' of interconnected capabilities. This means that the project team skill set must be enhanced and continually nurtured to provide a holistic approach to complex challenges.

The ever present 'human factor' in the dynamics of interconnected systems is a central driver of complexity. The people involved, the ways in which they communicate and the relationships that they forge constitute the behaviour and combined culture of any organisation or project. Only by developing leadership that can transform dysfunctional attitudes, behaviours and culture can complex project execution the be improved.

The interviews and research behind Kaye's book reinforce the point that Complex Projects demand outcome-focussed and multi-disciplinary leadership that is possessed of a broad enough repertoire to face the unknown – the ability to lead in the face of ambiguity and uncertainty. Her book is an important 'touch stone' for reinforcing what effective leadership can achieve and the importance of appropriate organisational structures to support such leadership

This outstanding work makes an important contribution to the global complex project management community by providing a practical guide for those involved in complex project leadership. I believe this book is required reading for those already working as complex delivery leaders as well as those engaged in the pursuit of developing such leaders and I strongly recommend it's inclusion in your professional library.

Stephen Hayes MBE
Chief Executive Officer
International Centre for Complex Project Management

Introduction:
Leadership for Complex Projects

 *Some books are to be tasted, others to be swallowed, and some few to be chewed and digested; that is, some books are to be read only in parts; others to be read but not curiously; and some few to be read wholly, and with diligence and attention. Some books also may be read by deputy, and extracts made of them by others.*
Francis Bacon, (1625) Of Studies.

I hope this book does some credit to those who contributed and that it fits at least one of Francis Bacon's categories of readership.

This Book is About Leadership for *Complex* Projects

It is not about leadership per se. It draws directly from the experience of practitioners associated with all aspects of complex projects, across industries, through interviews with project leaders who are in the 'thick of it' everyday. Research data on leadership has been used to explain and contextualise what highly experienced project leaders, from all levels, are saying. Above all, the book aims to provide a practical guide for everyone concerned with project leadership, from project manager to executive sponsor, from team leader to end user, owner, client and specialist consultant.

As the topic is specifically about leadership for *complex* projects, not any project, it is important first, to discuss how a complex project can be differentiated from a complicated or difficult one. This is the focus of the first chapter. Within both professional and academic worlds questions about project complexity are still highly contested. If you have picked up this book you might already have come to the conclusion that some projects do not seem to respond even to best practice project management. The easy, and often quoted, answer to why this is so goes something like 'it's all about the people', or 'if you get the right people it will be OK'. To some extent that is true, the people matter enormously, however, there are times when even the right people can't work the miracles expected of them because the support is not there to enable them to act appropriately, or because the project is changing so rapidly that anything we do makes things worse, not better. Complex projects require leaders with what Stacey (1993; 1996) describes as *extraordinary* leadership capabilities. These projects also require the support structures that enable exceptional leaders to lead.

Given the realities faced by complex projects many executives now recognise that some projects behave in such unexpected and unpredictable ways that unusual actions are required for delivery of anything remotely resembling the initial requirements. Evidence from research and practice now indicates that leadership for these so-called complex projects differs considerably from leadership that works for functional operations or simple projects or projects with more stable contexts (Turner and Müller, 2005; Gehring, 2007). Additionally, the challenges are not only about delivering successful outcomes in the short term, but also ensuring that outcomes are sustainable and provide business and community benefits in the long term.

HIGHLY EXPERIENCED PEOPLE FROM DIFFERENT FIELDS SAID SIMILAR THINGS!

The research for this book has taken place over an extended period of seven years, draws upon about thirty years of observations by the author, in practice, and has tapped into innumerable years of knowledge and wisdom from many project practitioners, from many different fields. During my time in practice and teaching at universities I have had the pleasure of meeting scores of remarkable project leaders and I have met many others during preparation for this book. Their amalgamated insights form the practice basis for this book.

My research assistant, Jane Helm, and I interviewed 70 leaders. They included owners, sponsors, project/programme directors, project managers, client managers, HR directors, general managers, directors of project management offices and senior consultants. They came from such disparate discipline areas as defence, mining, transport, construction and engineering, IT, telecommunications, environmental management, chemical manufacturing, public policy, criminal justice, health and zoology. The commonality derives from the fact that the projects were perceived by major stakeholders to be complex and of high risk (financial and/or reputational) and our interviewees had taken key leadership roles in steering those projects to successful conclusions, often against all odds. In spite of the differences in background we were encouraged by the fact that repeated themes began to emerge quite quickly. A lot of highly experienced people from different fields were saying similar things!

As a research team we were very impressed by the calibre of the individuals whom we had the pleasure to interview. They came across as exceptional people as well as exceptional leaders. Our impressions of them as a whole can be found in the final section of this book. The samples for both studies (2004, 2005 and 2010, 2011) were selective and therefore to some degree the results are biased. We searched for successful leaders, seeking recommendations from customers, owners, peers and other key stakeholders.

HOW WE DEFINED COMPLEXITY INITIALLY FOR THE STUDY

For the sake of the research, when seeking leaders to interview, we used a very simple definition of a complex project. We defined a complex project as one characterised by uncertainty and ambiguity. The projects had also to be designated as high risk projects, either measured in terms of return on investment or reputation to the sponsoring organisation(s). Budget was not used as a criterion for selection because we have encountered many low budget projects that were extremely complex, success being vital to the reputations of the sponsoring organisations: international aid projects, organisational change projects and projects with a cultural sensitivity are examples. Some leaders also spoke candidly about complex projects that had gone wrong. Extracts from the interviews have been included throughout the book to illustrate, support, contest or contextualise findings from the research literature. In order to preserve the anonymity of the projects and the people who so generously contributed their knowledge, leaders interviewed are referred to by code numbers and any identifying characteristics of the projects have been removed.

Not all the findings are specific to complex projects. Many of our findings are consistent with organisational complexity leadership research (Marion and Uhl-Bien, 2001; Plowman and Duchon, 2008; Schwandt, 2008). However, the characteristics and themes explored throughout the book were consistently reported by those whom we interviewed.

Who is the Leader?

When this book was still a germ of an idea, Jonathan Norman, from Gower Publishing, posed an important question about leadership of complex projects. He asked: 'Who is the leader?'

The answer to that question, strongly supported by the results from our research, is that in a complex project or programme there is rarely one leader. A complex project or programme is a multi-level endeavour involving numerous different groups and individuals, a kind of macro-team activity. Although certain individuals might be required to take overt leadership roles at critical times, the command-control notion of a single leader stems from a simpler world view. The many levels of leadership in a complex programme or project must somehow coalesce – individuals, teams, organisations and environment. Highly networked groups interact, each group having a small but significant impact on the overall carriage of the project. Leadership under these circumstances will be a more diffuse concept, obvious only when it is absent, the exception being times of crisis when leadership should be very obvious. Effective leadership depends upon the good will and capability of all the parties involved with the project but it will only work if the organisational structures are there to support. Understanding how these roles are performed and how they interact seems to be crucial to understanding how leadership in a complex project actually functions.

Beliefs and Myths About Leadership

Some recent thinking on complexity and leadership in organisations challenges some long-held understanding about what leaders actually do.

Many of these beliefs such as, leaders being able to control outcomes, leaders being able to define and deliver a vision, leaders' role in minimising conflict and leaders using their influencing skills to direct others are underpinned by a linear rational view of the world. Complexity theorists dispute many of these views. Instead they argue that organisations are characterised by emergence and non-linearity, where cause and effect are often difficult to connect. Leadership in these organisations might need to be different; flexible, responsive, adaptive, inclusive and richly communicative.

MYTH: ILLUSIONS OF CONTROL

In 2004 I wrote a paper with a colleague entitled 'Illusions of Control' (Remington and Crawford, 2004). The aim was to raise awareness and question some of the convictions underpinning project management thinking at the time; beliefs that were grounded in command-control notions. About that time other authors were also beginning to argue that project management methods stemming from a command-control paradigm may indeed apply to small, straightforward projects with short durations but probably do not work when projects become more complex, where uncertainty abounds (see Ivory and Alderman, 2005; Jaafari, 2003; Williams, 2002; De Meyer et al., 2002; White 2001; Baccarini, 1996). As projects become more complex the possibility for a leader to be in full control, at any point in time, rapidly diminishes. There are too many dimensions, any of which could interrupt control, to make it possible to achieve full and consistent control of outcomes all the time. The fact that many of these complex projects are brought in close to budget and schedule is all the more remarkable and a credit to the project leaders. Often, however, at times the best leaders can do is create an *illusion of control*.

Nevertheless, an expectation remains strong in parts of the organisational literature that reducing or eliminating disorder to return to a pre-determined status quo is the role of a leader and that this kind of control is possible. One fundamental flaw in this logic is the assumption that a goal once set is the right goal and remains relevant as time progresses; presupposing that learning is not taking place. Only an unchanging, static system does not learn and evolve over time. In 1973 Minzberg (p. 78) writes of leadership: 'A disturbance occurs, a correction is necessary.' This idea of leadership stems from a military metaphor; an aircraft or a missile pursues a search path with the aim of eventually hitting a target. Ideas like these have dominated traditional approaches to project management until fairly recently.

MYTH: CREATING AND DELIVERING THE VISION

Some writers, Plowman and Duchon (2008) for example, question the idea that leaders can actually specify desired futures at all. It has been assumed for some time that the task of creating a vision for an organisation is one of the key leadership roles (see Kotter, 1999; Nanus, 1992). This constructed 'picture of the future' (Kotter, 1996, p. 68) is believed to be the key to defining what the organisation will be in the future and how it will perform. In any complex adaptive system ideas are likely to emerge from anywhere in the system.

Marion and Uhl-Bien (2001) argue that in complex situations leaders focus less on controlling or pre-determining the future and more on enabling a positive future, whatever that may be. 'Leaders provide linkages to emergent structures by enhancing connections among organizational members.' (Plowman and Duchon, 2008, p. 139)

Does this idea apply to complex projects? Many of our interviewees stressed the need to embrace a 'few very clear goals' or 'a clear vision' as an essential way of focusing attention on the project and clearing away obstacles. In any complex adaptive system ideas are likely to emerge from anywhere in the system. From our conversations with senior project leaders, it was apparent that much of their work involved providing linkages, creating connections and ensuring information flows (see also Marion and Uhl-Bien, 2001). With the exception of some programmes of very long duration, that have been described as 'temporary organisations' (Lundin and Söderholm, 1995), compared with organisational life cycles most projects are relatively short in duration. The vision seems to be important as a distant goal to channel energy and motivate. However, the project leaders interviewed focused less on controlling the pathways and more on enabling flexible paths towards the vision and being responsive to adaptation.

MYTH: MINIMISING CONFLICT

Another widely held belief is that leaders should seek to minimise conflict. Minimising conflict is desirable if the conflict is destructive, however, the uncertainty and instability that occurs during constructive conflict stimulates idea generation and growth (Maguire and McKelvey, 1999; Prigogine and Stengers, 1984; Stacey, 1996), even if parts of the programme or project might, at times, appear chaotic to outside observers. Some researchers (Plowman et al., 2007) observe that effective leaders play an important role in destabilising a system where they see complacency. This kind of system disturbance can encourage followers to look at issues from different perspectives. This vital role of project leaders, particularly at the level of sponsor, in challenging project teams was clearly identified early in our research. Senior project managers interviewed expected executive sponsors to challenge them to think differently.

MYTH: LEADING THROUGH DIRECT INFLUENCING

Directing progress through influencing others is also considered by many to be an important role in leadership (Yukl, 2006). While influencing was a key strategy used by the leaders we interviewed, influencing as a strategy needs to be placed in perspective. One assumption that should be challenged is a belief in a direct, linear connection between the person engaged in influencing and the intended result. As with communicating and creating a vision, implicit in this idea is the assumption that people in leadership roles really do know what needs to be done all the time. As many of the leaders interviewed observed, in reality any person in a leadership role has only a very limited perspective of what is happening, both internally and externally. All complex adaptive systems have the capacity to learn and evolve. That also means at any time different parts of the system will be behaving differently and reacting differently to their immediate environments. In other words some groups in the project will know things that other groups don't. If the information is being used constructively the groups who know more or are experiencing stronger environmental pressures will be learning faster, faster perhaps than their leaders (Schwandt, 2008). Partnering is a preferable strategy in complex situations partly because it encourages collaborative sharing of information, problem-solving and learning.

Leading a complex programme or project requires leadership that fosters sharing of mental models and information across the entire project. Researchers have found that when leaders and followers share the same information and the same understanding about processes and how decisions are made, performance is better overall (Solansky, 2008). Plowman and Duchon (2008) suggest that leaders in complex environments should focus more on clarifying processes rather than specifying outcomes. This resonates with some other research on effective leader communication, which will be discussed in Chapter 2.

HOW OUR LEADERS LED

This is the subject of the final section of this book. Suffice to say at this stage they seem to understand how best to lead in complex environments.

How Does This Apply to Complex Projects?

Much of the recent research about complexity leadership might seem inappropriate for project management, which is by nature a goal driven activity. Nevertheless, the reality is that for many complex projects, or programmes, a fixed goal is an illusion rather than a hard reality. What the goal really looks, sounds and feels like is often not understood or shared by those who are expected to deliver the goal, or indeed by other leaders. Even if the goal is understood and agreed, the goal-paths, the means of achieving the goal, might be unclear, particularly to those who are expected to lead the implementation.

> *A project with which some of my colleagues were involved several years ago springs to mind as a perfect example. The vision was to inculcate 'a culture of trust' in a large regional police force. It is a good example of a vision that the people tasked with implementing soon realised was very, very nebulous. It took the project teams many months to arrive at a shared understanding of the goal and years to carry out the hundreds of projects that were needed to shift the culture towards the vision. In the process the expectations changed and the nature of the 'simple' initial goal went through significant mutations. In the end, sharing decision-making and processes were fundamental to finding the ways forward. Interview 62 GM.*

This was a very 'soft' project but even so-called 'hard' projects, like building a submarine, can be affected by uncertainty and nonlinearity. At a high level the brief might be to build a top-of-the-range submarine within a certain budget and time-frame. These projects tend to have durations of several years. During the life cycle of the project it is almost certain that the initial specifications will need to be altered, as new technology becomes available or as technical problems are encountered. Setting aside political and economic pressures, changes in leadership, changes in executive structures, changes in project teams, and countless other sources of complexity, the goal-paths are circuitous and emergent. On completion of the project the initial specifications might seem to have been almost absurd, however more likely than not the initial goal, to deliver a state-of-the-art submarine, will have been achieved – now it just looks nothing like what was initially envisaged because both technology and requirements will have emerged and adapted.

How complexity and uncertainty impact project leadership and how successful project leaders have handled complexity is the focus of this book.

This Book is Set in Three Sections:

Section One: *What effective leadership achieves* in complex project environments forms the bulk of the book. The chapter themes within are derived directly from what was 'top of mind' for those senior leaders who took part in our studies.

Section Two: *What effective leadership needs* in complex project environments discusses some of the structures that are required to support effective leadership, without which leadership would not work.

Section Three: *How effective leadership performs* in complex project environments,the final section, summarises our observations of the leadership styles of the 70 project leaders interviewed. The chapters in this section come from a synthesis of individual reflections by the research team.

I hope that what follows rings true for project leaders at all levels!

References and Further Reading

Baccarini, D. (1996) The Concept of Project Complexity – A Review. *International Journal of Project Management*, 14(4), pp. 201–204.

De Meyer, A., Loch, C.H. and Pich, M.T. (2002) Managing Project Uncertainty: from Variation to Chaos. *MIT Sloan Management Review*, 43(2), pp. 60–67.

Gehring, D.R. (2007) Applying Traits Theory of Leadership to Project Management. *IEEE Engineering Management Review*, 35(3), pp. 109–109.

Ivory, C. and Alderman, N. (2005) Can Project Management Learn Anything from Studies of Failure in Complex Systems? *Project Management Journal*, 36(3), pp. 5–16.

Jaafari, A. (2003) Project Management in the Age of Complexity and Change. *Project Management Journal*, 34(4), pp. 47–57.

Kotter, J.P. (1999) *What Leaders Really Do*. Ma: Harvard Business School Press.

Kotter, J.P. (1996) *Leading Change*. Boston, Ma: Harvard Business School Press.

Lundin, R. and Söderholm, A. (1995) A Theory of the Temporary Organization. Scandinavian. *Journal of Management*, 11(4), pp. 437–455.

Maguire, S. and McKelvey, B. (1999) Complexity and Management. Moving from Fad to Firm Foundations. *Emergence: A Journal of Complexity Issues*, 1(2), pp. 19–61.

Marion, R. and Uhl-Bien, M. (2001) Leadership in Complex Organizations. *Leadership Quarterly*, 12(4), pp. 389–418.

Mintzberg, H. (1973) *The Nature of Managerial Work*. New York, NY: Harper and Row.

Nanus, B. (1992) *Visionary Leadership: Creating a Compelling Sense of Direction for Your Organization*. San Fransisco: Ca: Jossey-Bass.

Plowman, D., Thomas, S., Beck, T., Baker, L., Kulkani, M. and Travis, D. (2007) The Role of Leadership in Emergent, Self-organization. *The Leadership Quarterly*, 18, pp. 323–339.

Plowman, D.A. and Duchon, D. (2008) Dispelling the Myths About Leadership: From Cybernetics to Emergence. In: Uhl-Bien, M. and Marion, R. (eds) *Complexity leadership. Part I: Conceptual Foundations*. Charlotte, North Carolina: Information Age Publishing Inc., pp. 129–153.

Prigogine, I. and Stengers, I. (1984) *Order Out of Chaos: Man's New Dialogue with Nature*. New York, NY: Bantam Books.

Remington, K. and Crawford, L. (2004) Illusions of Control, IRNOP VI Conference, Published in IRNOPVI Conference Proceedings, August, 2004, Finland.

Schwandt, D.L. (2008) Individual and Collective Co-evolution: Leadership as Emergent Social Structuring. In: Uhl-Bien, M. and Marion, R. (eds) *Complexity Leadership. Part 1: Conceptual Foundations*. Charlotte, NC: Information Age Publishing, pp. 101–128.

Solansky, S.T. (2008) Leadership Style and Team Processes in Self-managed Teams. *Journal of Leadership & Organizational Studies*, 14, pp. 332–341.

Stacey, R.D. (1996) *Complexity and Creativity in Organizations*. Berrett-Koehler Publishers.

Stacey, R.D. (1993) *Strategic Management and Organizational Dynamics*. London. Pitman.

Turner, J.R and Müller, R. (2005) The Project Manager's Leadership Style as a Success Factor on Projects: A Review. *Project Management Journal*, 36(2), pp. 49–61.

Uhl-Bien, M. and Marion, R. (2008) Complexity Leadership – A Framework for Leadership in the Twenty-first Century. In: Uhl-Bien, M. and Marion, R. (eds) *Complexity Leadership. Part 1: Conceptual Foundations*. Charlotte, NC: Information Age Publishing (xi-xxiv).

White, L. (2001) Effective Governance Through Complexity Thinking and Management Science. *Systems Research and Behavioral Science*, 18, pp. 241–57.

Williams, T. (2002) *Modelling Complex Projects*, (Sussex, UK: John Wiley & Sons).

Yukl, G. (2006) *Leadership in Organizations, 6th Edition*. Upper Saddle River, NJ: Prentice Hall.

SECTION ONE:

What Good Leadership Does When Projects Are Complex

The chapter headings in this section reflect the key themes from our interviews. They describe what the leaders we interviewed actually did to lead themselves and their teams through almost impossible situations to deliver positive outcomes for their key stakeholders. The chapters are presented roughly in the order of frequency of theme from the interviews. The emphasis is on what worked for them. The chapters then explore current knowledge from research and practice around each of the major themes. Some of the themes will be familiar to readers. Chapter 1 announces a repeated view by the leaders we interviewed, that leader and key stakeholders must recognise that they are dealing with a complex project, rather than just a difficult or challenging one, and that they need to understand why it is complex. Chapter 2 is entitled: 'Communicate, Communicate, Communicate.' It reflects the enormous emphasis placed on communication by those whom we interviewed. Nevertheless, the focus is communication in complex environments, rather than project communication in general. Chapter 3 explores another frequently cited theme; that a complex project depends on the interaction of teams at many different levels, from the executive teams to those actually doing the work. Chapter 4 discusses the value of conceptualising the project as a programme; part of a business portfolio. Chapter 5 reflects a key theme in our studies (2004–2011); the value of challenging others to develop innovative approaches to management. Chapter 6 explores how leaders use critical and reflective thinking skills to help them to navigate complex environments. Chapter 7 also reflects a common theme, the critical understanding of disparate organisational, national and generational cultures and how differences can affect project teams and their interactions. Chapter 8 has been built around the acute awareness of the need to manage organisational politics by the project leaders in our sample. Chapter 9 explores crises, from the perspective of complexity theory, and how leaders guide both their teams and their key stakeholders through major risk events.

Chapter 1: Comprehend Complexity

Chapter 2: Communicate, Communicate, Communicate

Chapter 3: Cultivate the Right Teams *from Project Teams to Executive Board*

Chapter 4: Employ Portfolio-programme Thinking

Chapter 5: Challenge Through Innovation

Chapter 6: Think About Thinking

Chapter 7: Consider Culture

Chapter 8: Exercise Political Skills

Chapter 9: Pilot Project Through Crises

1

Comprehend Complexity

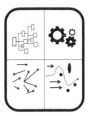

I understand, if we are on the one-hundred-eightieth meridian, we are at the Solomon Islands. But how do you know we are actually on the one-hundred-eightieth meridian?…You find the Solomon Islands and you have learned where is the hundred-eightieth meridian, and you know where are the Islands of Solomon! But why must those islands lie on that meridian?
Umberto Eco, The Island of the Day Before, (p. 253).

The notion of comprehending complexity might appear to be somewhat incongruous. Many writers argue that it is impossible to understand something which is truly complex. Nevertheless, people do lead and manage projects that are extraordinarily challenging; projects exhibiting characteristics that are associated by scientists with complexity. The ability to comprehend that the project is something out of the ordinary seems to be the first step in being able to deal with it effectively.

Key Points in This Chapter:

- Importance of early recognition of complexity by all stakeholders.

- The difference between complex and complicated projects.

- Indicators of project complexity.

- Project specific factors contributing to project complexity.

Part 1: The Importance of Recognising Complexity ASAP

There appears to be a positive correlation between project success and the capacity of the executive sponsor and other key project leaders to recognise complexity and support the project manager and project team in managing the complexity (Helm and Remington, 2005; Crawford et al., 2006). There is also generally agreement amongst experienced project leaders that if you can get as many key players recognising that the project or programme is more than just complicated or challenging, the better the chance of achieving desired outcomes. This was a strong point of agreement amongst leaders of complex projects at all levels. It was one that was brought up again and again, particularly when discussing projects that had gone wrong. The act of early recognition by key players that the project is likely to be complex has the beneficial effect of alerting decision-makers to the need for special consideration, and hopefully also of engaging them in constructive problem-solving.

> *The early phase of that programme, the requirements, was a very good example of a few people really grasping the complexity issue. Interview 63.*

As the project director of a very successful international defence project observed, experienced project leaders often know in advance when a project is likely to be extraordinarily challenging. On the other hand, others associated with the project might not have the same level of experience, either with complexity, or projects, or both. Tools to help identify and assess the level of complexity are very useful, especially if they also engage key decision-makers in ownership of the complexity through recognition and comprehension.

NOT ALL KEY STAKEHOLDERS UNDERSTAND COMPLEXITY

However, it cannot be assumed that all key players will understand the complexity. Inability to comprehend the level of complexity might be related to experience or to personal characteristics, such as learning style or the way the person comprehends the world as the following extract from an interview with a senior IT project manager reveals:

> *The project on paper actually looked easier than it was, and [the sponsor] hated that ambiguity. And it was very conceptual as well. It wasn't one plus one equals two, at all … so they [senior executive] struggled with it. So you'd deliver pieces of information in small chunks, so they could go okay I understand that, let's move on to the next step. Interview 17 PM.*

Unfortunately, in the first part of our study (Helm and Remington, 2005a, 2005b) this kind of response was the rule rather than the exception. For that part of the study we focused on experienced project managers who had successfully delivered projects that also had been deemed by colleagues and other key stakeholders as complex. Unfortunately the vast majority of the senior project managers interviewed reported that they managed in spite of senior executives' unwillingness or inability to recognise the level of complexity exhibited by the project. They were 'managing around' senior project executives!

The implications from the first study are quite serious. If experienced project managers believe they have to simplify and filter information for executive leaders, who might be unwilling or unable to address the true complexity of the project, opportunities for conversations with senior executives that might have important implications for the project are effectively reduced or even eliminated. Theoretically, senior executive leaders are the ones who have most immediate access to knowledge about wider environmental and organisational changes that might impact the success of the project or programme. A few project leaders reported better experiences.

> *The sponsor, who was at a particularly high level in the organisation, would regularly email me or send messages via her colleagues to alert me to something which was going on in the organisation, which might potentially have some impact on the project. In such a large and diverse organisation, I [PM] could not possibly have access to her knowledge at an organisational level. This was invaluable. Interview 11 PM.*

Without access to this important information it can be very difficult for a project leader to negotiate the field and successfully deliver the project or programme. While the senior project managers found ways to deal with ineffective senior executives, the same could not be expected of less experienced project managers.

TEAM PERCEPTIONS

It is also important that leaders acknowledge complexity with project teams. Teams may experience complexity as confusion, distress or loss of confidence in themselves and the leadership. The most frequent response at the team level is aversion to complexity – 'that's too complex; it's all too much; let's try and simplify it'; but some problems are not simple and the act of simplification can involve making selections and choosing pathways at dangerously early stages of a complex undertaking or project.

Recognising that a project is complex and then determining how complex and in what way, is the first key. The first part of this research also provided some input for the first book in this series, *Tools for Complex Projects* (Remington and Pollack, 2007). In preparation for that book we looked for special ways in which experienced project managers were working with complexity; tools, methods and approaches that were non-standard. For that book, my colleague, Julien Pollack, and I developed a method to help practitioners to identify and analyse project complexity based on the source of the complexity.

Part 2: How Are Complex Projects Different From Complicated Ones?

A number of authors have demonstrated that projects, like organisations, can be likened to the complex adaptive systems found in nature (see for example: Ivory and Alderman, 2005; Jaafari, 2003; Williams, 2002; White 2001; Baccarini, 1996; Stacey, 1991). When we look at many of the recommended practices in the project management literature it becomes apparent that, although projects are often thought of as systems, they are treated as simple systems. In a simple system, like a straightforward project, we can assume a problem can be defined properly and completely at the start of a project. As we monitor the project we might observe that there is a variation from the goal-path. Usually we then take some remedial action to return the project to the goal-path. We call that monitoring and controlling. If we are lucky the project more or less reaches its initially defined goal. It behaves like a simple system (Figure 1.1). But let's face it how many projects really behave like this?

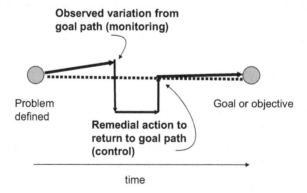

Figure 1.1   **A diagrammatic representation of a simple, goal-seeking system**

COMPLEX SYSTEMS

Likening complex projects to the complex adaptive systems found in animals and plant systems incorporates the notion that projects exist in the social world, which is a complex adaptive system (Eisner, 2005; Axelrod and Cohen, 2000). Implicit in the notion of a complex adaptive system are questions about whether all projects can be expected to behave in predictable ways, the way we expect a mechanical system (or simple system) to behave. A simple mechanical system, like a car, has a very high likelihood of getting us from A to B if we can guarantee certain conditions: the mechanical parts are in good working order; it is filled with the right kind of fuel; the roads are in a passable condition and there are no physical barriers like traffic jams, fierce storms or landslides and the driver is competent. If all these requirements are fulfilled there is a high likelihood that we will arrive at our destination within a reasonable time-frame.

When systems become more complex, the level of certainty of achieving our goals decreases. Even expectations around the simple car journey can become less predictable when we add in human error. Perhaps someone forgot to fill the car up with petrol, or the driver was chatting to passengers and missed a turn, or much, much worse, missed some ice on the road and the car skidded causing an accident. Or, other drivers on the road were not careful and the driver rolled the car trying to miss an oncoming vehicle. The very fact that all projects involve people means that all projects might legitimately be described as complex systems. Nevertheless, it is important to acknowledge that there are degrees of complexity and it is even more useful to be able to distinguish in advance projects that require extraordinary efforts to manage from those that are routine.

SIMPLE, COMPLICATED, COMPLEX OR CHAOTIC

One of the questions that vex both practitioners and academics is how is a complex project is different from a complicated or difficult project and when does a project become chaotic, or out of control?

As Figure 1.2 illustrates, depending on whether the outcomes can be controlled precisely, we can think of projects or parts of projects as being anywhere on a continuum between control and chaos, with simple projects at the control end and out of control projects at the chaotic end of the spectrum. The majority of projects exist in the complicated or complex space. Thankfully not many projects enter the turbulent, chaotic space. If, having entered the chaotic space, they cannot be quickly brought back into the complex space, they usually collapse. Not many projects are really simple because all projects involve people and people have a tendency to make things complicated. Complicated projects can be very challenging but there is usually a way through if we can get the right experts working on the problems. Once we move into the complex space the connections between causes and effects are more difficult to discern, people become anxious and outcomes are extremely difficult to predict with any degree of certainty. However, projects do not remain in one space, they can quickly move from the control end to the chaotic end. Also, as we shall explore later, parts of projects can be in control while other parts can be complex or even chaotic.

At this point the sceptics might ask whether complexity in relation to projects is just a matter of semantics. In a practical sense, whether or not a project is considered to be complex, or just very complicated, *is* a matter of perception, related to experience and familiarity. Lack of experience can increase the apparent complexity or difficulty of a project because a less experienced person does not have access to the range of responses available to a highly experienced person. When a project, or part of a project, moves into the complex space events follow each other very rapidly. Then, making the wrong decision at key points, or avoiding action, really matters.

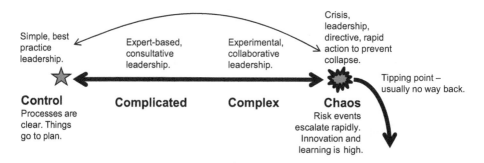

Figure 1.2   **Most projects exist on a continuum between control and chaos (developed and adapted by the author for projects from Snowdon, 2002)**

Part 3: Indicators of Project Complexity

There are several indicators that experienced people can use to gauge the level of complexity of a project. It is important to remember that indicators are contextually sensitive. Whether a project or programme is perceived to be complex depends on the people concerned, their experience, the environment and other pressures, such as tight deadlines.

UNCERTAINTY

One way of differentiating a complex project or programme from a difficult, but ultimately manageable one, involves identifying the point in time at which the exact nature of the deliverables or how to get there is no longer clear or certain. In the quote at the very beginning of this chapter from the book, *The Island of the Day Before*, Umberto Eco's characters are expressing the kind of uncertainty that people experience in a complex world as their own deeply held versions of reality are challenged. Uncertainty can occur when information is lacking or inadequate; when the details are ambiguous, complicated or unpredictable. It can also occur when people feel unsure about their own knowledge or available knowledge in the field as a whole (see Babrow et al., 2000; Babrow et al., 1998). Because the perception of uncertainty is a subjective perception based on a person's ability to know or understand the world, 'a person who believes himself or herself to be uncertain is uncertain' (Brashers, 2001, p. 478). From an objective standpoint, the required knowledge might be available, but if a person believes that s/he cannot make a decision on the basis of that knowledge then s/he might still be uncertain. Therefore, feelings of uncertainty depend both on the knowledge available to the people concerned and their own perceptions of their ability to access it or use it. Perceptions of uncertainty can also be related to a person's assessment of the probability of an event. When people relate the probability of an event to their feelings of uncertainty the relationship is not linear (Babrow, 1992).

TRUST

Uncertainty reduces people's confidence in themselves and in the leadership. It therefore contributes to lack of trust in people associated with the project (see Geraldi and Adlbrecht, 2007; Geraldi, 2008). Feelings of discomfort due to uncertainty can be to do with the scope or direction of the project, or technical, budgetary and schedule risks. Reduction of confidence negatively impacts on our ability to deliver and can adversely affect the trust in those on whom you depend. When uncertainty prevails and trust diminishes, otherwise competent leaders and managers can behave poorly. People start running for cover and blame begins to be hurled in all directions.

DIFFICULTY IN LINKING CAUSE AND EFFECT OR NON-LINEARITY

Difficulty in linking cause and effect has a important effect on the project team and key stakeholders (Scudder et al., 1989). The complicated information pathways in many large projects involving multiple decision points and multiple players can result in, what complexity theorists refer to, as non-linearity; cyclical chains of events that reinforce each other, as opposed to predictable, linear chains of cause and effect. Factors which contribute to the uncertainty due to non-linearity might include technical complicacy, unclear or untimely decision-making, unexpected environmental changes and many others. The uncertainty, or ambiguity, that follows can present itself as loss of faith in the technology management of the project and in other parties involved in the project (Geraldi and Adlbrecht, 2007; Geraldi, 2008; Müller and Geraldi, 2007). In these situations uncertainty and associated reactions, such as loss of faith and trust, are contingent factors. They are consequences of the technical challenges or decision-making structure associated with the project.

Figure 1.3 is a simplified illustration of the decision network in a project that went horribly wrong, a delay in decision-making at the decision point E had such a profound impact on so many other parts of the project to make the outcomes uncontrollable. In the following diagram the reinforcing loops, implying cycles of re-work, that kept compounding the initial delay, can be seen.

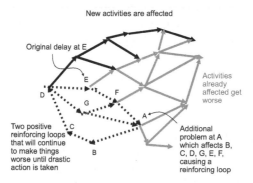

Figure 1.3   **A decision network for a complex project illustrating reinforcing loops that compound the problem due to non-linear effects**

A significant delay in one activity in a dense network of activities like this one can have an effect on many different activities in the project. This is simply due to high levels of interconnectivity and interdependence that produce cycles of rework which are often difficult to anticipate at the outset of a project.

Part 4: Project Specific Factors Contributing to Project Complexity

Complexity associated with projects has been attributed to a number of factors. As mentioned earlier some causes are directly related to who is involved with the project, the capabilities, motivation and commitment of the key personnel (executive sponsors, clients, user representatives, project managers and project team members). Other causal factors stem from the physical nature of the project, such as its size, the organisation structure, the technical challenges and how the project is affected by deadlines and time-related issues. However, there is rarely just one causal factor and perceptions of the complexity of the project are more likely to be influenced by an intersection of these aspects.

For example, in one very large project we investigated in the energy sector, theoretically avoidable complexities were traced back to poor cost and time estimates during the feasibility phase that were related to pressure from senior executives to get the project started. A culture of optimism was accompanied by an unwillingness by senior executives to acknowledge the seriousness of the risks that had been identified and reported by project personnel. This situation was underpinned by a lack of relevant expertise at senior executive levels and apparent unwillingness to co-op others who did have the right expertise. Technical challenges that were impossible to solve in the time-frame led to wildly inaccurate guesses and inappropriate choice of procurement systems for the level of complexity of the project. Some of these conditions, such as over-optimism, pressure on project personnel to get started, sponsors' inability to acknowledge the levels of risk when reported by the project manager, sponsors' lack of understanding of the need for highly experienced project support personnel and so on are directly related to leadership capability and behaviour. Other causal factors were related to the nature of the project itself – innovative, technically challenging, involving a multitude of authorities with contradictory requirements, the public visibility of the project and public concern over environmental issues associated, the scale of the project and the lack of appropriate support structures in place within the owner organisation.

It is the intersection of the leadership capability at all levels of the project and the nature of the project itself that can seriously affect how complexity is addressed. Uncertainty about how to proceed, ambiguity about what is happening at any one time, loss of trust in colleagues and key stakeholders and loss of faith are consequences. These characteristics might also provide us with ways of assessing the level of the complexity for the organisation and context.

In our previous book, *Tools for Complex Projects* (Remington and Pollack, 2007), we offered a model and tools for identifying and categorising the complexity based on contributing or causal factors. Organisation specific tools are currently being developed by large organisations for their own use in differentiating complex projects from standard ones. Whatever methods a leader uses, the purpose is the same, to help others recognise the nature and degree of the complexity early enough so that the best decisions can be made to assist project delivery. Putting our heads in the sand is not an option with a complex project or programme.

HOW COMPLEXITY IS AFFECTED BY PROJECT ORGANISATION OR STRUCTURE

Project organisations can be considered to be networks of information exchange. It is theoretically possible to measure the number of possible pathways in a complex network but it is often very difficult or even impossible to predict how the pathways might be affected when changes are imposed from outside the system, for example, Figure 1.3 illustrates a project decision network in a defence industry project which had many interdependent and co-dependent activities. When a delay occurred in pathway E (due in this case to a key stakeholder withholding approval due to political issues about the scope, but it could equally have been due to a supplier monopoly or a technical design issue) there was a knock-on effect that impacted the whole project. This effect alone could have been dealt with by a schedule variation but in a complex system there is the propensity for cyclical reinforcement where delays in later pathways start to influence and make redundant tasks and processes that have already been completed – the classic rework syndrome.

In large projects with many interrelated and interdependent activities this kind of effect, resulting in excessive amounts of rework, is not uncommon. Often called 'vicious cycles', these patterns result in what complexity theorists call 'emergence'. The system starts to turn into something different and the outcomes can be altered considerably. In the case of the project in the example above cost budgets and the schedule started to get out of hand until the only option was to shut down the project causing substantial embarrassment to key stakeholders. Unfortunately this is also when litigation takes over and relationships between parties can become nasty.

TECHNICAL DIFFICULTIES THAT CONTRIBUTE TO COMPLEXITY

One expected source of project complexity is technical difficulty (Turner and Cochrane, 1993; Payne, 1995; Williams, 2002). Technological novelty, task uncertainty and the ability of the organisation to cope with technological novelty have been cited as specific causes of complexity (Taikonda and Rosenthal, 2000; Pundir et al., 2007). Technical and design challenges are commonplace in projects, however, if they appear to be insurmountable, or at least insoluble within an acceptable time-frame, they contribute to uncertainty and lack of trust between key stakeholders, which might increase the perception of complexity (Müller and Geraldi, 2007). Also, design and creative activity is by definition nonlinear. Inherent in the design process are positive reinforcing loops, hopefully 'virtuous cycles', leading to new ideas and knowledge (Kokotovich and Remington, 2007), rather than 'vicious cycles' leading to potential disaster (Williams, 2002). However, there can be many frustrating dead-ends when trying to solve technical design problems. Jones and Deckro (1993) add another aspect to technical complexity, that of instability of the assumptions upon which the tasks are based. Williams (2004) also refers to 'aleotoric uncertainty', which is inherent uncertainty relating to the reliability of calculations and what he calls 'epistemic uncertainty', stemming either from poor mental models or lack of knowledge within the technical field.

TIME AND PROJECT COMPLEXITY

By definition projects are time-driven. However, the degree to which time affects the project is relevant here. A number of authors (Clift and Vandenbosch,1999; Williams, 2002) argue that an increasing desire to reduce time to market is an important source of complexity. How pressure due to time affects decision-making in teams and amongst other key stakeholders is not well understood at all (see Chapter 6).

The way different key stakeholders experience time is, in itself, a source of complexity. We know that time is perceived differently at the beginning of project, in the middle, and at the end. It is also perceived differently by different people associated with the project (Remington and Söderholm,

2010). For project team members, sensitivity to the passage of time changes throughout a normal project, with time perceived as more at the start of a project, contracting as the project progresses (Gersick, 1988). For stakeholders who are not actually involved in managing the project, time can be perceived differently. Entrepreneurs, for example, might be more conscious of time at the beginning of the project when there is pressure to commit to key financiers. Project financiers are likely to be highly conscious of time towards the end of schedule when benefits are close to realisation. This is a common phenomenon in the property development field where buildings need to be leased quickly in order to achieve satisfactory returns on investment, or in manufacturing industries where time to market is critical to the success of a product.

Particularly as many projects last for extended periods, over several years, they become increasingly subject to effects which might be avoided in projects of a shorter duration. These projects are affected by a range of environmental impacts, including political upheavals, local and worldwide economic crises, major regulation changes, mergers and replacement of key personnel. At the time of writing a major rail extension project was summarily cancelled in Sydney, Australia, due to a change in Premier and Cabinet and a crisis in confidence, partially related to global economic pressures. The repercussions for contractors and other stakeholders, such as affected local businesses, are serious.

LACK OF CLARITY ABOUT GOALS

Apart from being the most identifiable symptom of complexity, uncertainty itself, can also be a primary cause of complexity. At project initiation, a lack of a shared understanding about goals and goal-paths, or goals that are understood differently by individual stakeholders, can contribute to feelings of uncertainty. If not recognised and addressed early decision-making can be affected and the level of uncertainty may increase as the project progresses (Remington and Pollack, 2007; Remington et al., 2009). Uncertainty as a causal factor has been explored by a number of authors (Williams, 2002, 2005; De Meyer et al., 2002).

COMPLEX PROJECTS IN A NUTSHELL

Briefly we can describe a complex project as one which involves abnormally high levels of uncertainty, ambiguity and associated reactions, such as decreasing levels of trust. These characteristics might stem from some or all of the following characteristics (see Remington and Pollack, 2007):

- Highly networked, interdependent and co-dependent tasks.

- Complicated and interdependent communication pathways, often found where there are many different reporting pathways and diffuse or conflicting authority.

- High levels of technical uncertainty such that suitable technical solutions might not be available within the time.

- Many disparate groups of stakeholders with competing agendas that are difficult to understand, track and manage, as found in projects with political or societal implications and multi-owner projects.

- Several different work or national cultures involved, as often found in multi-national and cross-agency projects.

- Lack of clarity, shared understanding or vision about goals and goal-paths at any level of the project.

- External environmental changes, political, regulatory, technical or organisational, that are unusually difficult to predict in terms of impact and time.

- Other time-related pressures that have abnormal impacts.

- Unexpected emergent behaviour resulting in rapidly escalating risks due to the triggering of a series of small events which might be previously have been thought to be unrelated.

Projects afflicted by any or all of these conditions are likely to behave in ways that make reliable prediction of outcomes, (in terms of costs, budgets, scope, quality and value) difficult, if not impossible. Often these projects are plagued by negative behaviour that comes with uncertainty and eventual undermining of previously good relationships. If these projects are not led effectively at all levels they can fail in many ways.

The majority of interviewees in our research were working on large scale and mega projects but there were also interviewees who were working on relatively low budget projects that also fit our definition. Most of these smaller projects were culturally or politically sensitive and the reputation of the project owners and other key stakeholders rested heavily on their success.

Understanding many of the factors that contribute to complexity in a project matters because practitioners can be forewarned and therefore forearmed. More importantly project leaders can forewarn key stakeholders, such as the project owners, clients, executive sponsors, end-users and champions. The ability to predict that a project might become complex, even if the exact nature of the complexity cannot be exactly, was acknowledged as very important by many of our respondents.

In Summary

Complex projects, like complex adaptive systems, are characterised by high levels of:

- Uncertainty

- Ambiguity

- Decreasing levels of trust.

Risk events are likely to have emergent, non-linear characteristics which increase the level of uncertainty.

Event pathways are often not predictable. Therefore, early recognition that risk events might escalate in a non-linear, unpredictable way might encourage decision makers to make sensible and timely decisions about communication, key role capabilities and governance. It has the affect of raising the general level of alertness and an atmosphere of preparedness develops.

Nevertheless, as indicated by some of the interview reports from our research, getting key senior stakeholders to understand and acknowledge the likelihood of the effects of complexity is not always easy.

In spite of the uncertainty many complex projects are led and managed successfully and this book endeavours to explore those factors that have contributed to their successful leadership.

References and Further Reading

Axelrod, R. and Cohen, M.D. (2000) *Harnessing Complexity. Organizational Implications of a Scientific Frontier*. New York, NY: Basic Books.

Babrow, A.S. (1992) Communication and Problematic Integration: Understanding Diverging Probability and Value, Ambiguity, Ambivalence, and Impossibility. *Communication Theory*, 2, pp. 95–130.

Babrow, A.S., Hines, S.C. and Kasch, C.R. (2000) Managing Uncertainty in Illness Explanation: An Application of Problematic Integration Theory. In: Whaley, B. (ed.) *Explaining Illness: Research, Theory and Strategies*. pp. 41–67, Hillsdale, NJ: Erlbaum.

Babrow, A.S., Kasch, C.R. and Ford, L.A. (1998) The Many Meanings of Uncertainty in Illness: Toward a Systematic Accounting. *Health Communications*, 10, pp. 1–23.

Baccarini, D. (1996) The Concept of Project Complexity – A Review. *International Journal of Project Management*, 14(4), pp. 201–204.

Brashers, D.E. (2001) Communication and Uncertainty Management. *Journal of Communication*, International Association, Sept. pp. 477–497.

Clift, T.B. and Vandenbosch, M.B. (1999) Project Complexity and Efforts to Reduce Product Development Cycle Time. *Journal of Business Research*, 45(2), 187–198.

Crawford, L., Cooke-Davies, T., Labuschagne, L., Hobbs, B. and Remington, K. (2006) 'Exploring the Role of the Project Sponsor,' PMI Research Conference, 18 July, Montreal.

Crawford, L., Hobbs, B. and Turner, J.R. (2006) Aligning Capability with Strategy: Categorizing Projects to do the Right Projects and to do Them Right. *Project Management Journal*, 37(2), pp. 38–51.

De Meyer, A., Loch, C.H. and Pich, M.T., (2002) Managing Project Uncertainty: From Variation to Chaos. *MIT Sloan Management Review*, 43(2), pp. 60–67.

Dooley, K.J. and Van de Ven, A. (1999) Explaining Complex Organizational Dynamics. *Organization Science*, 10(3), pp. 358–372.

Eco, U. (1995) *The Island of the Day Before*. (Trans. W. Weaver) New York, NY: Penguin Books.

Eisner, H. (2005) *Managing Complex Systems: Thinking Outside the Box*. (Hoboken, NJ: John Wiley and Sons).

Eriksson, M., Lilliesköld, J., Jonsson, N. and Novosel, D. (2002) How to Manage Complex, Multinational R&D Projects Successfully. *Engineering Management Journal*, 14(2), pp. 53–60.

Geraldi, J. (2008) Patterns of Complexity: The Thermometer of Complexity. Project Perspectives 2008. *The Annual Publication of International Project Management Association*, pp. 4–9.

Geraldi, J. and Adlbrecht, G. (2007) On Faith, Fact and Interaction in Projects. *Project Management Journal*, 38(1), pp. 32–43.

Gersick, C.J.G. (1988) Time and Transition in Work Teams: Toward a New Model of Group Development. *The Academy of Management Journal*, 31(1), pp. 9–41.

Griffin, D., Shaw, P. and Stacey, R. (1999) Knowing and Acting in Conditions of Uncertainty: A Complexity Perspective. *Systemic Practice and Action Research*, 12(3), pp. 295–309.

Helm, J. and Remington, K. (2005a) 'Adaptive Habitus – Project Managers' Perceptions of the Role of the Project Sponsor'. Proceedings of EURAM Conference, May, Munich: TUT University.

Helm, J. and Remington, K. (2005b) Effective Sponsorship, Project Managers' Perceptions of the Role of the Project Sponsor. *Project Management Journal*, 36(3), 51–62.

Hobday, M. (1998) Product Complexity, Innovation and Industrial Organization. *Research Policy*, 26, pp. 689–710.

Ivory, C. and Alderman, N. (2005) Can Project Management Learn Anything from Studies of Failure in Complex Systems? *Project Management Journal*, 36(3), pp. 5–16.

Jaafari, A. (2003) Project Management in the Age of Complexity and Change. *Project Management Journal*, 34(4), pp. 47–57.

Jones, R. and Deckro, R. (1993) The Social Psychology of Project Management Conflict. *European Journal of Operational Research*, 64, pp. 216–228.

Kokotovich, V. and Remington, K. (2007) Enhancing Innovative Capabilities Developing creative thinking approaches with tomorrow's project managers, IRNOP VIII, Brighton, UK, Conference Proceedings.

Langton, C.G. (1990) Computation at the Edge of Chaos. *Physica*, D, 42.

Müller, R. and Geraldi, J.G. (2007) Linking complexity and leadership competences of Project Managers. IRNOP VIII Conference (International Research Network for Organizing by Projects). Conference papers. Brighton, UK.

Payne, J. (1995) Management of Multiple Simultaneous Projects: A State-of-the-Art Review. *International Journal of Project Management*, 13(3), pp. 163–168.

Payne, J.H. and Turner, J.R. (1999) Company-wide Project Management: The Planning and Control of Programmes of Projects of Different Type. *International Journal of Project Management*, 17(1), pp. 55–59.

Pundir, A.K., Ganapathy, L. and Sambandam, N. (2007) Towards a Complexity Framework for Managing Projects. *E:CO*, 9(4), pp. 17–25.

Remington, K. and Pollack, J. (2007) *Tools for Complex Projects*. Aldershot, UK: Gower Publishing.

Remington, K., Zolin, R. and Turner, J.R. (2009) A Model of Project Complexity: Distinguishing Dimensions of Complexity from Severity, IRNOP IX Conference Papers, Berlin, Germany.

Remington, K. and Söderholm, A. (2010) Time is of the Essence: One Factor Influencing the Project Management of Change. *International Journal of Organization and Management*, Special Edition.

Scudder, G.D., Schroeder, R.G., Van de Ven, A.H., Seiler, G.R. and Wiseman, R.M. (1989) Managing Complex Innovations: The Case of Defense Contracting. In: Van de Ven, A.H., Angle, H.L., Poole, M.S. (eds) *Research on the Management of Innovation*. NY: Harper and Row, pp. 401–438.

Shenhar, A.J. (2001) One Size Does Not Fit All Projects: Exploring Classical Contingency Domains. *Management Studies*, 47(3), pp. 394–414.

Snowden, D. (2002) Complex Acts of Knowing: Paradox and Descriptive Self-Awareness. *Journal of Knowledge Management*, 6(2).

Stacey, R. (1991) *The Chaos Frontier: Creative Strategic Control for Business*. Oxford, UK: Butterworth-Heineman.

Taikonda, M.V. and Rosenthal, S.R. (2000) Technology, Novelty, Project Complexity and Product Development Project Execution Success: A Deeper Look at Task Uncertainty in Product Innovation. *IEEE Transactions on Engineering Management*, 47(1), pp. 74–87.

Turner, J.R. and Cochrane, R.A. (1993) Goals-and-Methods Matrix: Coping with Projects with Ill Defined Goals and/or Methods of Achieving Them. *International Journal of Project Management*, 11, p. 93.

White, L. (2001) Effective Governance Through Complexity Thinking and Management Science. *Systems Research and Behavioral Science*, 18, pp. 241–57.

Williams, T. (2005) Assessing and Moving on from the Dominant Project Management Discourse in the Light of Project Overruns. *IEEE Transactions on Engineering Management*, 52(4), pp. 497–508.

Williams, T. (2004) Why Monte Carlo Simulations of Project Networks can Mislead. *Project Management Journal*, 25(3), pp. 53–61.

Williams, T. (2002) *Modelling Complex Projects*. Sussex, UK: John Wiley and Sons.

Williams, T. (1999) The Need for New Paradigms for Complex Projects. *International Journal of Project Management*, 17, pp. 269–73.

2

Communicate, Communicate, Communicate

The problem with communication ... is the illusion that it has been accomplished.

Attributed to George Bernard Shaw (1856–1950)
Author, Nobel Laureate

Communication was a word used by almost every project leader we interviewed. A general manager from the defence industry used a wonderful metaphor – 'like water to a plant!'

> *In a nutshell, the principle that I live by is let your communication be like water to a plant. Communication is a positive leading quality for project performance. It starts and stops with it. If you water it, it grows. Once it starts growing, you provide support. But communication, even though it's the very soft side of things, if it's not there, or wrong, the plant dies, or if you water it too much, it floods the plant and can kill it as well. So it has to be the right amount, pitched correctly, to the right client, if it's a seedling growing or if it's a full grown plant. Know who you're talking to and frame your communication that way. Interview 55 GM.*

Many authors have noted that communication is central to leadership (see for example, Awamleh and Gardner, 1999; Den Hartog and Verburg, 1997; Frese et al., 2003; Kirkpatrick and Locke, 1996; Riggio et al., 2003; Shamir et al., 1994; Spangler and House, 1991; Towler 2003). 'Communication' is the most widely used word in management and remains the toughest to achieve effectively. What does effective communication really mean for leadership of a complex project and what does it look and sound like?

Key Points in This Chapter:

- Communication to suit the complexity.

- Working with uncertainty.

- Communication networks.

- Leadership communication styles.

- Knowledge sharing.

- Information transfer during uncertainty.

- Communication planning.

Part 1: Communication to Suit the Complexity

In large projects communication effectiveness will be driven by needs for accuracy, timeliness and appropriateness of information throughout a complex network of layers of leadership. Formal processes and informal processes will be important. As the following project director, also working in the defence industry, argued:

> *Communication within the leadership layers is all important; if you get that, so much else follows, and all of the other ingredients that need to coalesce start to happen. If you say it will happen, people will understand and respond – you don't always know exactly what the response will be, but if communications are effective you can trust the response will be appropriate. Interview 54 PD.*

The ideas within this statement were reiterated in different ways by several project leaders from other industries.

COMMUNICATION TO FIT THE COMPLEXITY

When a project is complex the approach to communication is influenced by the source of project complexity and how the complexity is being managed. Complexity in large projects with tight deadlines, but reasonably short durations, may be due to non-linear effects and emergence occurring because an enormous number of activities are interlinked and interdependent. However, the vision might be very clear from the beginning and the outcomes defined clearly and early in the project life cycle. This kind of project suits a top-down approach that seeks to achieve communication that will concentrate on aligning people to goals quickly in order to maintain focus and motivation. It is a valid approach for many commercial organisations.

> *This programme was led by the sales area of the business and therefore the leader on the business side was the Executive General Manager from that area. You won't be successful doing that. It needs to be led from the top. You need a business strategy that will deliver the value and the aspirational targets you've defined in the next three years. The only way you'll be successful is if you lead it, drive it through your people, I'll drive it from the top down and you lead it from the top down and together we'll drive the change. I don't think they've got the stomach for what really needs to be done so I think they'll take an easier option where they define the high level strategy and some tactical pieces of work, and I do some work around the edges to ensure there's alignment between strategy and those pieces of work, and there's a bucket load of integration activity that needs to be done around every piece of work to ensure it's consistent and delivering across the entire business. Educating the executive is the biggest issue to be addressed in all significant change programmes. They generally have defined high level financial metrics and operational targets like increasing market share by 5 per cent without understanding what that means. I've also found a lot of them get together in their teams and build aspirational goals in isolation without validating the assumptions that sit under their aspirations. So they get two years down the track and wonder why it hasn't delivered what they expected it to deliver. Interview 63 CPM.*

Nevertheless, it is important to recognise that in spite of apparent control of communications from the top, when a project is characterised by complexity, communication is always multi-layered with temporary pockets that appear to be chaotic, as countless parties interact at many levels.

For projects that do not begin with clear goals, or goal-paths that are unable to be understood or are unknowable in the short term, what and how to communicate is more problematic. When clear goals and goal-paths are unknown, leaders may only be able to communicate vague vision statements, raising more questions than answers. It can be unwise to try to communicate certainty when none exists. Lack of apparent direction can be demotivating to followers and reduce trust in the leadership's ability to lead.

Or a project might be complex because it is exposed to external pressures, such as political upheavals or volatile market forces, which are difficult to predict with certainty. These kinds of complexity demand different approaches to communication. Leaders may need to have teams with several options developed, ready to act in the best direction as soon as the environmental constraints change.

Because communication is such an enormous topic the remainder of this chapter will address communication and information transfer under conditions of uncertainty when the landscape is far from stable.

Part 2: Working with Uncertainty

FEELINGS OF UNCERTAINTY – A USEFUL SIGN

Uncertainty is a feature of complex projects. As discussed in Chapter 1 the perception of uncertainty is the main means by which people can assess the level of complexity associated with the project. An impression that things are not quite right can be a very useful gauge for leaders. Although an impression is a subjective assessment, projects are fundamentally social undertakings. Therefore, subjective impressions can be meaningful 'measures' for gauging the level of complexity.

To some extent we can produce an objective measure of the complexity of an information system by ascertaining the number of relationships, the number of potential pathways, roadblocks and blind alleys (Girmscheid and Brockman, 2008; Moldoveanu, 2004; Williams, 2002; Simon, 1962). The more sophisticated scheduling software systems will help us to identify time critical components and potential bottlenecks. Beyond a certain point, however, this all becomes academic. We cannot predict with certainty how key decision-makers will behave at those bottlenecks. Will the executive team expedite the decision-making process or will personal political agendas get in the way, causing further delays? We cannot predict with certainty how a design team will respond to a particular design challenge. Will they produce a 'satisficing' solution (one that meets most of the criteria within the time and budget constraints) or will one key designer tenaciously insist on perfecting his/her part of the design no matter how much the others want to proceed with their parts of the design and no matter how much the project manager insists on keeping to the schedule? If the majority of people in the team are very uncertain about project outcomes then the project is moving into complex space, even if the cause of the uncertainty is due to lack of experience.

THE EMPHASIS HAS BEEN ON REDUCING UNCERTAINTY

The health sector has been the source of a great deal of research on the subject of communication under conditions of uncertainty, and with very good reason (for example, Babrow, Hines and Kasch, 2000). People who face life-threatening illnesses would be expected to be anxious, and the anxiety is closely coupled with feelings of uncertainty about their futures and the impact of their ill-health on their loved ones. Another source of research about uncertainty and communication comes from the organisational change literature; studies about the anxiety people feel when experiencing change during corporate mergers or acquisitions (for example, Kitchen and Daly, 2002). The other major field of research investigating anxiety under conditions of uncertainty is relationship research; why some people feel more anxious than others when meeting new people or joining a new team, for example (Kramer, 1993; Berger and Calabrese, 2006; Sunnafrank, 2006).

Much of this research is founded on the belief that uncertainty causes anxiety. This leads to the assumption that uncertainty is fundamentally a negative condition, an assumption that has been challenged by a number of authors (for example, Brashers, 2001; Giarni and Stahel, 1989; Eisenberg, 1987). People can experience anxiety under conditions of uncertainty that can affect decision-making (see Chapter 9) but uncertainty is also a catalyst for creative problem-solving. All breakthroughs have been characterised by obstacles (uncertainties) that had to be overcome.

MANAGING PERCEPTIONS OF UNCERTAINTY

An important leadership communication skill, therefore, centres around 'managing' perceptions of uncertainty, understanding when to help people to feel more comfortable and when to resist the urge to simplify matters. Managing uncertainty is vital to interpersonal communication (Berger and Bradac, 1982; Marris, 1996). There are many personal and interpersonal sources of uncertainty of which leaders must be aware. People may feel uncertain about goals but also their knowledge, their ability to deal with a situation, or their beliefs (Berger, 1995). In projects that involved a number of cultures, uncertainty can also stem from limited knowledge of the language or cultural practices (Goldsmith, 2001). Obviously there are some situations when reduction of uncertainty is the best course. However, dangers can result from routinely attempting to reduce perceptions of uncertainty. They nearly all relate to how information is filtered.

EFFECTS OF REDUCING UNCERTAINTY ON INFORMATION FLOW

Not Knowing What Information is Needed

Stemming from a reasonable desire to clarify the situation the leader or the leadership team can make unilateral decisions about what information they perceive to be important for the receivers. In a truly complex project we may not know what information will be needed when and by whom. Early filtering and simplification by a leadership team carries the danger of making enormous and far reaching mistakes if information that later proves to be vital is left out.

Stifling Creative Thinking

Uncertainty can breed anxiety but it can also stimulate creative thinking and be used productively to challenge a team, often bringing the additional advantage of unifying teams to overcome adversity – how do we get ourselves out of this situation? In order to arrive at innovative solutions we need 'rich' information rather than poor or thin information.

Reducing Trust

Another potentially damaging result from restriction of information, even if it is done with the 'best possible motives', is that people start to distrust the leadership. They might assume that there are hidden agendas. As the general level of trust is diminished people start to distrust not only information relating to a particular issue but there is a flow on effect to other information. Indeed, access to a narrow band of information might increase anxiety and distrust as people begin to believe that they are not being told all the facts. Distrust becomes endemic.

Promoting Dependency

Inappropriate filtering of information can also foster dependency in followers, the 'let's just wait until they tell us' syndrome.

SOME PEOPLE THRIVE ON UNCERTAINTY

How people cope with uncertainty varies. There is some anecdotal evidence that people who elect to follow certain career paths, like project management, may seek a degree of uncertainty in their working lives, and the challenges that brings. Reducing uncertainty for these people might mean taking the excitement out of the job.

> *It just got to be so routine – so boring that I quit and went to another organisation that tackled the big, interesting projects. Interview 30 PM.*

We do know that people have varying thresholds of ability to cope with uncertainty and individual thresholds are also affected by the situation. Ability to cope with uncertainty is influenced by prior experience, physiological health, social resources and external factors, like support (adapted from Smith and Liehr, 2008). And there is now evidence that people can increase their ability to cope with uncertainty through developing higher personal resilience. Leaders' communication styles can influence development of resilience in followers.

RESILIENCE IN UNCERTAINTY

One approach is to manage communication of uncertainty with the aim of building resilience in followers. Resilience is the process of adapting well in the face of uncertainty and adversity. What a leader communicates and how the leader chooses to communicate information plays a key role in helping teams and key stakeholders to remain resilient during times of uncertainty. Recent studies suggest there is no single means of maintaining equilibrium following highly aversive events, but rather there are multiple pathways to resilience (for example Luthar, et al., 1993). Some attributes seem to be clearly linked to resilience.

The most obvious is the personality trait of hardiness (Kobasa, Maddi, and Kahn, 1982) that helps to buffer a person's exposure to extreme stress. Hardiness is defined by scholars in terms of three dimensions:

- Being committed to finding a meaningful purpose in life.

- The belief that one can influence one's surroundings and the outcome of events.

- The belief that one can learn and grow from both positive and negative life experiences.

Armed with this set of personal constructs, hardy individuals have been found to appraise potentially stressful situations as less threatening than others who are less hardy, thus minimising the experience of distress. Hardy individuals are also more confident and better able to use active coping and social support, thus helping them deal with the distress they do experience (Florian, Mikulincer, and Taubman, 1995).

Positive emotion and laughter are other signs that indicate that people are coping with adversity (Keltner and Bonanno, 1997). Laughter used to be considered a form of unhealthy denial (for example, Bowlby, 1980). Recently, however, research has shown that positive emotions can help reduce levels of distress following aversive events either by quieting or undoing negative emotion (Fredrickson and Levenson, 1998; Keltner and Bonanno, 1997) and by increasing access to and support from other people.

A third, very interesting, finding is that resilience seems to be linked to the desire and practice of self-enhancement. The need for self-enhancement has been associated with benefits, such as high self-esteem, but in its extreme form it is also associated with other negative traits such as narcissism (Paulhus, 1998).

COMMUNICATING RESILIENCE

There are certain behaviours that a leader can encourage when communicating uncertainty to teams and other key stakeholders. Nevertheless, it goes without saying that a leader also has to model resilience in his/her interaction with others. The following behaviours have been identified as important in informing a leader's communication content and style during uncertainty:

Self-reflection

Self-reflection is the ability to stand back and look at our own thinking, emotions and behaviour, and articulate a reflective approach to problem-solving. Self-reflection invariably leads to inquiry. It is important that leaders demonstrate in their communication that they are *not* making ill-considered decisions.

Let's stand back and take a look at this.

Emotions

Identify what others are feeling about the issue and articulate it, thereby giving others permission to own their own feelings and talk about them – a great stress reliever. This process serves to normalise emotional responses to uncertainty and expose them so that they can be addressed, if necessary with expert help. Expressing emotions (without collapsing in a heap of tears) allows others to acknowledge their doubts and invites problem-solving dialogue.

> *I am feeling really unsure about some of this, is everyone here feeling the same way?*

Problem/Challenge Frame

When leaders expose their own feelings of doubt and insecurity, it is important that they are willing to take the next step and address the emotions from a problem-solving perspective. This models resilience as opposed to resignation or withdrawal. Guiding others in how to approach the problem also models problem-solving behaviour and coaches others in problem-solving skills.

> *I wonder if we start to look at this from this angle first ...? Or if one of the team comes up with a way forward, Great idea, let's explore that one and see where it takes us.*

Use of Appropriate Tools to Help Continue the Dialogue to Explore the Issue

This is a good time to introduce some simple problem-structuring tools that stimulate creative thinking and problem-solving (see *Tools for Complex Projects*, Remington and Pollack, 2007).

Mistakes

It is also very powerful, and it helps to breed a climate of trust, when leaders can own mistakes and setbacks and make it clear that they are finding ways of working with them.

> *I (we) made the wrong call on this one. Let's see what we can do better next time.*

Naming Correctly

Calling loss or misfortune by its correct name – naming the misfortune – has a very strong clarifying effect on the people involved. Finding the correct name for an action, loss or mistake enhances shared comprehension. Often people do not take appropriate action in response to an issue because it is couched in 'soft' words. Then either the impact becomes diluted because listeners or readers do not grasp the true meaning or people fail to act at all. People may use 'soft' language because they do not want to be the one to make the call, or they are trying to be nice. The problem remains and it can become a pattern.

Distinguish Past From Present

It is helpful to clearly distinguish the past from the present when describing the causes of uncertainty. During periods of uncertainty people may resort to stories of past events that might have had similar outcomes. We usually remember the disasters and they always make good stories. This can be misleading as the past events might have significant differences from the present situation. It is important that those aspects of the past that are relevant to the present situation are clearly separated from those that are not.

> *In 2003, we had a seemingly similar situation, but it differed from the situation we are facing now in the following ways … we shouldn't assume that we will have the same outcomes … however we do need to make sure we learn as much as possible from the bits that are relevant.*

MEANING AND PURPOSE

It is important to continue to emphasise the meaning and purpose behind the endeavour. This has a strong motivating effect as it keeps people focused on the overarching goals, the purpose for which they are there, even if the means of getting there is unclear at the time.

> *Remember we are here to do a job that is critical to the success of …*

USE EXAMPLES FROM THE PAST TO SUPPORT THE QUEST

Use examples of former struggles and explain how they were surmounted.

Some of you will remember that project we did in 1999 … We thought then that there was no way we could get there … But we did! We did it by …

COMMUNICATE TO BUILD RESILIENCE ACROSS ALL STAKEHOLDERS

Often we forget about building resilience amongst all the key project stakeholders, not just the project teams. It is easy to make the mistake of assuming that senior people automatically come to the project with high personal levels of resilience.

Generally speaking senior executive leaders do have high levels of personal resilience or they would not be where they are. However, like many other attributes, resilience can be context specific. The project might require a very different area of experience and expertise than that held by executive leaders or key stakeholders. Or this project might be just one of many they have to deal with and therefore they have not given the project the attention it needs. Lack of knowledge is closely linked with feelings of anxiety; with anxiety comes reduced levels of resilience. Very few people have been closely involved with a truly complex project.

Part 3: Communication Networks

Our interviews clearly demonstrated that the leaders in all types of complex projects consciously used informal as well as formal networks to make sure communication was effective. Complex projects involve complex communication networks. The idea that communication is simply filtered down from a top leadership echelon has long been contested. Much of the real work happens *despite* the formal communication structure (Krackhardt and Hanson, 1993).

In a complex environment it's very difficult to have a total view, and a lot of people put effort and time into establishing a total view, and by the time they get that total view, things have changed. That's the worst feature of a complex project. You have to accept that there's a degree of incompleteness in the view, but if you communicate effectively, you have a reason to trust the responses will be appropriate. Communications in a complex environment are complex in their own right. It has to be tailored. One of the great mistakes that project managers can make

is when they're dealing with lot of different stakeholders they try to
shoehorn them into one type of communication. Interview 54 PD.

SOCIAL NETWORKS

Informal communication in complex projects can be understood in terms of
complicated social networks. A social network is made up of 'nodes' (people or
groups of people) who are tied together by specific types of interdependency,
such as friendship, common interests, financial exchange, beliefs, knowledge
or status.

Social communication networks operate on many levels from small groups
up to nations and they play a critical role in the way problems are solved. The
density of the network can be used as a measure of *social capital*. Social capital
is generated from the number and strength (importance) of the ties or links
within a network.

Leaders need a great deal of social capital, which means a rich communication
network involving each of the many layers of a complex project. Figure 2.1
(simplified) illustrates some of the informal connections that existed on a large
infrastructure project in the Middle East. When we investigated the project we
found that there were many informal connections between project leaders and
other key players but there were significant ones that were absent, between the
major contracting firm A and local supplier, for example. In a culture where
informal communication is vital to being able to conduct business effectively
this meant that relationships with local suppliers were never properly
established. Also there were no effective informal communications with the
client organisation, with the result that the client did not really appreciate some
of the challenges that the project team were facing. Some members of the project
team who were sourced locally did have connections but not at a high enough
level for the host country's stratified society. The project team attempted to
operate by establishing 'single points of contact' however they neglected to
'assist' the official points of contact through a strategically developed informal
network.

USE OF INFORMAL COMMUNICATION NETWORKS

Informal networks can cut through formal reporting procedures to jump-start
stalled initiatives and meet extraordinary deadlines. Tapping into informal
communication networks allows the leadership to tap into established norms.
This can be important when lobbying for support over an issue.

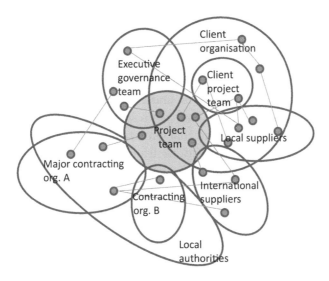

Figure 2.1   Simplified map of informal communication pathways in project under stress

Speaking about a very large infrastructure project in the Middle East, a project director's major concern was finding out 'who really makes the decisions' (Interview 32 PD). In some societies, particularly those which stress group rather than hierarchical decision-making, decision-making might more accurately be ascribed to a *complex web of influencers* rather than a single, indentifiable focal point.

PROBLEMS WITH INFORMAL NETWORKS

Informal networks can just as easily sabotage best-laid plans by blocking communication and stirring up opposition to proposed actions or by simply not functioning at optimal levels of efficiency. Also informal communication networks organise themselves on the basis of like attracts like. As Aristotle explained in the Rhetoric Nichomachean Ethics – people 'love those who are like themselves' (Aristotle, 1934, p. 1371). Relying on informal networks for communication exchange might also have the effect of favouring established norms with a stultifying effect on transport of new information that might challenge the status quo.

UNDERSTANDING INFORMAL COMMUNICATION NETWORKS

Krackhardt and Hanson (1993) found that leaders and managers often thought they had a good understanding of their informal communication networks but when they investigated leaders' understanding of the informal networks operating in their organisations they were surprised by how far from reality their pictures were. They argue that understanding the informal networks is so vitally important that they advise leaders to take some time to map the informal networks in their organisation. They found that as leaders became more sophisticated in analysing communication networks they could use them to spot a number of patterns.

Extending recommendations by Krackhardt and Hanson (1993) to the project environment, the following informal networks might be worthwhile investigating:

Advice Network

This informal network shows the prominent players on whom others depend for advice to solve problems and provide technical information. These networks reveal the most influential players in the project teams and within the stakeholder groups.

Trust Network

This informal network shows which team members and other stakeholders share political information and back one another in a crisis. They can reveal the causes of non-routine problems such as poor performance by individuals and teams.

Work Communications Network

This informal network reveals those people who talk about work-related matters on a regular basis. They can help to identify gaps in information flow, inefficient use of resources and failure to generate new ideas.

Power and Influence Communications Network

Who has the power might already have been investigated as part of the stakeholder analysis for the project, nevertheless the decision to add this in the form of a network has been shown to be of great assistance when power and influence are diffuse, when it is difficult to find the key decision-makers.

Maps can be constructed from simple anonymous questionnaires, which include questions such as:

Who do you talk to about work?

Whom do you go to for help and advice?

Whom would you recruit to support a proposal or idea of yours?

Whom would you trust to keep in confidence your concerns about a work issue?

Constructing power and influence network maps usually requires much devious detective work and many informal conversations.

As many of these network maps contain potentially sensitive information, names of people and groups should always be coded, with codes kept securely elsewhere, or preferably, in the heads of a couple of trustworthy people associated with the project. There are some spectacular examples of leaks with severe political ramifications when uncoded information about key players has been leaked to the press or to competitors. The many embarrassing leaks in recent years attest that the adage 'what hasn't been written hasn't been said' only applies if the message has not been recorded.

COMMON PATTERNS FOUND IN INFORMAL COMMUNICATION NETWORKS

Krackhardt and Hanson (1993) also found that when leaders and managers were asked to construct the informal communications networks themselves from their own knowledge, their versions were often disparate from those constructed from surveys of staff and generally connections were not as rich. Leaders often did not realise that subcultures associated with advice, trust and work communication were different.

They found that as leaders became more sophisticated in analysing communication networks they could use them to spot a number of patterns (Krackhardt and Hanson, 1993).

Imploded Communication Networks

These apply to teams or groups that have few links to other groups. Imploded groups neglect to cultivate relationships with other groups with possible serious implications about how effectively information is integrated. Or managers can guard connections with other groups by denying team members access to other groups. Thus all information is filtered through the manager with potentially limiting affects on the team's performance.

Once detected, leaders can intervene to make sure that the manager's hegemony is broken down, for example, by partnering with the manager in meetings to make sure that information is more widely networked.

External Communication Preferences

Sometimes team members communicate with members of other groups but do not communicate amongst themselves. This can be due to friction within the team or simply due to individual work-communication styles. For example, an engineer who likes to work alone on highly specialised problems (without 'unnecessary' contact with other team members) might happily communicate with another specialist engineer from another team.

If the problem is team friction, some external help to identify the causes and rebuild the team might be needed. If the cause is due to the communication preference of a key specialist, intra-team communication can be improved dramatically when people become aware and respect individual members' communication needs and collaborate to support them. Not everyone is a natural team player! Not everyone sees value in being part of a team! Sometimes the remedy is as simple as getting the specialist to agree to a couple of short, well-structured, weekly meetings so that s/he can inform the others in the team about progress and issues, allowing them the freedom to work alone the rest of the time.

Fragile Communication Structures

In these kinds of communication patterns information can be exchanged only with one or two other teams, whilst effectively ignoring other teams, with the result that information exchange is biased.

Often these patterns emerge because of past associations or similarity in knowledge and expertise. Discipline-specific teams generally find it easier to communicate with others from the same discipline, so they do just that.

> *Speaking about an international tax evasion project, the project manager reported that '... the police teams all talk to each other internationally, the Government corporate, markets and financial services regulators all talk to each other, the taxation departments of the various countries all talk to each other as do the finance people and the IT people ... because they all talk the same language ... but it is really difficult to get the police to talk to the customs people and the tax people and the finance people and the IT people ... in this project the problem is less to do with the fact that they are from different countries and more to do with professional focus and they all have their own jargon.' Interview 50 PM.*

In this kind of situation a key task for the project leader is 'structuring the dialogue'. Providing opportunities for cross-fertilisation of information and making it easier for people to exchange information. It is important, however, not to be fooled into thinking that once information exchange is achieved through facilitation that it will continue. It rarely does. Effective information exchange, especially between teams from different disciplines, requires constant attention by the project leader.

Holes in the Network

A map might reveal gaps where communication ties would be expected but do not exist. The cause might be personality differences, physical barriers or knowledge differences. This requires investigation, diagnosis and action to remedy.

Unilateral Dependency

Krackhardt and Hanson (1993) describe these as 'bow-ties' – a network in which many people are dependent upon a single person but not on each other.

Either the result of a key person acting as gatekeeper, or the 'hero syndrome' in which one person becomes the problem-solver or trouble-shooter, this situation is detrimental to effective communication. If the gatekeeper or 'hero' leaves, connections between isolated groups might collapse. If they remain they might become overstressed, further reducing effective communication.

A great deal of research has established the influence of central figures in informal networks.

There is some evidence that being at the centre of a dense communication network makes it easier to diffuse technical innovation (Czepiel, 1974). Often referred to as a socio-gram, a map of an informal network can be a useful exercise in revealing potential problems and also opportunities associated with informal communication links.

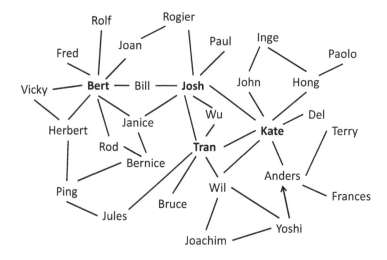

Figure 2.2   **A socio-gram indicating informal communication networks. A diagram like this can be overlaid with fields of influence, either as in Figure 2.1 or as suggested by Krackhardt and Hanson (1993)**

Part 4: Leadership Communication Style

Although communicative behaviours can be regarded as part of a leader's personality, what exactly constitutes this vital aspect has not really been properly investigated until recently. Most research separates human-oriented leadership from task-oriented leadership. Researchers have concluded that human-oriented leadership is mainly communicative, while task-oriented leadership is much less so (Penley and Hawkins, 1985). This makes sense because building relationships implies communication that promotes warmth, concern and trust. Leadership that is task-oriented on the other hand, is much more concerned with the content of the information rather than the style of communication.

If, as this book argues, project leadership is different in certain very distinct ways from leadership in general, project leadership would be expected to be more task-oriented, because of the goal-centred nature of projects themselves. Therefore, it is reasonable to assume that this task orientation might be reflected in the kind of communication style used by project leaders, with a tendency to focus on information content rather than relationship building. However, in our study we found the reverse to be the case.

LEADERS TALKED ABOUT PEOPLE RATHER THAN TASK

One very important observation from our research was that the majority of the leaders we interviewed were what might be called, 'human-oriented'. This impression was verified by both researchers and was based purely on the nature of the communication between the leaders and our research team. For example the references to people – relationships, teams, team members and clients – and stories of interactions with these people vastly outweighed the references to task, structure and organisation. The term 'human-oriented' applied to all interviewees, and some leaders exhibited characteristics that could also be called 'charismatic' (see Chapter 14).

Both charismatic and human-oriented leadership styles are expressed through the communication styles chosen by the leader. In contrast, task-oriented leadership is much less communicative and is regarded by some more as a managerial rather than a leadership style (see for example Daft, 2003; McCartney and Campbell, 2006).

VERBAL COMMUNICATION STYLES

De Vries et al., (2009) investigated verbal communication style by analysing the words used during communication. From this they developed communication style dimensions which they labelled:

- Expressiveness

- Preciseness

- Niceness

- Supportiveness

- Verbal aggressiveness

- Assuredness

- (Expressed) emotional tension (or reversed, assuredness)

- Argumentativeness.

A more recent study by De Vries et al., (2010) found that human-oriented leadership is strongly associated with the communication style *supportiveness*, to a lesser extent with leader's *expressiveness* and, as would be expected, does not match at all with the category labelled *verbal aggressiveness*. In contrast charismatic leadership communication was found to be *assured*, *supportive*, *precise*, and *verbally non-aggressive*. *Argumentativeness* may also work for charismatic leaders. De Vries et al., (2010) found that the quality of argumentativeness was more related to charismatic leadership. Some aspects of charismatic leadership styles refer to visionary and intellectually stimulating leadership, which may involve an argumentative communication style.

Table 2.1   A summary of the relationship between communication style and leadership style based on various findings (De Vries et al., 2010; Awamleh and Gardner, 1999; Pennebaker et al., 1996)

Communication style	Most frequently associated with leadership style		
(de Vries et al., 2010)	Charismatic	Human-oriented	Task-oriented
Argumentativeness	Yes	No	Somewhat
Assuredness	Yes		Yes
Preciseness	Yes		Yes
Supportiveness	Yes	Yes	Possibly
Expressiveness	Varies with context	Somewhat	
Niceness	No	No	No
Emotional Tension			Somewhat
Aggressiveness	Somewhat		Somewhat

Surprisingly De Vries et al., (2010) found 'expressiveness' also to be unrelated to charismatic leadership. It is possible that charismatic leaders do not need to be particularly expressive to reach their desired effect as less expressive but notable charismatic leaders, such as Mahatma Gandhi, have shown. On the other hand, cultural preferences might be important. The subjects from this study were in the Netherlands where people value a less 'expressive' style of interaction than for instance people from Southern Europe (Pennebaker et al., 1996). Also using a different sample, Awamleh and Gardner (1999) found that an expressive (enthusiastic) delivery style had a much stronger effect than the content of the speech particularly when articulating a vision.

De Vries et al., (2010) also found that task-oriented leadership is much less strongly related to communication styles than charismatic leadership and human-oriented leadership. Task-oriented leaders are characterised by assuredness and, more than the other styles, by preciseness. However, they also found that in contrast with human-oriented and charismatic leadership, task-oriented leadership is also characterised by the presence of (some) verbal aggressiveness. An explanation of this finding might simply be the focus of communication, which for task-oriented leaders is content (for example, rules, planning, and goal-setting) as opposed to relationship (for example, friendliness, trust, and inspiration) for human-oriented leadership and charismatic leadership communication.

PRECISENESS

De Vries et al., (2010) also found that a leader's preciseness in communication positively influenced how they were perceived as a leader and this applied to any of the three leadership styles. Precise, or structured, communication is regarded as an important leadership communication skill in many disciplines (Yedidia et al., 2003).

SUPPORTIVENESS

No matter what style leaders' exhibited, supportiveness seems to be the most important communication attribute across the board that is associated by followers with effective leadership. It seems that if leaders communicated supportiveness to followers it compensated for other failings (De Vries et al., 2010).

ASSUREDNESS

Under conditions of uncertainty leaders may have to rely on more general 'conversation models' (Van der Molen and Gramsbergen-Hoogland, 2005) to deal with different situations. In a complex project there are often few fixed rules for leaders to follow to help them handle specific situations in a precise way. Hence communicating with self-assuredness, a characteristic that De Vries et al., (2010) found to be linked with both human-oriented and charismatic leadership, might be an important way of promoting confidence during uncertainty. Assuredness comes from a strong sense of self and appears be more related to the leader's ability to communicate that aspect of their personality rather than the content of the message itself.

CLARITY ABOVE DIRECTION – AN IMPORTANT FINDING

There is evidence, particularly with respect to the political arena (Dewan and Myatt, 2008), that clarity of communication is more important than communicating direction. This is an important finding in relation to complex projects because there will be times when the direction is unclear. Given a choice, they found that people tended to follow the leader who communicated clearly in preference to the leader who had the best understanding of direction but was less clear in enunciating that direction.

Under conditions of uncertainty, leaders might be well placed to focus on expressing themselves with clarity, even if they don't have the answers. It seems that being able to state clearly and concisely that you don't know where the project is going is preferable to having a good plan but communicating it in a complicated or unclear manner. In this respect the De Vries et al., (2010) category of *preciseness*, which is important for all leadership styles, confirms findings by Dewan and Myatt (2008) and, in some respects, those of Awamleh and Gardner (1999), about the importance of clarity.

BREVITY AND REPETITION

Dewan and Myatt (2008) also emphasise the importance of brevity which is related to conciseness and clarity. The message must be repeated in the same format at every venue and across different media and it must be short enough so that people remember it and for it not to become distorted with repetition.

SPEECH IMAGERY AND METAPHOR

Naidoo and Lord (2008) found that imagery in speech was more likely to be used by leaders that were described by followers as charismatic. This was because speech imagery connects more effectively with people's emotional experiences. Charismatic leaders tend to be seen as having a 'vision for the future' Awamleh and Gardner (1999).

FRIENDLINESS

Friendliness is often associated with follower satisfaction but niceness was not necessarily associated with effective leadership. On the other hand this communication style can be associated with performance, but only in some instances, and it might also encourage dependency in some followers.

Table 2.2   Essential communication styles associated with productivity in conditions of uncertainty, amalgamating findings by Awamleh and Gardner (1999); Dewan and Myatt, (2008); Naidoo and Lord (2008)

Communication styles and uncertainty	Very important	Less relevant
Clarity	Yes (all styles)	
Direction		Less important than clarity if direction unclear
Brevity of message/ preciseness	Yes (all styles)	
Repetition of key message	Yes (all styles)	
Speech imagery and metaphor	Yes (for communicating project vision)	
Argumentativeness		Only works with charismatic styles
Supportiveness, niceness	Yes (strongly associated with performance but not with perceptions of effective leadership)	Exception (not productive with dependent followers)

Part 5 Knowledge Sharing

KNOWLEDGE SHARING AND LEADERS' COMMUNICATION STYLES

Knowledge sharing has been defined as the process where individuals mutually exchange their (tacit and explicit) knowledge and jointly create new knowledge (Van den Hooff and De Ridder, 2004). Knowledge management in the project environment is a vast subject which is beyond the scope of this book. However, leaders' communication styles do seem to influence how knowledge is shared in a project.

> You've got to target communication to the audience that you're working with ... have alternatives to put up and encourage people to explore those with you, having hopefully got them to agree that existing thinking is sub-optimal in terms of what we've got to do. I think it's just a style that you have, you're not just sitting there mute, you're actually expressing a view and you're prepared to challenge an alternative view if you don't agree with it. You don't just sit there and nod and accept it. If you don't think something is appropriate or right, you say so, and explore it together. You're trying to establish a rapport and a relationship, and building on that. Interview 65 PM.

Complex projects often move very fast and decision-making is critically dependent upon effective knowledge sharing. Knowledge sharing is relevant to communication style because the exchange of knowledge assumes a communication process. Even when people have ready access to the Internet or a firm's intranet, people are more likely to turn to other people for information than to impersonal sources (Levin and Cross, 2004).

Leadership styles may play a central role in inspiring and supporting knowledge sharing behaviours (see De Vries et al., 2006; Srivastava et al., 2006). Knowledge sharing has been found to be highest with human-oriented leaders. Knowledge sharing behaviours have also been found to relate to higher perceptions of leader performance, satisfaction with the leader, and higher levels of subordinate team commitment and satisfaction (Srivastava et al., 2006).

Encouragement of self-management, a concept akin to empowering leadership, has been found to be very strongly related to human-oriented and charismatic leadership (De Vries et al., 2002). Srivastava et al., (2006) found that empowering leadership had a positive effect on knowledge sharing, which suggests that both human-oriented and charismatic leadership styles will be related to knowledge sharing.

Additionally, the preciseness of the leader's communication together with leader's supportiveness, were the most important factors in whether a subordinate was able to obtain knowledge from a leader. Consequently, leader's preciseness seems to be an important construct. This is consistent with the importance of clarity, discussed earlier in this chapter (Dewan and Myatt, 2008).

Supportive communication by a leader enhances the capacity of the subordinate to offer knowledge to the leader and as well as obtain knowledge from the leader. On the other hand the quality of assuredness in a leader was related to perceived leader performance, satisfaction with the leader, and subordinate's team commitment, but *not* to knowledge sharing. Having a leader who is very certain may help to give a team direction and purpose, but it might also cancel some of the positive creative effects that knowledge sharing in uncertainty can bring. Or a leader who is very certain might inhibit potentially valuable conversations with subordinates about their own uncertainties or anxieties about the project, thus limiting problem-solving opportunities.

Table 2.3   Leaders' communication styles and knowledge sharing tendencies, adapted from studies by De Vries et al., 2002, 2006; Srivastava et al.; 2006 Dewan and Myatt (2008)

Leader's communication style	Capacity to offer knowledge to the leader	Capacity to receive knowledge from leader	Associated leadership style
Communicating empowerment	Yes	Yes	Charismatic and Human-oriented leadership
Preciseness, clarity		Yes	All styles
Supportiveness	Yes	Yes	Charismatic and Human-oriented leadership
Assuredness	No	No	Charismatic and Task-oriented leadership

TEAM COMMUNICATION STYLE AND KNOWLEDGE SHARING

The communication style of a team member is likely to have an effect on the willingness and eagerness of team members to share knowledge with each other. In another study by De Vries et al., (2006), team members were found to be more likely to be willing to share knowledge with those team members who were more agreeable and extraverted in their communication style. Specifically they found that team members' agreeableness, team members' extraversion, job satisfaction and an individual's performance beliefs all have a positive effect on the willingness to share knowledge with team members. Eagerness to share knowledge with peers is mainly determined by one's own performance beliefs and job satisfaction and the extraversion of one's team members.

There are several possible reasons for these findings. In a team whose members have more agreeable communication styles, people are probably more likely to be willing to share knowledge with each other as an extension of normal social communication. A willing attitude, in turn, may set into motion a cycle of reciprocity, in which team members are more likely to exchange (that is both donate and collect) knowledge with each other. Reciprocity (a cycle in which one favour is returned by another favour) may explain the relationship between agreeableness and willingness to share knowledge. Trust also plays an important role in the willingness to share knowledge (Inkpen and Tsang, 2005; Reagans and McEvily, 2003). Agreeable communication styles may also engender trust in the recipient. As would be expected trustworthiness has been found to increase the likelihood to cooperate and share knowledge (Insko, et al., 2005). More generally agreeableness creates a positive impression in the recipient of the communication (Williams et al., 1998) and may create stronger emotional attachment and commitment to the relationship (Reagans and McEvily, 2003), both of which stimulate a willingness to reciprocate.

Both talkativeness and enthusiasm are common components of an extraverted communication style. Groups that have an extraverted communication style are more likely to generate the sort of enthusiasm that is present in transformational teams (Avolio et al., 1996). Transformational behaviours, in turn, may generate a number of positive effects, such as extra effort and motivation of other employees (Podsakoff et al., 1990; Yammarino and Bass, 1990). Thus this type of team communication may be contagious, inspiring a similar style in others (Cherulnik et al., 2001). Consequently, team extraversion may engender talkativeness and enthusiasm in the other team members and increase their willingness to share own experiences and knowledge with the extravert communication partner.

De Vries et al., (2006) also found that both job satisfaction and self-rated performance were related to willingness and eagerness to share knowledge. They suggest that this could be explained by the fact that these two attributes are associated with performing well on satisfying tasks. Self-esteem has been found to be related to altruism and a desire to help and mentor others (Pierce and Gardner, 2004). Mentoring others is a key activity in knowledge sharing.

Enthusiasm and status are probably the key reasons behind willingness to share knowledge without direct gain or return (De Vries et al., 2006). Performing well means one is an expert in the particular knowledge area, and the desire to confirm and maintain the status of expert is strong. For individuals who are willing to share, these mechanisms may be much less important. However, as De Vries et al., (2006) point out, enthusiasm is not enough because individuals who are not necessarily team oriented can also be enthusiastic about their work. They argue that willingness to share may be more strongly associated with orientation toward the group and reciprocity in knowledge sharing. Therefore, high self-esteem about work might be more likely to inspire greater eagerness to share knowledge than job satisfaction by itself. People who perform better because they possess valuable information and skills are more likely to be in a position to share knowledge (Borgatti and Cross, 2003). Additionally, a high level of self-esteem associated with job performance may stimulate people to want to share their knowledge in order to show their mastery of the subject matter, irrespective of whether they get any information in return.

Part 6: Information Transfer During Uncertainty

INFORMATION CAN BE USED, DISTORTED AND MISUSED

Information can be used to manipulate uncertainty in a desired direction (to decrease, increase or maintain feelings of uncertainty). Information gathering, for example, helps people in differentiating options, finding options and creating options (Langer, 1994). People seek information in order to increase their knowledge of a situation or to confirm or reject their current understanding of a situation. Information is used to help people to distinguish between options but it also helps to decrease uncertainty by allowing people to develop meaning (Brashers, 2001). On the other hand feelings of uncertainty can be increased by information that contradicts the current state of knowledge or beliefs (Frey et al., 1996; Kruglanski, 1989). As successful politicians know, in order to reduce uncertainty, information does not need to be absolutely correct but it does need to be coherent for the people concerned. Knowledge that people hold with certainty is often inaccurate (Planalp and Honeycutt, 1985).

SELECTING INFORMATION DURING UNCERTAINTY

How people select information is also important during uncertainty. Some sources may have greater credibility than others or might be simply chosen because they are available, whether it be on the web or from the next person encountered. Preferences for different sources and types of information may be linked to various forms of uncertainty (Teboul, 1994; Morrison, 1995). When it is not easy to obtain information or there are competing tasks people often become quite selective in what they seek (Brashers, et al., 2006).

One relatively common reaction when people feel overwhelmed or distressed by the uncertainty is avoidance. Whether conscious or unconscious avoidance maintains the uncertainty at one level, but at another creates an illusion of increased certainty. Selection can include selective attention (Ratneshwar et al., 1997), selective ignoring (Mishel, 1988), withdrawal from social interaction and thought suppression (Wenzlaff and Wegner, 2000), intentional forgetting (Golding and MacLeod, 1998) or discounting negative information, or discrediting the source . Comparing the current situation with failures in the past is also a way of avoiding information.

According to Merry (1995), people can also buffer themselves by developing routines. This builds a perception of certainty to protect themselves from the complexity. Two common behaviours are stereotyping (Kramer, 1999) or reverting to familiar processes to provide structure. Returning to well understood structures and processes can be a very useful way of reducing anxiety due to uncertainty, however, it is important that leaders do not respond to uncertainty by applying more rules and procedures and increasing constraints. In a turbulent environment it is important that the leader monitors the relevance of structure, balancing the anxiety reducing effect of structure and processes with dependence on structure that might stultifydevelopment of important new knowledge.

Organisational crisis research has confirmed that ambiguity is regularly used as a strategic weapon (Eisenberg, 1987) by putting up smoke screens that are intended to obscure, confuse or distract people's attention away from some aspects of an issue or towards information that is more favourable (Messick, 1999). As some interviewees have revealed, a high level of sensitivity to organisational politics is essential (see Chapter 8).

Effective leadership manages uncertainty by being aware of the level of uncertainty and consciously using communication behaviours and messages to increase or decrease the uncertainty (Albrecht and Adelman, 1987; Ford et al., 1996). These might include (adapted from Brasher, 2001):

- Providing access to information.

- Collaborating to gather information.

- Validating information.

- Assessing the credibility of information sources.

- Comparing and evaluating conflicting sources.

- Identifying inconsistencies in information.

- Vigilant of our propensity for sublimating goals, avoiding information and so on.

- Providing opportunities for venting.

- Encouraging people to focus on the key issues or questions.

- Reappraising the level of uncertainty without trivialising it.

- Using firm rather than hesitant communication styles.

- Being aware of smokescreens, confusing for distracting information.

FORMAL INFORMATION EXCHANGE BETWEEN PROJECT PARTNERS

Especially in early stages of cooperation, relationships between project partners are frequently characterised by relatively high levels of ambiguity and uncertainty (Carson et al., 2006), particularly at an inter-organisational level. Problems of understanding can be aggravated when cooperating parties come from disparate backgrounds, work in different industries, or hold dissimilar belief systems (Sutcliffe and Huber, 1998). In these situations parties tend to develop distinct and separate interpretations and understandings of the same phenomena (Porac et al., 2002; Vaara 2003) and the likelihood for misinterpretations and misunderstandings increases (Shankarmahesh et al., 2004).

Vlaar et al., (2006) suggest that formal information exchange may function as one means to make sense of differences, enabling participants in collaborative relationships to cope with problems of understanding. For example, contracting processes may be consciously used with the intention of increasing mutual understanding (Blomqvist et al., 2005). Kaghan and Lounsbury (2006: 260) argue that formal written contracts provide a structure 'within which on-going relationships can proceed sensibly over time'. Blomqvist et al., (2005: 502), for example, found that a global machine and equipment supplier and a small metal engineering company 'got to know each other through the lengthy contracting process', indicating that this process enabled them to make sense of their partner.

In projects that involve more than one organisation it has been shown that formal communications processes have several important functions (adapted from Vlaar et al., 2006):

- Formal communication processes help participants from different organisations or cultures to focus their attention, thereby affecting their ability to make sense of their partners, the relationships in which they are engaged and the collaborative contexts in which these are embedded.

- Formal communication processes help participants from different organisations to articulate, deliberate, and reflect upon issues, thereby affecting their ability to make sense of their partners, the relationships in which they are engaged and the collaborative contexts in which these are embedded.

- Formal communication processes not only signify the start of the relationship but also help to maintain interaction among participants in relationships that include more than one organisation.

- Formal communication processes can also reduce the impact of individual biases and judgement errors.

However, under conditions of uncertainty formal communication processes can have negative consequences. Because formal processes help to make situations seem more comprehensible and controllable than they really are, sense-making may be stopped too early due to an illusion of management control (Brown 2004; Yakura 2002). Furthermore, excessively formal communication processes may serve to constrain thinking (Snell 2002), so that subsequent sense-making activities are restricted within decision-making boundaries that are too narrow (Ring 2000). In these situations, formal processes can allow teams to ignore or overlook critical factors because the focus of attention is either too rigid or inappropriate (Hill and Levenhagen, 1995; Sutcliffe and McNamara, 2001). As Weick (2001, p. 460) argues, 'once a sense of the situation begins to develop, that sense can be terribly seductive and can resist updating and revision'. It may also result in a loss of systemic focus – seeing the trees but not the forest (Putnam 2003).

Apart from normal organisational requirements associated with procurement and risk, formal communication processes can be usefully employed in complex projects, to prolong negotiations in order to allow sense-making to take place and relationships to develop between parties. However, leadership teams should be careful that the processes do not seek to simplify the complexity too early by channelling thinking and contributing to risk patterns later in the project that might be much more difficult to manage.

Part 7: Communications Planning

Finally all projects and, above all, complex projects need rigorous communications planning. Even though the plan will be altered as the complexity requires, the very act of planning encourages participants to analyse and plan to manage communications risks. It is vital preparation.

> *One important thing that contributed to the success of such a complex project – we recognised that for a big complex project with multiple parties you need a very complex communications plan. Even though every project manager will say comms is vital, if you ask them have they planned the comms or how they intend to measure comms performance they look at me blankly. I tell our project managers: 'I want you to do your communications planning to the same rigorous standard of that you use for technical things'. Interview 47 GM.*

ASSESSING COMMUNICATIONS RISKS

Invariably communications issues are cited when things go wrong. Nevertheless, in spite of the stress on project communications planning in the literature, it is rarely given the attention it needs in practice. The high levels of uncertainty expected in a complex project means that a huge degree of effort must be placed on planning the communications for the project. In this sense communications refers to the full gamut of project communications from formal reporting to informal chats face-to-face or via electronic media. The following check-list provides a basis for questions that might inform communications planning for a complex project, taking into account the expected sources of complexity. The questions take the form of a risk assessment but with the focus on communications. The communications plan should address the risks identified.

As you can see from the list of questions below communications planning is a central activity that should drive other processes, rather than being left 'in the lap of the Gods'.

Table 2.4   Questions to assist communications planning

Potential communication barriers	Questions for discussion when constructing the plan	Some prompt questions to answer when planning communications strategies	Measures
Structural/ organisational barriers.	Are there groups who, for various reasons, might block or hold up communications? Are there processes which might block or hold up communications? When are they likely to affect the schedule?	Do we need to develop relationships with blockers in advance to ascertain their needs and what might prevent them from expediting communication (such as issues management)? Do we need to rethink or renegotiate process or procedures that might get in the way of smooth issues resolution?	What indicators will tell us that communications are effective in the short term and in the long term? What indicators should we be alert to that might give us early warning of issues associated with communications? What will we see, hear or sense?

Table 2.4 *Continued*

Potential communication barriers	Questions for discussion when constructing the plan	Some prompt questions to answer when planning communications strategies	Measures
	Is more than one organisation involved in delivering the project? What differences in work practices exist between the collaborating organisations? Do work practices differ substantially from one organisation to another? Do employees have different expectations about workloads, deadlines, timeliness and different ways of working?	How can we align reporting requirements to suit each organisation's communication protocols? How can we come to agreement about differences in expectations about working methods? How can we resolve differences in expectations about work practices?	
	Are approval pathways clear? *In many complex projects, particularly those involving multiple owners or international consortia it is difficult to ascertain who has sign-off. Knowledge can be withheld for political and cultural reasons or because the pattern of accountability within one or more of the organisations is historically diffuse.*	Can we identify who has sign-off at for each element that requires approval? If we cannot identify with confidence who has sign-off for each element (stage or issues), with whom to we need to develop informal relationships in order to understand the pattern of influence affecting the project or programme? What are their communication requirements (format, content, medium)?	

Table 2.4   *Continued*

Potential communication barriers	Questions for discussion when constructing the plan	Some prompt questions to answer when planning communications strategies	Measures
Dysfunctional behaviour.	Are there any individual (or group) behaviours that might inhibit communications? These could include: personnel who might restrict information in order to retain power for themselves; people who are defensive of a position and construct barriers to keep work for themselves; groups, or influential individuals who do not trust others and might try to ostracise or marginalise them; people who distrust the professional expertise of others associated with the project. It is important to remember, however, that some behaviours which might be seen as deliberately disruptive are due to misunderstandings – linguistic or cultural.	How do we identify potential dysfunctional behaviours? Who do we need to talk to (informally) in the other participating organisations in order to identify potential disruptive behaviours? How do we address these behaviours before they disrupt the project? What do we do if any of these behaviours are encountered? Who needs to be notified? Where can we get help if disruptive behaviours are encountered?	

Table 2.4   *Continued*

Potential communication barriers	Questions for discussion when constructing the plan	Some prompt questions to answer when planning communications strategies	Measures
Linguistic barriers.	Does the project use only one language for communication? Even when project participants use the same language there can be a number of barriers to communication. *Interviewees have noted communications difficulties in projects that involve the United Kingdom, the USA, Australia, New Zealand and Canada. All countries have English as a national language and in spite of this there are many examples of misunderstanding due to local jargon or colloquialisms. By way of a trivial example of how English usage has changed globally, car boot in the UK and Australia is known as a trunk in the USA. A trunk in the UK and Australia is a large container that was once used in travel but nowadays is used as a piece of storage furniture.*	What national differences can we find/be alert to with regard to: colloquial expressions, professional jargon, meanings of words and phrases? Do we expect all participants to be expert in the selected language for the project? What standard of language skill is required? Do we require both written and spoken expertise with the chosen language? What actions do we need to take if people in the project cannot understand? What special considerations and actions do we need to take to eliminate potential misunderstanding? What training is needed for project personnel to help them communicate more effectively with each other?	
	Is the project trans-national and cross-lingual?	How will translation be achieved to make sure that all parties have a full understanding of what the other parties really mean?	

Table 2.4   Continued

Potential communication barriers	Questions for discussion when constructing the plan	Some prompt questions to answer when planning communications strategies	Measures
Cultural barriers.	What cultural communication barriers are expected that might inhibit development of productive working relationships based on trust? *People can infringe cultural norms without knowing. For example, English (as spoken in the UK, Australia and New Zealand) is a relatively polite language because of the number of modal operators used in a sentence. For example: 'would you mind tossing me that file please'. These cultures 'soften' the command or request with extra words like 'would you mind' and 'please'. Other language cultures might not use so many modal operators and the sentence becomes contracted to: 'give me that file'. Not intended to be impolite from the speaker's point of view but it could be considered quite rude from the position of the receiver. Many non-English speakers learn their English from watching American TV shows. When they come to work in other English speaking countries they do not realise that their use of English is not as effective as it could be.*	How do we communicate that we wish to build a trusting relationship with the other parties? Are project personnel and key stakeholders aware of cultural differences that might affect relationships and communications? What training is needed for project personnel to help them understand different cultural practices and expectations? How are newcomers to the project informed about what is culturally acceptable or not for this project?	

Table 2.4   *Continued*

Potential communication barriers	Questions for discussion when constructing the plan	Some prompt questions to answer when planning communications strategies	Measures
	Are teams communicating mainly electronically rather than face-to-face?	How do we initiate and manage communications in order to build relationships and understanding between teams that will communicate electronically? How will we monitor and support team communications? How will we ensure that information transmitted electronically is received and interpreted as the sender intended?	
	What cultural differences exist with regard to deference to and access to senior executives? *Some cultures (national and organisational) support an open-door policy. Other cultures prefer a more hierarchical access structure which might result in approvals taking much longer to obtain than with 'open door' access.*	Is our access style to senior executive leadership compatible with those of our partners? What allowances in our plan (schedule and communications) do we need to make to accommodate differences in access to decision makers?	
	Do we/they live up to what we/they espouse? *For example, some organisations might state that they have an open door policy but the reality is quite different.*	With regard to communications do we do what we say we do? Do we mislead newcomers to our project by our rhetoric?	

Table 2.4   *Continued*

Potential communication barriers	Questions for discussion when constructing the plan	Some prompt questions to answer when planning communications strategies	Measures
Time related issues.	Does the project involve multiple time zones?	How do we make communications effective when key parties are distributed over more than one time zone?	
	Do the participating organisations or groups operate using different time protocols?	Do participating organisations have differing work practices around time – arrival at meetings, availability in the office, availability after office hours? Do participating groups have different expectations about deadlines? What conversations should we have with participating groups and organisations in order to moderate differences in expectations about time and timeliness?	
	Does the project involve geographically distributed teams?	What protocols need to be in place to ensure that teams can effectively exchange information in a timely manner across time zones?	
Reporting protocols.	Are all parties agreed on what needs to be reported and the frequency?	Is the protocol for communicating issues, exceptions and risks fully understood by all parties? How do we check to see that reporting protocols are being adhered to?	

Table 2.4   *Continued*

Potential communication barriers	Questions for discussion when constructing the plan	Some prompt questions to answer when planning communications strategies	Measures
Technical.	What technical barriers exist to information exchange?	Do all parties have the required level of access to communication tools and technology? Are Internet and software protocols in alignment? Are all parties skilled in using the technology?	
Security.	Are all parties agreed on security protocols?	Do these protocols cover verbal as well as written information exchange? How do we check that security protocols are being adhered to?	
Knowledge sharing.	What barriers are there to rapid and effective knowledge sharing? *Barriers can take the form of vertical or horizontal silos or the actions of individuals. Barriers to knowledge sharing can also occur due to fear of criticism or due to impending litigation.*	How do we make sure that important information is transferred to all people who need accessas quickly as possible? How best can leaders learn about issues that might affect the project from: team members, external stakeholders, suppliers and contractors? If we have addressed all the barriers above, are there any additional barriers that might prevent knowledge required for timely problem-solving to be transferred to the appropriate people?	

Table 2.4　　*Concluded*

Potential communication barriers	Questions for discussion when constructing the plan	Some prompt questions to answer when planning communications strategies	Measures
Flexibility	Does the communication plan allow for flexibility and emergence? *A complex project morphs and changes in response to a wide variety of stimuli. Communication needs will likewise change as the project progresses.*	Are mechanisms in place that will allow us to make rapid adjustments to communications protocols, tools and approaches in response to the project needs as they emerge? What processes, attitudes and tools do we have to assist us to make sure that the communications strategies are kept up to date with the changing nature of the project or programme?	

In Summary

Communications matters. This chapter is large because communications is the most frequently cited cause of project failure and was most frequently cited by the senior project people who took part in the study. From various leadership perspectives, the chapter addressed some, but by no means all, aspects of project communications as experienced in complex projects environments.

Adverse effects of reducing uncertainty on information flow include:

- Not knowing what information is needed.

- Stifling creative thinking.

- Reducing trust.

- Promoting dependency.

Managing communication under uncertainty is related to building enough resilience in team members and key stakeholders to support them through conditions of uncertainty.

Communicating to build resilience is vital under conditions of uncertainty. It can be communicated by leaders through their ability to model:

- Self-reflection.

- Acknowledging and addressing emotions.

- Using a problem/challenge frame.

- Use of appropriate tools to help continue the dialogue to explore the issue.

- Acknowledging and learning from mistakes.

- Naming issues correctly.

- Distinguishing past from present.

- Articulating meaning and purpose.

- Communicating to build resilience across all stakeholders, including senior executive stakeholders.

Communication can be understood in terms of formal and informal networks. The section covers:

- Use of informal communication networks.

- Mapping informal networks to discover gaps and barriers.

- Sensitivity and security.

- Common patterns found in informal communication networks.

Effective leadership communication is shown to be related to the following aspects of communication style:

- Preciseness.

- Supportiveness.

- Assuredness.

- Clarity above direction.

- Brevity and repetition.

- Argumentativeness may work for charismatic leaders.

- Speech imagery and metaphor.

- Friendliness (with some reservations).

Knowledge sharing is affected by communication and communication styles. This section discusses:

- Leadership styles and knowledge sharing.

- Team communication style and knowledge sharing.

Information transfer for complex projects is discussed, in terms of how information is perceived during periods of uncertainty.

Positive and negative outcomes from formal communications are explored.

Finally, a section on communications planning in complex projects emphasises that much more effort needs to be placed on planning the communications for the project. A list of questions to assist communications planning is provided.

References and Further Reading

Albrecht, T.L. and Adelman, M.B. (1987) *Communicating Social Support.* Thousand Oaks, CA: Sage.

Aristotole (1934 trans.) *Rhetoric. Nichomachean Ethics.* Trans. Rackman. Cambridge: Harvard University Press.

Avolio, B.J., Jung, D.I., Murry, W. and Sivasbramaniam, N. (1996) Building Highly Developed Teams: Focusing on Shared Leadership Process, Efficacy, Trust, and Performance. In: Johnson, D.A. and Beyerlein, M.M. (eds) *Advances in Interdisciplinary Studies of Work Teams: Vol. 3. Team leadership*, pp. 173–209. Greenwich, CT: JAI Press.

Awamleh, R. and Gardner, W.L. (1999) Perceptions of Leader Charisma and Effectiveness: The Effects of Vision Content, Delivery, and Organizational Performance. *The Leadership Quarterly*, 10(3), pp. 345–373.

Babrow, A.S., Hines, S.C. and Kasch, C.R. (2000) Managing Uncertainty in Illness Explanation: An Application of Problematic Integration Theory. In: Whaley, B. (ed.) *Explaining Illness: Research, Theory and Strategies*, pp. 41–67. Hillsdale, NJ: Erlbaum.

Baldwin, T.T. (1992) Effects of Alternative Modeling Strategies on Outcomes of Interpersonal-skills Training. *Journal of Applied Psychology*, 77(2), pp. 147–154.

Berger, C.R. (1995) Inscrutable Goals, Uncertain Plans, and the Production of Communicative Action. In: Berger, C.R. and Burgoon, H.M. (eds) *Communication and social influence processes*, pp. 1–28. East Lansing: Michigan State University Press.

Berger, C.R. and Bradac, J. (1982) *Language and Social Knowledge.* London; Edward Arnold.

Berger, C.R. and Calabrese, R.J. (2006) Some Explorations in Initial Interaction and Beyond: Toward a Developmental Theory of Interpersonal Communication. *Human Communication Research*, 1(2), pp. 99–112.

Blomqvist, K., Hurmellina, P. and Seppänen, R. (2005) Playing the Collaboration Game Right: Balancing Trust and Contracting. *Technovation*, 25, pp. 497–504.

Borgatti, S.P. and Cross, R. (2003) A Relational View of Information Seeking and Learning in Social Networks. *Management Science*, 49(4), pp. 432–445.

Bowlby, J. (1980) *Loss: Sadness and Depression: Vol. 3. Attachment and Loss.* New York: Basic Books.

Brashers, D.E. (2001) Communication and Uncertainty Management, *Journal of Communication*, International Association, Sept. pp. 477–497.

Brashers, D.E., Hsieh, E., Neidig, J.L. and Reynolds, N.R. (2006) Managing Uncertainty About Illness: Health Care Providers as Credible Authorities. In: R.M. Dailey and B.A. Le Poire (eds), *Applied Interpersonal Communication Matters*, pp. 219–240. New York: Peter Lang.

Brown, A.D. (2000) Making Sense of Inquiry Sensemaking. *Journal of Management Studies*, 37(1), pp. 45–75.

Brown, A.D. (2004) Authoritative Sensemaking in a Public Inquiry Report. *Organization Studies*, 25(1), pp. 95–112.

Carson, S.J., Madhok, A. and Wu, T. (2006) Uncertainty, Opportunism and Governance: The Effects of Volatility and Ambiguity on Formal and Relational Contracting. *Academy of Management Journal*.

Cherulnik, P.D., Donley, K.A., Wiewel, T.S.R. and Miller, S.R. (2001) Charisma is Contagious: The Effect of Leaders' Charisma on Observers' Affect. *Journal of Applied Social Psychology*, 31, pp. 2149–2159.

Czepiel, J.A. (1974) Word of Mouth Processes in the Diffusion of a Major Technical Innovation. *Journal of Marketing Research*, 11, pp. 172–180.

Daft, R.L. (2003) *Management* (6th ed.). Cincinnati, OH: South-Western.

Den Hartog, D.N. and Verburg, R.M. (1997) Charisma and Rhetoric: Communicative Techniques of International Business Leaders. *The Leadership Quarterly*, 8(4), pp. 355–391.

De Vries, R.E., Bakker-Pieper, A., Alting Siberg, R., Van Gameren, K. and Vlug, M. (2009) The Content and Dimensionality of Communication Styles. *Communication Research*, 36, pp. 178–206.

De Vries, R.E., Van der Hooff, B. and De Ridder, J. (2006) Explaining Knowledge Sharing. The Role of Team Communication Styles, Job Satisfaction, and Performance Beliefs. *Communication Research*, 33(2), pp. 115–135.

De Vries, R.E., Bakker-Pieper, A. and Oostenveld, W. (2010) Leadership = Communication? The Relations of Leaders' Communication Styles with Leadership Styles, Knowledge Sharing and Leadership Outcomes. *Journal of Business Psychology*, 25, pp. 367–380.

De Vries, R.E., Roe, R.A. and Taillieu, T.C.B. (2002) Need for Leadership as a Moderator of the Relationships Between Leadership and Individual Outcomes. *The Leadership Quarterly*, 13(2), pp. 121–137.

Dewan, T. and Myatt, D.P. (2008) The Qualities of Leadership: Direction, Communication and Obfuscation. *The American Journal of Political Science Review*, 102(3), pp. 351–368.

Driskill, L.P. and Rymer, J. (1986) Uncertainty: Theory and Practice in Organizational Communication. *Journal of Business Communication*, 23, pp. 41–56.

Eisenberg, E.M. (1987) The Strategic Uses of Ambiguity in Organizations. *Communication Monographs*, 51, pp. 227–242.

Florian, V., Mikulincer, M. and Taubman, O. (1995) Does Hardiness Contribute to Mental Health During a Stressful Real-life Situation? The Roles of Appraisal and Coping. *Journal of Personality and Social Psychology*, 68, pp. 687–695.

Ford, L.A., Brabrow, A.S. and Stohl, C. (1996) Social Support and the Management of Uncertainty: An Application of Problematic Integration Theory. *Communication Monographs*, 63, pp. 189–207.

Fox, C.R. and Irwin, J.R. (1998) The Role of Context in Communication of Uncertain Beliefs. *Basic and Applied Social Psychology*, 20, pp. 57–70.

Frese, M., Beimel, S. and Schoenborn, S. (2003) Action Training for Charismatic Leadership: Two Evaluations of Studies of a Commercial Training Module on Inspirational Communication of a Vision. *Personnel Psychology*, 56(3), pp. 671–697.

Friedman, S.M., Dunwoody, S. and Rogers, C.L. (1999) *Communicating Uncertainty: Media Coverage of New and Controversial Science*. Mahwah, NJ: Erlbaum.

Fredrickson, B.L. and Levenson, R.W. (1998) Positive Emotions Speed Recovery from the Cardiovascular Sequelae of Negative Emotions. *Cognition and Emotion*, 12, pp. 191–220.

Frey, D., Schulz-Hardt, S. and Stahlberg, D. (1996) Information Seeking Among Individuals and Groups and Possible Consequences for Decision-making in Business and Politics. In: Whitte, E.H. and David, J.H. (eds) *Understanding Group Behaviour*, pp. 211–225. Mahwah, N.J. : Erlbaum.

Giarni, O. and Stahel, W.R. (1989) *The Limits to Certainty: Facing Risks in the New Service Economy*. Dordrecht, The Netherlands: Kluwer Academic.

Girmscheid, G. and Brockman, C. (2008) The Inherent Complexity of Large Scale Engineering Projects. Project Perspectives. *The Annual Publication of International Project Management Association*, pp. 22–26.

Golding, J.M. and MacLeod, C.M. (eds) (1998) *Intentional forgetting: Interdisciplinary Perspectives*. Mahwah, NJ: Erlbaum.

Goldsmith, D.J. (2001) A Normative Approach to the Study of Uncertainty and Communication. *Journal of Communication*, 51(3), pp. 514–533.

Gouldner, A.W. (1960) The Norm of Reciprocity: A Preliminary Statement. *American Sociological Review*, 25, pp. 161–178.

Hill, C.A. (2001) A Comment on Language and Norms in Complex Business Contracting. *Chicago-Kent Law Review*, 77, pp. 29–57.

Hill, C.A. and Levenhagen, M. (1995) Metaphors and Mental Models: Sensemaking and Sensegiving in: Innovative and Entrepreneurial Activities. *Journal of Management*, 21(6), pp. 1057–1074.

Inkpen, A.C. and Tsang, E.W. (2005) Social Capital, Networks, and Knowledge Transfer. *Academy of Management Review*, 30(1), pp. 146–165.

Insko, C.A., Kirchner, J.L., Pinter, B., Efaw, J. and Wildschut, T. (2005) Interindividual-intergroup Discontinuity as a Function of Trust and Categorization: The paradox of Expected Cooperation. *Journal of Personality and Social Psychology*, 88, pp. 365–385.

Kaghan, W.N. and Lounsbury, M.D. (2006) Articulation Work, Collective Mind, and the Institutional Residue of Organizational Artifacts. In: *Artifacts and organizations*. Rafaelli, A. and Pratt, M.G. (eds), Mahwah, NJ: Lawrence Erlbaum.

Keltner, D. and Bonanno, G.A. (1997) A Study of Laughter and Dissociation: Distinct Correlates of Laughter and Smiling During Bereavement. *Journal of Personality and Social Psychology*, 73, pp. 687–702.

Kirkpatrick, S.A. and Locke, E.A. (1996) Direct and Indirect Effects of Three Core Charismatic Leadership Components on Performance and Attitudes. *Journal of Applied Psychology*, 81, pp. 36–51.

Kitchen, P.J. and Daly, F. (2002) Internal Communication During Change Management. *Corporate Communications: An International Journal*, 7(1), pp. 46–53.

Kobasa, S.C., Maddi, S.R. and Kahn, S. (1982) Hardiness and Health: A Prospective Study. *Journal of Personality and Social Psychology*, 42, pp. 168–177.

Krackhardt, D. and Hanson, J.R. (1993) Informal Networks: The Company Behind the Chart. *Harvard Business Review*, July-August. Reprint no. 93406.

Kramer, M.W. (1993) Communication and Uncertainty During Job Transfers: Leaving and Joining Processes. *Communication Monographs*, 60, pp. 178–198.

Kruglanski, A.W. (1989) *Lay Epistemics and Human Knowledge: Cognitive and Motivational Bases*. New York: Plenum.

Langer, E. (1994) The Illusion of Calculated Decisions. In: Schank, R.C. and Langer, E. (eds) *Beliefs, Reasoning and Decision-making: Psycho-logic in Honor of Bob Abelson*, pp. 33–53. Hillsdale. N.J: Erlbaum.

Levin, D.Z. and Cross, R. (2004) The Strength of Weak Ties You Can Trust: The Mediating Role of Trust in Effective Knowledge Transfer. *Management Science*, 50(11), pp. 1477–1490.

Luthar, S.S., Doernberger, C.H. and Zigler, E. (1993) Resilience is not a Unidimensional Construct: Insights from a Prospective Study of Inner City Adolescents. *Development and Psychopathology*, 5, pp. 703–717.

Marris, P. (1996) *The Politics of Uncertainty: Attachment in Private and Public Life*. New York: Routledge.

McCartney, W.W. and Campbell, C.R. (2006) Leadership, Management, and Derailment: A Model of Individual Success and Failure. *Leadership and Organization Development Journal*, 27(3), pp. 190–202.

Merry, U. (1995) *Coping with Uncertainty: Insights from the New Sciences of Chaos, Self-organization and Complexity*. Westport, CT: Praeger.

Mishel, M.H. (1988) Uncertainty in Illness. *Image: Journal of Nursing Scholarship*, 20, pp. 225–232.

Moldoveanu, M. (2004) An Intersubjective Measure of Organisational Complexity: A New Approach to the Study of Complexity in Organizations. *Emergence: Complexity and Organization*, 6(3), pp. 9–16.

Morrison, E.W. (1995) Information Usefulness and Acquisition During Organizational Encounter. *Management Communication Quarterly*, 9, pp. 131–155.

Naidoo, L.J. and Lord, R.G. (2008) Speech Imagery and Perceptions of Charisma: The Mediating Role of Positive Affect. *The Leadership Quarterly*, 19, pp. 283–296.

Paulhus, D.L. (1998) Interpersonal and Intrapsychic Adaptiveness of Trait Self-enhancement: A Mixed Blessing? *Journal of Personality and Social Psychology*, 74, pp. 1197–1208.

Penley, L.E. and Hawkins, B. (1985) Studying Interpersonal Communication in Organizations: A Leadership Application. *Academy of Management Journal*, 28(2), pp. 309–326.

Pennebaker, J.W., Rimé, B. and Blankenship, V.E. (1996) Stereotypes of Emotional Expressiveness of Northerners and Southerners: A Cross-cultural Test of Montesquieu's Hypotheses. *Journal of Personality and Social Psychology*, 70(2), pp. 372–380.

Pierce, J.L. and Gardner, D.G. (2004) Self-esteem Within the Work and Organizational Context: A Review of the Organization-based Self-esteem Literature. *Journal of Management*, 30, pp. 591–622.

Planalp, S. and Honeycutt, J. (1985) Events that Increase Uncertainty in Interpersonal Relationships. *Human Communication Research*, 11, pp. 593–604.

Podsakoff, P.M., MacKenzie, S.B., Moorman, R.H. and Fetter, R. (1990) Transformational Leader Behaviors and Their Effects on Followers' Trust in Leader, Satisfaction, and Organizational Citizenship Behaviors. *The Leadership Quarterly*, 1, pp. 107–142.

Porac, J.F., Ventresca, M.J. and Mishina, Y. (2002) Interorganizational Cognition and Interpretation. In: *The Blackwell Companion to Organizations*. J. Baum (ed.) pp. 579–598. Oxford: Blackwell.

Putnam, L.L. (2003) Dialectical Tensions and Rhetorical Tropes in Negotiations. *Organization Studies*, 25(1), pp. 35–53.

Putnam, L.L. and Cooren, F. (2004) Alternative Perspectives on the Role of Text and Agency in Constituting Organizations. *Organization*, 11(3), pp. 323–333.

Ratneshwar, S. Warlop, L., Mick, D.G. and Seeger, G. (1997) Benefit Salience and Consumers Selective Attention to Product Features. *International Journal of Research and Marketing*, 14, pp. 245–259.

Reagans, R. and McEvily, B. (2003) Network Structure and Knowledge Transfer:
    The Effects of Cohesion and Range. *Administrative Science Quarterly*, 48,
    pp. 240–267.
Riggio, R.E., Riggio, H.R., Salinas, C. and Cole, E.J. (2003) The Role of Social and
    Emotional Communication Skills in: Leader Emergence and Effectiveness.
    Group Dynamics: Theory, Research, and Practice, 7, pp. 83–103.
Ring, P.S. (2000) The Three T's of Alliance Creation: Task, Team and Time.
    European Management Journal, 18, pp. 153–162.
Roloff, M.E. (1987) Communication and Reciprocity Within Intimate
    Relationships. In: Roloff, M.E. and Miller, G.R. (eds) *Interpersonal Processes:
    New Directions in Communication Research*, 14, pp. 11–38. Newbury Park, CA:
    Sage.
Rutter, M. (1987) Psychosocial Resilience and Protective Mechanisms. *American
    Journal of Orthopsychiatry*, 57(3), pp. 316–331.
Shamir, B., Arthur, M.B. and House, R.J. (1994) The Rhetoric of Charismatic
    Leadership: A Theoretical Extension, a Case Study, and Implications for
    Research. *The Leadership Quarterly*, 5, 25–42.
Shankarmahesh, M.N., Ford, J.B. and LaTour, M.S. (2004) Determinants of
    Satisfaction in Sales Negotiations with Foreign Buyers: Perceptions of US
    Export Executives. *International Marketing Review*, 21(4), pp. 423–446.
Simon, H.A. (1962) *The Architecture of Complexity*. Reprinted in H. Simon, 1982.
    The Sciences of the Artificial. Cambridge, MA: MIT Press.
Smith, M.J. and Liehr, P.R. (2008) *Middle Range Theory for Nursing*, 2nd Ed.
    Springer Publishing.
Snell, R.S. (2002) The Learning Organization, Sensegiving and Psychological
    Contracts: A Hong Kong Case. *Organization Studies*, 23(4), pp. 549–569.
Spangler, W.D. and House, R.J. (1991) Presidential Effectiveness and the
    Leadership Motive Profile. *Journal of Personality and Social Psychology*, 60,
    pp. 439–455.
Srivastava, A., Bartol, K.M. and Locke, E.A. (2006) Empowering Leadership
    in Management Teams: Effects on Knowledge Sharing, Efficacy, and
    Performance. *Academy of Management Journal*, 49(6), pp. 1239–1251.
Sunnafrank, M. (2006) Predicted Outcome Value During Initial Interactions.
    A Reformulation of Uncertainty Reduction Theory. *Human Communication
    Research*, 13(1), pp. 3–33.
Sutcliffe, K.M. and McNamara, G.M. (2001) Controlling Decision-making
    Practice in Organizations. *Organization Science*, 12(4), pp. 484–501.
Sutcliffe, K.M. and Huber, G.P. (1998) Firm and Industry as Determinants of
    Executive Perceptions of the Environment. *Strategic Management Journal*, 19,
    pp. 793–807.

Teboul, J.C.B. (1994) Facing and Coping with Uncertainty During Organizational Encounter. *Management Communication Quarterly*, 8, pp. 190–224.

Towler, A.J. (2003) Effects of Charismatic Influence Training on Attitudes, Behavior, and Performance. *Personnel Psychology*, 56(2), pp. 363–381.

Van den Hooff, B. and De Ridder, J.A. (2004) Knowledge Sharing in Context: The Influence of Organizational Commitment, Communication Climate and CMC use on Knowledge Sharing. *Journal of Knowledge Management*, 8(6), pp. 117–130.

Van der Molen, H.T. and Gramsbergen-Hoogland, Y.H. (2005) *Communication in Organizations: Basic Skills and Conversation Models*. Hove, East Sussex: Psychology Press.

Vaara, E. (2003) Post-acquisition Integration as Sensemaking: Glimpses of Ambiguity, Confusion, Hypocrisy, and Politicization. *Journal of Management Studies*, 40, pp. 859–894.

Vlaar, P.W.L., Van den Bosch, F.A.J. and Volberda, H.W. (2006) Coping with Problems of Fomalization as a Means to Make Sense. *Organizaton Studies*, 27, pp. 1617–1638.

Weick, K.E. (2001) *Making Sense of the Organization*. Oxford, UK: Blackwell.

Wenzlaff, R.M. and Wegner, D.M. (2000) Thought Suppression. *Annual Reviews of Psychology*, 51, pp. 59–91.

Williams, S., Weinman, J. and Dale, J. (1998) Doctor-patient Communication and Patient Satisfaction: A Review. *Family Practice*, 15, pp. 480–492.

Williams, T. (2002) *Modelling Complex Projects.* John Wiley and Sons, Ltd.

Yakura, E.K. (2002) Charting Time: Timelines as Temporal Boundary Objects. *Academy of Management Journal*, 45(5), pp. 956–970.

Yammarino, F.J. and Bass, B.M. (1990) Transformational Leadership and Multiple Levels of Analysis. *Human Relations*, 43, pp. 975–995.

Yedidia, M.J., Gillespie, C.C., Kachur, E., Schwartz, M.D., Ockene, J., Chepaitis, A.E. et al., (2003) Effect of Communications Training on Medical Student Performance. *JAMA: Journal of the American Medical Association*, 290(9), pp. 1157–1165.

Yukl, G. (1999) An Evaluation of Conceptual Weaknesses in Transformational and Charismatic Leadership Theories. *The Leadership Quarterly*, 10(2), pp. 285–305.

3

Cultivate Effective Teams from Project Teams to Executive Board

I don't feel that the conductor has real power. The orchestra has the power, and every member of it knows instantaneously if you're just beating time.
                    Itzhak Perlman, conductor, composer and musician.

Complex projects involve macro-leadership. They are large, temporary, organic systems, like orchestras. Symphony orchestras comprise musicians who have reached the peaks of their musical talent. They are all of soloist standard but still must work as an integrated team. There needs to be just the right balance of players and instruments. Orchestras are regularly reconfigured to suit the piece to be performed. A symphony by Tchaikovsky features massive augmentation of woodwind and brass sections compared with a Mozart symphony, which has a more intimate sound. An orchestra also has several levels of leadership; the public see the conductor and the concert master, but most orchestra leaders will say that the real leadership happens off-stage, before the performance.

For a complex project the leadership needs to be local, timely, and appropriate. Many teams of people work either in synergy or not. The leadership exercised by the various teams is different and specific, but without effective leadership at all key levels of the project, it will not work. The success of the project rarely rests with one leader.

> *I won't say leader because it's the construct; multi faceted invariably, without exception, on successful projects I've seen ... where there's general acknowledgement that the project achieved what it intended to achieve. Interview 54 PD.*

This chapter draws not only from interviews with successful project leaders but also from our observations of how project leaders appear to work in practice to build and nurture teams at all levels of the project, from the individual work teams to teams at executive level.

In both our research studies (2004, 2005 and 2010, 2011) building and sustaining the right teams for the leadership task was a frequently cited theme. The chapter structure follows the main sub-themes from our interviews.

Key Points in This Chapter:

- Match the people to the project.

- Build trusting relationships (with all stakeholders).

- Avoid micromanagement.

- Energise the executive.

Part 1: Match the People to the Project

PERSONALITY AND BEHAVIOUR STYLES

It was surprising to discover that many leaders we interviewed engaged in a kind of psychological profiling, even if subconscious, when putting teams together. One managing director we interviewed, a project manager with many years of experience, described how he and his team consciously went about selecting people for a very sensitive, high-risk and extremely complex project, not just on the basis of their experience and education, but after an astute assessment of their personalities, strengths and weaknesses:

> We had to find someone to lead the project who could work with a diverse group of academics from different research backgrounds and who would also have credibility with environmental lobby groups, like Greenpeace. We found the right person but, after a number of interviews we realised that he might become over-zealous, to the point of aggression, if he didn't like the way things were going. It was critical that we got all the various groups, government, commercial, local

residents and environmental groups to work together harmoniously under his leadership. We kept him very well informed – we worked to understood his motivations and drivers and we were careful about who we put with him. He always looked good because we supported him. We paired him with an older,more experienced guy, a project manager who really knew the ropes, but someone he would respect and we gave him team members who were not only competent but who were also peacemakers by nature. We made sure that he was never in a position where his weaknesses would be exposed. There was always someone there to step in if he went too far. Interview 46 GM.

Some might think that this kind of profiling is Machiavellian; that it comes from the belief that individuals can be sacrificed for the good of the project. However, the people who worked on the project described above have very positive memories of the project and the project was hailed as a great success. The challenge for many executive project leaders is how to get the best out of people by allowing them to work to their strengths and not be forced to expose their weaknesses. That the workplace includes people who exhibit extreme and often antisocial personalities, including many people who are in senior leadership positions, is now well documented by research (Clements and Washbush, 1999; Maccoby, 2000; McCabe, 2005; Burke, 2006; Kellerman, 2004a, 2004b). However, many of these people have skills that are essential to a project. If the counterproductive aspects of their behaviour can be accommodated in some way, it can be of benefit to all.

Most work places do not address these kinds of differences effectively. We were interested that several of the project leaders interviewed paid so much attention to how they put teams together, not just in terms of skill sets and expertise, but also in terms of personality; how people would work together. When a project is complex team members must be able to work effectively to support each other because the project is only as strong as its weakest link.

We had encountered this kind of informal psychological profiling in our earlier research (Helm and Remington, 2004a, 2004b). Some executive project leaders placed great emphasis on constructing teams. Taking into account the characters and foibles of key people, they carefully matched them with people who would work harmoniously with them. Particularly in the construction industry, matching clients' personalities with project managers' personalities seems to be a regular practice.

My last boss actually said the hardest part in managing projects for her was matching us [project managers] to clients. Not our ability to do the job, we could all do the job, we did it in different ways, but she said matching the right project manager to the right client guarantees its success. If I get that wrong, she said, you'll have angst the whole way through. Interview 2 PM.

You have to be compatible. We have the luxury of being a large organisation - if we start off with a client or sponsor and if the project manager's not compatible with the client then we can change. Because we have enough project managers to be able to chop and change. Interview 6 PM.

It is important to note that compatibility did not exclude the desire by senior project managers to be challenged (see Chapter 4) by their leaders. However when compatibility and behaviour differences were not considered, the consequences could be serious as this segment demonstrates. Projects led by this executive sponsor had very high staff turnover as project managers struggled to meet their KPI's:

Adherence to basic social norms on the part of the executive sponsor, like not having tantrums with customers ... it's the extreme self-centredness that's both a curse and a blessing. It's handy when you want something done, but otherwise not ... [The executive sponsor], if he wanted someone in his team to come into his office would pick up the hands free and say 'here boy' and hang up. It's like he's treating people like a dog. Interview 3 PM.

There are strong links between personality and communication style which can affect information exchange and, in the following case, willingness to provide information to the executive sponsor. As discussed in Chapter 2, information is filtered when the recipient is unwilling or unable to engage, with potentially serious consequences for the project. In the following case the project manager avoided unnecessary contact with the executive sponsor and in so doing the project did not have the benefit of potentially important information that the executive sponsor might have been able to provide:

I provide the documentation reporting and status reports as he requires. Other than that, I'm not going to go and pester him. You don't wake up a sleeping tiger do you? Interview 10 PM.

Team selection practice that takes into account how people interact requires exceptional perception. Constructing compatible teams is generally much easier to achieve when project teams are dedicated to the project. Effective project team selection seems to be more difficult to achieve in large functional organisations. Nevertheless a focus on team harmony at all levels affecting the project must become priority for senior leadership . The incentives are there for executive leaders to be more proactive in this respect as clear evidence now directly links happiness at work to productivity (Pryce-Jones, 2010).

UNDERSTAND PERSONALITIES, STRENGTHS AND WEAKNESSES

Because projects are usually discipline specific and many are highly technical in nature, specialist engineers or IT specialists may find themselves leading complex projects. Leading a complex project is a higher order undertaking that requires a broad range of mature interpersonal capabilities. Lack of awareness by executive leadership of personality differences can lead unbalanced teams like this example noted by a general manager in defence:

> When they looked at themselves they found they had a whole organisation of ME's [the Belbin (2010) category for a person who has a high preference for analysis and judgement] so they know their problem very well but they lack innovator/creators that can design their way out and they lack the organisers who can get people to go in one direction – hugely unbalanced workforce – self-selected group of ex-military people ... Interview GM 47.

Individual behavioural and learning characteristics matter enormously in how well a team functions at any level of an organisation. Many organisations train people in various personality instruments but, in my experience, few organisations actively use the knowledge to select teams in the way described earlier. Several interviewees mentioned that they actively used various personality instruments or models in helping them frame their daily interactions with people and teams.

In over 40 years working on projects, at senior management level in a range of organisations and later teaching Masters of Project Management students, I have found two instruments to be particularly useful: Dr. Meredith Belbin's Team Role Profile (Belbin, 1981, 2010) inventory helps leaders to understand how to compose teams and work groups; and the Strength Deployment Inventory based on Dr. Elias Porter's Relationship Awareness Theory (Porter,

1950,1953; 1973/1996), a very easily remembered instrument that helps leaders to understand personality differences, work style preferences, communication styles and conflict patterns from the dual perspectives of behaviour and motivation. Practice with instruments like these helps leaders to observe and anticipate personality imbalances within teams and across organisational boundaries.

Whichever instruments are chosen, they must become part of the language of the team and the organisation. A pervasive and active language that identifies and celebrates differences in personality, work style preferences and capability helps leaders to make appropriate team choices. Shared understanding of instruments, like those by Belbin (1981) and Porter (1973) give key people the knowledge and the permission to create teams and manage others so that personal strengths are highlighted and weaknesses supported and not exposed unnecessarily.

MAKE SURE THE SKILL SETS ARE APPROPRIATE IN PROJECT TEAMS

Complex projects operate outside organisational boundaries. Skill sets need to be specific to the project. Referring to a very complex project in the oil and gas sector, that ended up in trouble, the senior project manager was vehement about this point. Those responsible for assigning personnel to the project had no idea of the special skills required for a complex project of this size. In spite of repeated requests from the project manager, the executive leaders' lack of experience in delivering a project of this complexity in-house meant that at an organisational level there was little appreciation of the special skills sets needed. For example, purchase officers were assigned to the project when project controllers were requested.

> You can't use asset officers who process invoices as project control officers ... The project had to be managed hourly or at least daily and not remotely ... lack of contract competency was an issue ... they would issue instructions without an understanding of the consequences. Interview PM 45.

As experienced project managers are aware, project control requires advanced knowledge of techniques like Earned Value Management that allow reporting of work achieved and forecasting of work to be done in a way that accurately links scope, time and budget. Reporting and forecasting may be required on a daily basis when a project is complex. Organisational monthly reporting schedules do not address project requirements. Things move much too fast in a complex project and leaders need to be able to respond quickly with accurate, up to the minute, information. Assigning people with the right skill set is critical.

MAKE SURE THE TEAM STRUCTURE IS FLEXIBLE

> *The team of people you have around is vital – making sure you have people with the right mix of experience and that you have the flexibility to change the team of the project through different phases. Quality of the team you select and flexibility is vital. Interview PD 48.*

As the project director for a highly successful and extremely complex public housing project emphasised, team flexibility is a vital ingredient. The project in question involved delivering 6300 units of accommodation located in 502 projects across the state of New South Wales in Australia. New South Wales occupies an area of 800, 642 km², about 3.5 times the area of the United Kingdom and nearly twice that of California. At the time of interview the project team had delivered 4500 of the accommodation units within 18 months. The extremely compressed time-frame for delivery was a result of the nature of the funding, being part of the Australian Government's stimulus package in response to the Global Financial Crisis (GFC).

> *... we will make it just – other states have thrown in the towel – we got the team selection right and nobody has ever thought for one minute about giving up ... Interview PD 48.*

Due to the nature of complexity, project requirements might change frequently. Complexity involves emergent behaviour. The project, like any complex adaptive system, flexes in response to external and internal environmental pressures. The larger the project the more these effects will be apparent. Projects which are extremely time-driven, like this one, or projects that are of very long duration, are highly sensitive to environmental impacts. In this case, impacts that were difficult to control or plan for included – unpredictable, unseasonal weather patterns resulting in extremely heavy rainfall and violent storms that delayed building progress, a domestic construction industry experiencing high instability due to the effects of the GFC, extreme levels of media scrutiny fuelled by a very active opposition party, an embattled State government needing a 'show stopper' and an impending State election with no funds to support budget blowouts. The success of this project has been an extraordinary achievement.

ENERGY, OWNERSHIP AND SKILL

Project management, particularly when the project is complex, is a higher order management activity. This is not recognised widely enough in the business world. During the first set of interviews (2004a, 2004b) we discovered that it was not unusual for executive sponsors with little or no experience, either in the role of sponsor or with projects, to be assigned to complex projects. An organisational merger, in the gaming industry was such an example:

> *I don't think anyone realised just how much work was involved. Because this is one of the largest entertainment and gambling organisations in the world now. And people just think 'yeah that'll be pretty easy', but it's not, there's so much work involved bringing two organizations together like that. It's a cultural issue as well. We do things differently from what they do. Interview 10 PM.*

Managing a complex project and working on a project team in this kind of project is a high stress activity. Project personnel work long hours; 15 hour days and 7 day weeks are not uncommon when things reach critical stages. As a senior project manager in the oil and gas industry stated:

> *A lot of people want to get into project management because it is a buzz thing and they don't understand the level of stress involved and energy and resources required ... I need three things in a project manager for a complex project of this kind.*

> *Energy – if you don't have the energy to keep going to meet the deadlines to be in a high performance team it doesn't work – you don't want a bunch of cake-eaters sitting in the corner on a high performance project.*

> *Ownership – they need to own the task and be resourceful enough to find out how to do it if they don't know – ownership is intricately linked with pride in what they do.*

> *Skill – they need the competency to do the task – it needs to be project specific competency. For example, the procurement team – organisations set policy but don't do anything – in corporations people talk about assurance and don't take responsibility – for example when you ask 'can you follow this up – you have actually approved the purchase can*

you keep track of it' and the answer is 'no we don't do that you need an expediter to follow stuff up and make sure it gets to you' it doesn't work. Interview 45 PM.

However, project executive leaders need to understand the stress that people in highly complex projects may experience. Not everyone has the extraordinary stamina exhibited by the interviewees quoted above. Allowing people to work under continued stressful conditions has been identified with poor leadership (Kelloway et al., 2005).

Part 2: Build Trusting Relationships with All Key Stakeholders

Strong trusting relationships with everyone; project team members, contractors, suppliers, anyone affected by the project and/or executive sponsors was repeatedly mentioned as the ideal position from which to lead a project. One of the defining aspects of a complex project, however, is the number and diversity of stakeholder groups. Stakeholder management is a key theme in any good project management text (see for example, Cleland, 2008; Turner, 2008). Nevertheless, it is not always achieved as well as it might be and one reason for this is that achieving excellent stakeholder management is difficult. In a complex project it will be difficult to identify all key stakeholders, difficult to anticipate how certain stakeholders might react and difficult to keep a track on changes in stakeholder requirements or emerging groups or factions. As one project director in charge of an otherwise extremely successful but technically complex engineering project reported:

> *We got it wrong. We thought that the residents from … [a very affluent suburb] would give us the most trouble because we were going to block their million dollar views for several months and also create a lot of noise. But all we did was conduct a couple of community meetings. They were really happy when we agreed to paint the equipment in camouflage colours and delay start times until late on Saturday mornings so they could sleep in. However we thought the residents from … [a much less affluent community] wouldn't give us any problems because they were going to get a new park as part of the project and the area would be cleaned up. All we wanted to do was to locate one small … [structure] in their area. What we didn't know is that this particular community had defeated the government on several other occasions and they were highly organised politically. It didn't matter what the government*

proposed, they were going to fight it. In the end we had to go to court.
We won the court case but we consider it was a failure on our part
because we failed to manage that stakeholder group. Interview 32 PD.

Building trusting, co-operative relationships is a huge task for large complex projects, one that should not be assigned as an afterthought. It takes a depth of research about what motivates each stakeholder (group) and individualised management approaches need to be developed. When we think of stakeholders we often focus on external stakeholders. Key internal stakeholders, such as project sponsors, also need to be managed in order to develop trusting and productive relationships.

She [the sponsor] was nervous at first. I [PM] was an unknown
quantity for her and she is not a naturally trusting person. It took a
while to gain her trust. I had to work hard. Interview 26 PM.

It was clear that many leaders interviewed worked very hard to build trusting relationships that were also sustainable. At all levels of the project, within teams and with external stakeholders, strong relationships were seen to be the key to success, especially when things got tough. When asked what were the most important attributes for a leader, the following project leader, with 30 years international experience in the mining industry, said the following:

Integrity, truthfulness, being able to listen deeply, giving people a
fair hearing, fairness, we are all human beings, respect is essentially
important. We can be frustrated by certain behaviours but we still
need to be leaders and refrain from getting into slinging matches
– just because you think the other party is not being honest
there is no excuse for those who want to be leaders to follow suit.
Leadership is about having a clear goal or vision and then articulating it
in such a way that others join in wanting to realise that vision. It often
requires taking a less than easy path. Good leadership involves being
an effective decision maker and then following through on delivery.
Interview 56 PM?

The organisational leadership research clearly demonstrates that a leader's ability to develop trusting relationships is a key success factor (Bennis, 1999). High levels of trust in a leader have been shown to have important positive outcomes for the leader, his/her associates and teams. These include improved individual and team performance (Dwivedi, 1983; Earley, 1986; Rich, 1997), enhanced cooperation (Lindskold, 1978), increased employee trust in top management and the CEO (Costigan, et.al., 2004), increased perceptions of fairness (Wech, 2002), increased job satisfaction (Driscoll, 1978; Wech, 2002), improved organisational citizenship behaviours (Podsakoff, et al., 1990; MacKenzie, et al., 2001), higher likelihood that people will disclose important information rather than hold back, more willingness to work interdependently with colleagues, and greater acceptance of higher level goals and methods of execution (Zand, 1972).

TRUST CAN BE UNDERMINED BECAUSE OF DIFFERENT UNSTATED AGENDAS

The need to understand your stakeholders' real motivation is vitally important. We tend to make assumptions based on our own world views and assume that those practices also apply to others. As a project manager working in the engineering manufacturing industry illustrates with this tale of woe, an initially positive relationship broke down very quickly because they didn't think about the sub-contractor's drivers and how the work culture might be different from their own, before settling the contract. They did not 'step into the sub-contractor's shoes' to try and see the world from their perspective.

> Our organisation used to do all of its manufacturing in house but because we did not have the in-house capability to deliver the beat-rate [unit production over time] required by the client we outsourced production of a major component to an off-shore sub-contractor. At first this appeared to be a Godsend. The off-shore sub-contractor invested in new machinery and they built a new manufacturing hall for the operation. It was only later that cracks appeared in the relationship. Our operation was run by highly skilled technicians who were used to dealing with changes in design, based on test results – they would always find a way to make it work. There is a low turnover of staff and a great deal of knowledge rests with individuals. While our in-house technicians could readily respond to design changes, the off-shore operation was geared towards fast delivery of a stable design and there was virtually no capability to respond to change. This allowed the sub-contractor to employ a changing workforce of low-skilled workers. One of the expectations on the part of the off-shore company, which we didn't pick up until too late, was that they were expecting to get training and skill development out of the project to invest in their workforce. Our company had assumed that the sub-contractor would provide fully

trained staff. Because we had not stipulated stability of workforce in the contract, the off-shore sub-contractor regularly moved the people, trained by us, on to other projects of their own so the workforce on the project was continually staffed with unskilled people. This rapidly lead to relationship breakdown. Interview 31 PM.

TRUST CAN ALSO BE CONTEXTUALLY DEPENDENT

It is important for leaders to understand that their behaviour contributes to developing trust in different ways depending on the context. Knowing the differences helps practitioners to better understand why an individual may trust them in one situation but not in another. In her research study DePaolo (2005) found that trust develops differently in task-based contexts compared with relationship-oriented contexts. Not unexpectedly she found that predominantly in task-oriented situations the leader should make it a priority to demonstrate both *competence* and *consistency* in order to develop trust. Doing so is more likely to foster willingness to comply with the leader's task-related directives, assurances and plans of action. Where trust is needed to encourage problem-solving collaboration between leaders and others, expertise needs to be coupled with a more *human-oriented, supportive* and *encouraging* approach (see Chapter 2 for a discussion of leadership styles and communication; De Vries et al., 2006; Srivastava et al., 2006).

DePaolo (2005) found that in relationship-oriented situations (compared with task-oriented situations), perception of the leader's motivation matter more. Thus, when the focus is more about the relationship rather than the task the person will be more willing to rely upon the leader if s/he thinks leader's motivational intentions are positive. When leaders are in positions where relationship-oriented trust is needed, they should clearly consider how benevolent or exploitative their actions are perceived by colleagues and subordinates. If people think that leaders are out for themselves or willing to use information against them, it is unlikely they will engage in open communication because they will be unwilling to make themselves vulnerable to the leader. As discussed in Chapter 2, an unfortunate result of this unwillingness might be unclear and perhaps untrue information delivered to the leader.

These conclusions have multiple practical implications. As Galford and Seibold Drapeau (2003) note, some leaders may be honest, straightforward and competent and yet there are times when they are still clearly not trusted if they are not also seen as having positive intentions, or being supportive and encouraging. There is a danger, especially in relation to task-oriented undertakings like projects, that the focus will be more on building task-based trust than on building relationship-oriented trust. Projects, even though they are focused on tasks and goals, are social systems and much of what can or can't be achieved, particularly when things get tough, is based on the strength of the trusting relationships that have been established.

In short, to develop trusting relationships project leaders need to engage in activities that enhance others' perceptions that they are both competent and consistent, particularly when the issue is task-oriented, and on making sure that their motivational intentions are positive and clear.

Part 3: Refrain From Micromanagement

> But I think that was the beauty of him [the sponsor]. He only injected himself when he thought he was needed. Interview 6 PM.

The senior project manager who offered this comment about his project sponsor was referring to an executive leader who understood how important it was to demonstrate trust in the capability of the project manager and team, but still be available for advice when needed. Micromanagement requires that subordinates secure excessive permission and approval, particularly for routine choices. When optimal pathways and solutions are unclear, doubt and fear can be manifested in an increasing need to control processes and people, particularly if the tendency to micromanage is already present as a supervisory pattern. However, under these conditions, tightening of constraints is likely to be counterproductive. As things become more complex the need for freedom to explore and experiment increases. Leaders respond through micromanagement for both personal and organisational reasons. Ineffective leaders may 'lack self-confidence. They make up for it by micro-managing people' (Schafer, 2010; 742 – interviewee cited). Also, partly stemming from the litigious nature of today's society, organisations have emerged to support cultures in which people can avoid responsibility (Ross, 2000). In an attempt to mitigate liability risk, newly promoted leaders, struggling to delegate and demonstrate leadership, may default to bureaucratic management tactics (Krimmel and Lindenmuth, 2001) or highly focused styles of supervision. As the following sponsor from a large food manufacturing company notes, the temptation to micromanage is there but should be resisted:

I am now a sponsor – my role is in terms of guidance, to look at where the project is going, I coach and mentor, definitely part of my role to challenge. I am here to help and break down barriers. Secondly I am here to coach and mentor. It is easy for me to micromanage but I try not to. Interview 67 GM.

Micromanagement, which can manifest as requests for excessive reporting, might also increase when senior leaders lack appropriate interpersonal skills, preferring paperwork to discussion. Micromanagement can also arise when supervisors fear that empowered subordinates might outshine the leader's own accomplishments. Unfortunately, in our first study (2004a, 2004b) micromanagement by executive leaders was the rule rather than the exception. All project managers interviewed were highly experienced and it was clear that they perceived micromanagement by their executive sponsors to be insulting professionally. Schaffer (2010) also found that the practice negatively affected relationships with executive leaders.

Ideally he [the executive sponsor] needs to be removed, he needs to be external to the project. From my point of view, the sponsor should be someone who looks at the process of the project, not the actual project itself. Interview 28PM.

Schafer (2010) also found that micromanagement tends to slow the pace of organisational action and output. Such a heavy focus on controlling subordinate and routine actions can actually prevent desired outcomes because ineffective leaders 'fail to delegate authority [to subordinates] that is necessary for the success of desired results' (Schafer's, 2010: 742 – interviewee cited). A number of project managers in both our studies (2004, 2005, and 2010, 2011) cited micromanagement as a problem.

Micromanagement has a profoundly negative effect on trust. In a complex project, when people are experiencing high levels of stress, establishing and maintaining trust at all levels is critical to project success in a number of ways.

Leaders need to have faith in staff to do the right thing – having faith requires that staff have the appropriate skills, knowledge, and abilities to undertake the work required too. We need to have leaders that focus on being a leader rather than getting involved in the minute day to day details (as that is where they felt comfortable). If staff have been promoted into a job – make them do the job and not hand hold them for months. Interview PM 50.

Micromanagement can be problematic at all levels of the project leadership, the client being no exception. In line with Schafer's (2010) observations, a senior project manager noted the slowing down effect of micromanagement in property development projects, which have a critical time to market focus and work to tight schedules in order to deliver appropriate returns on investment. There is a fine line between micromanagement and ownership.

> The client wants to control all aspects including much of the detail, less delegation to competent team members. Parts of this are good as he takes ownership of the decision, however it slows the project and may affect programme objectives. Lack of understanding of the process, particularly the design phase can be problematic. This is not an issue if they are willing to take advice and accept they don't know everything. Interview PM 51.

Part 4: Energise the Executive

> On the other hand, once properly energised, the Board provided some good support at EC level. Interview 49 PD.

The comment above, by the project director of an international environmental clean-up project involving four countries, emphasises the importance of keeping the executive leadership fully engaged. The excerpt below refers to an international mobile telecommunications project:

> I would say that prior to signing it the head office wasn't particularly excited about the deal. I had to fight to get it recognized, and I had to face huge negativity from the sponsor and members of the sponsor's team to the level of personal insults and I had to politic like hell to push it through. The trick was to involve people, bring them in one at a time, and then one by one the key negative players started to come around, and the project gained momentum. But two years down the track it's one of our most profitable deals ever, and strategically important. Interview 3 PM.

Several of our interviewees noted that they had to work hard to engage executive leaders. Possibly based on the assumption that executives will be automatically motivated to fully support the project, the organisational literature tends to focus on energising workers. There are several reasons why key people at Board level might not be fully engaged. Whilst managing one large programme I became aware that the Deputy CEO had been nominated as project sponsor for over 200 projects. Even with the best of intentions it would have been impossible for him to have had more than a passing familiarity with most of them. Many of those projects had wilted and were dying for lack of appropriate executive energy and support. When projects are sponsored by government departments this can be particularly problematic.

> Governments have no idea how many projects they are running, how these projects align to strategic intent of policy and whether they have any chance of delivering on their goals. I'm sure this project has been forgotten about by all political parties who are funding it. Their attention will only be drawn when a public incident big enough to reach main stream press occurs. Interview 52 C.

The comment above was made by a senior consultant who had been engaged to provide expert advice to a water management project. Considering the criticality of the project to the area's water resources, it was surprising.

Executive boards comprise people with a range of personalities and skills that can make them either effective or ineffective board members. Individually they also have selective interests. For obvious reasons governments devolve executive responsibility to boards administered by senior public servants that meet periodically but rarely frequently enough to allow them to be fully engaged.

An energised executive project board is essential when the project is complex. Rapid but considered responses by executive teams may be needed to prevent the project from moving into chaos, past the tipping point, often a point of no return. Project leaders have gone to extreme lengths to make sure that boards are properly composed and have the requisite power to make timely decisions. As one highly experienced project manager stated about a programme to deliver five new prisons in five remote locations within a very tight timeframe; a hotly contested project with a media desperately looking for any issue that might be newsworthy:

> We knew this was going to be tough and we knew we might need very high level support at Board level, so we invited the ... [Head of the Government] to be on the project executive board, with the assurance that they would only be called upon in an emergency. We only needed

to call on them once but at that moment their support was critical to the
success of the project. Interview 45 PM.

Obviously not every project has access to executive board members with this
level of influence; however, it illustrates how important it is to make sure that
the project executive board comprises people who can make things happen
quickly if things get tough.

ADVICE FOR THOSE WHO NEED TO INFLUENCE UPWARDS

Obviously there should be a strong business case for the project which aligns
the project to the organisational objectives, but engaging and energising the
executive leadership often requires project leadership that goes far beyond
having a ratified business case.

Project leaders may not spend enough time managing upwards for a
variety of reasons. They may fail to appreciate how important it is. Almost
certainly they have other things to concentrate on. They might lack the skills or
the contacts to influence.

The following tips have been summarised from advice from leaders who
are very skilled in influencing upwards:

- Don't assume that people on the executive board will automatically
  be interested or engaged in the project.

- Ascertain who might be interested in the project and for what
  reasons, for or against – a stakeholder analysis of the Board.

- Learn about the Board members as people – their characters,
  strengths and shortcomings – couch your communication to fit
  their personality and communication style (see the Porter, E.H.,
  1973, 1996).

- Learn about their interests – frame your communication to get their
  attention by using language that draws upon their perspective of
  the world (see the Porter, E.H., 1973, 1996).

- Find out who they talk to – people whom you might be able to
  influence if it is inappropriate to contact the Board members
  personally.

- Make sure you understand the risks from their perspective and focus – viewed from the bigger picture and the implications from a wider perspective – for example: 'if this risk is triggered the implications for the return on investment for the organisation are as follows ...'; 'if these risks are not dealt with rapidly when they occur, adverse media will attract the attention of the opposition party which might in turn affect the outcome of the election'. In reality the project leader's immediate concern is the project, but a project Board member's immediate concern is much more likely to be the viability of the organisation or winning the next election.

- Be certain about what you want from the Executive Board and state it clearly – don't overload them with anything you and your team can handle – reserve their input for the critical moments.

- Keep supporters informed and enthused – provide them with very succinct updates regularly but certainly just before board meetings.

- Make sure that there are no surprises about issues that will need their support. No one likes to be placed in an embarrassing situation because of lack of information.

In Summary

Match the people to the project:

- Finding the right people is a priority for many of the senior project leaders interviewed. It becomes imperative if the project is complex.

- It is apparent that leaders who are successfully leading complex projects, consciously or unconsciously, profile team members at all levels of the project and actively intervene to match personalities, support perceived weaknesses and capitalise on people's strengths.

- In order to match people the leader needs a strong understanding of personality differences and how different people work together.

- Build trusting relationships.

- Building strong sustainable relationships with all stakeholders was another priority.

- Trust is the foundation for relationships which, if strong, can carry the team through when things get tough as they invariably do when a project is complex.

- If the context is task-oriented, development of trust appears to be related more to perception of competence and consistency in the leader.

- If the context is relationship-oriented the leader must demonstrate that his/her motivation is positive from the perspective of the other party.

- As most interactions involve a mixture of task and relationship, the wise leader would be better to focus on both these areas when building trust.

- Avoid micromanagement. As projects become more complex fewer, rather than more, constraints are needed so that team members can explore options.

- Micromanagement is linked with ineffective leadership.

- The role of the leader to is make sure people have sufficient information and skill to carry out their work and then be available for support, direction, challenge and encouragement when needed.

- Energise the executive. Don't assume that the executive leaders are engaged.

- The executive board often needs to be energised in order to deliver high level support at critical times.

References and Further Reading

Belbin, R.M. (2010) *Management Teams. Why They Succeed or Fail*, 3rd ed. Butterworth Heinemann.

Belbin, R.M. (1981) *Management Teams*. London; Heinemann.

Bennis, W. (1999) Five Competencies of New Leaders. *Executive Excellence*, 16(7), pp. 4–5.

Burke, R.J. (2006) *Why Leaders Fail: Exploring the Dark Side*. In: Burke, R.J. and Cooper, C.L. (eds) *Inspiring Leaders*, pp. 237–246. London: Routledge.

Cleland, D. (2008) *Project Management Handbook*, 2nd edition. New York, NY: Wiley Publishing.

Clements, C. and Washbush, J.B. (1999) The Two Faces of Leadership: Considering the Dark Side of Leader-follower Dynamics. *Journal of Workplace Learning*, 11(5), pp. 170–175.

Conger, J.A. (1989) *The Charismatic Leader: Behind the Mystique of Exceptional Leadership*. San Francisco: Jossey-Bass.

Conger, J.A. and Benjamin, B. (1999) *Building Leaders: How Successful Companies Develop the Next Generation*. San Francisco: Jossey-Bass.

Costigan, R.D., Insinga, R.C., Kranas, G., Kureshov V.A. and Ilter, S.S. (2004) Predictors of Employee Trust of Their CEO: A Three-country Study. *Journal of Managerial Issues*, 16(2), pp. 197–216.

DePaolo, C.A. (2005) Task and Relationship-oriented Trust in Leaders. *Journal of Leadership & Organizational Studies*, December 22.

De Vries, R.E., Van der Hooff, B. and De Ridder, J. (2006) Explaining Knowledge Sharing. The Role of Team Communication Styles, Job Satisfaction, and Performance Beliefs. *Communication Research*, 33(2), pp. 115–135.

Dotlich, D.L. and Cairo, P.C. (2003) *Why CEOs Fail: The 11 Behaviors That Can Derail Your Climb to the Top–and How to Manage Them*. San Francisco: Jossey-Bass.

Driscoll, J.W. (1978) Trust and Participation in Organizational Decision-making as Predictors of Satisfaction. *Academy of Management Journal*, 21, pp. 44–56.

Dwivedi, R.S. (1983) Management by Trust: A Conceptual Model. *Group and Organization Studies*, 8(4), pp. 375–405.

Earley, P.C. (1986) Trust, Perceived Importance of Praise and Criticism, and Work Performance: An Examination of Feedback in the United States and England. *Journal of Management*, 12, pp. 457–473.

Galford R. and Seibold Drapeu, A. (2003) The Enemies of Trust. *Harvard Business Review*, February, pp. 88–95.

Helm J. and Remington, K. (2004a) Adaptive Habitus, Project managers perceptions of the role of the project sponsor, EURAM Conference Papers, May: Munich.

Helm J. and Remington, K. (2004b) Effective Sponsorship, Effective Project Sponsorship: An Evaluation of the Role of The Executive Sponsor in Complex

Infrastructure Projects by Senior Project Managers. *Project Management Journal*, 36(3), pp. 51–61.

House, R.J. and Podsakoff, P.M. (1994) Leadership effectiveness: Past perspectives and future directions for research. In: J. Greenberg (ed.), *Organizational behavior: The state of the science*, pp. 45–82. Hillsdale, NJ: Lawrence Erlbaum.

Kellerman, B. (2004a) *Bad leadership: What it is, how it happens, why it matters*. Boston: Harvard Business School Press.

Kellerman, B. (2004b) Leadership: Warts and all. *Harvard Business Review*, 82(1), pp. 40–45.

Kelloway, E.K., Sivanathan, N., Francis, L. and Barling, J. (2005) Poor leadership. In: Barling, J., Kelloway, E.K. and Frone, M.R. (eds) *Handbook of work stress* (pp. 89–112). Thousand Oaks, CA: Sage.

Kets de Vries, M.F.R. (1993) *Leaders, fools and imposters: Essays on the psychology of leadership*. San Francisco: Jossey-Bass.

Krimmel, J.T. and Lindenmuth, P. (2001) Police chief performance and leadership styles. *Police Quarterly*, 4, pp. 469–483.

Lindskold, S. (1978) Trust development, the GRIT proposal, and the effects of conciliatory acts on conflict and cooperation. *Psychological Bulletin*, 85(4), pp. 772–793.

Lipman-Blumen, J. (2005) *The allure of toxic leaders: Why we follow destructive bosses and corrupt politicians — and how we can survive them*. New York: Oxford University Press.

Lord, R.G., De Vader, C.L. and Alliger, G.M. (1986) A meta-analysis of the relation between personality traits and leadership: An application of validity generalization procedures. *Journal of Applied Psychology*, 71, pp. 402–410.

Maccoby, M. (2000) Narcissistic leaders: The incredible pros, the inevitable cons. *Harvard Business Review*, 78(1), pp. 68–77.

Martin, R., Thomas, G., Charles, K., Epitropaki, O. and McNamara, R. (2005) The role of leader-member exchanges in mediating the relationship between locus of control and work reactions. *Journal of Occupational and Organizational Psychology*, 78, pp. 141–147.

McCabe, B. (2005) The disabling shadow of leadership. *British Journal of Administrative Management*, 46, pp. 16–17.

McCall, M.W., Jr. and Lombardo, M.M. (1983) *Off the Track: Why and How Successful Executives get Derailed*. Greensboro, NC: Center for Creative Leadership.

McCauley, C.D. (2004). Successful and Unsuccessful Leadership. In: Antonakis, J. Cianciolo, A.T. and Sternberg, R.J. (eds) *The Nature of Leadership*, pp. 199–221. Thousand Oaks, CA: Sage.

Peters, T.J. and Waterman, R.H. (1982) *In Search of Excellence: Lessons from America's Best Run Companies*. New York: Harper and Row.

Podsakoff, P.M., MacKenzie, S.B., Moorman, R.H. and Fetter, R. (1990) Transformational Leader Behaviors and Their Effects on Followers' Trust in Leader, Satisfaction, and Organizational Citizenship Behaviors. *Leadership Quarterly*, 1(2), pp. 107–142.

Podsakoff, P.M. and Organ, D.W. (1986) Self-reports in Organizational Research: Problems and Prospects. *Journal of Management*, 12(4), pp. 531–544.

Porter, E.H. (1973, 1996) *Relationship Awareness Theory. Manual of Administration and Interpretation*. Carlsbad, CA: Personal Strengths Publishing, Inc.

Porter, E.H. (1950) *An Introduction to Therapeutic Counseling*. Boston: Houghton Mifflin.

Porter, E.H. (1953) *The Person-relatedness Test*. Chicago, Science Research Associates.

Pryce-Jones, J. (2010) *Happiness at Work: Maximizing Your Psychological Capital for Success*. Chichester, UK: Wiley-Blackwell.

Ross, D.L. (2000) Emerging Trends in Police Failure to Train Liability. *Policing*, 23, pp. 169–193.

Schafer, J.A. (2010) The Ineffective Police Leader: Acts of Commission and omission. *Journal of Criminal Justice*, 38, pp. 737–746.

Srivastava, A., Bartol, K.M. and Locke, E.A. (2006) Empowering Leadership in Management Teams: Effects on Knowledge Sharing, Efficacy, and Performance. *Academy of Management Journal*, 49(6), pp.1239–1251.

Turner, J.R. (2008) (ed.) *The Gower Handbook of Project Management,* 4th edition. Aldershot, UK: Gower Publishing.

Wech, B.A. (2002) Trust Context. *Business and Society*, 41(3), pp. 353–360.

Zand, D.E. (1972) Trust and Managerial Problem Solving. *Administrative Science Quarterly*, 17, pp. 229–239.

Yukl, G. (2002) *Leadership in Organizations* (5th ed.). Upper Saddle River, NJ: Prentice Hall.

4

Employ Portfolio-programme Thinking

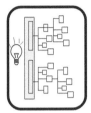

In order to manage these kinds of projects you need to see them from the highest possible perspective.

Interview 34 GM.

This chapter is not intended as a comprehensive guide to portfolio or a programme management. There are many excellent texts that cover that topic (see for example: PMI, 2008; APM, 2007; OGC, 2007; Reiss et al., 2006; Thiry, 2006). This chapter presents an argument for portfolio and programme management because currently this is the most effective way to work with complexity: to provide the necessary 'big picture' perspective; to allow for the degree of flexibility and to achieve the 'requisite variety' (Ashby, 1957) of responses needed. Under conditions characterised by complexity, single approaches are generally not the answer.

Key Points in This Chapter:

- Requisite variety and system stabilisation.

- Realising benefits from projects.

- Tailored implementation strategies.

- Projects, programmes and organisational knowledge management.

Part 1: Requisite Variety and System Stabilisation

In *An Introduction to Cybernetics* (1957) the English psychiatrist and pioneer of cybernetics, William Ross Ashby, formulated his law of Requisite Variety stating that only 'variety can destroy variety' (p. 207). The greater the number of parts, the greater the variety necessary. Using an analogy from the field of ecology, he further argues that:

> ... *when the system T is very large and the regulator R is very much smaller (a common case in biology), the law of Requisite Variety is likely to play a dominating part. Its importance is that if R is fixed in its channel capacity, the law places an absolute limit to the amount of regulation or control that can be achieved by R, no matter how R is re-arranged internally ... Thus the ecologist, if his capacity as a [regulatory] channel is unchangeable, may be able at best only to achieve a fraction of what he would like to do ... he may decide to control outbreaks rather than extensions, or virus infections rather than bacillary – but the* quantity *of control that he can exert is still bounded. (p. 245)*

> *When the system T is very large – when the organism as regulator faces a very large and complex environment with limited resources – there are various ways that* may *make regulation possible. (If regulation is not possible, the organism perishes ...). Sometimes regulation may be made possible by redefining of what is to be regarded as acceptable – by a lowering of standards. Another possibility is to increase the scope and power of R, until R's capacity is made adequate. (p. 246)*

In a nutshell, to stabilise the system, the number and variety of control mechanisms must be greater than or equal to the number of states in the system being controlled. If, by analogy, we extend this theory to complex projects, control is only possible if the number of ways of controlling are greater than or equal to the number of activities that can trigger risks. Projects as entities are not very flexible for a number of reasons. They have theoretically predetermined constraints such as scope, time, budget, quality, available resources and available communication channels. If the perspective can be expanded, as would be the case if the project were treated as part of a much larger programme, the project can be viewed as a small set of constraints within a larger system of interdependent activities. Therefore, the propensity for flexibility increases. In response to environmental changes to the larger system resources for individual projects can be added or removed as needed from a bigger pool. Also, there is a higher probability for access to a much wider variety of responses to manage the risks. From the perspective of complexity theory, these are two reasons why organisation or enterprise-wide benefits are more effectively delivered via programmes, which, in turn, are managed within portfolios.

Part 2: Realising Benefits From Projects

BENEFITS AND AN INTEGRATED APPROACH

Project outcomes contribute to realising business benefits as part of a comprehensive suite of activities (Reddington, et al., 2004). Most organisations have significant business portfolios, often comprising hundreds of programmes and projects, initiated to help realise business benefits as defined in the organisation's strategy documents (Bradley, 2006). The effects of complexity are most effectively managed through portfolios and programmes because they adopt a high level perspective rather than a project level view. In some cases, where the project is relatively small, programme management is not appropriate. Nevertheless, even relatively small individual projects are usually conceptualised as part of a business portfolio, with an executive sponsor or governance team, there to guide and mentor the project teams, and particularly to help the project leaders cope with externally imposed sources of complexity.

WHICH PART OF THE PICTURE DO YOU HAVE?

Our focus varies because of our interests and what we can see at any given time. Quite obviously strategic teams concentrate on the strategic direction and which projects are needed to help deliver the strategy, whereas project teams are focused on project implementation. At the strategic level this involves constant change in response to environmental volatility. Kooyman and Steel (2009) argue that the project teams are intrinsically resistant to change as change interferes with schedule and costs. Project managers monitor and control change in order to bring the project in on time and within budget as originally specified. In so doing they might actually prevent changes that are necessary for the business to respond to emergent events.

As Fonseca (2002) argues, leaders at any level work with only part of the picture. It is impossible for anyone to see the whole picture. A telecommunications project illustrates:

> *When PLATO moved from being a simple solution for a well-articulated problem to a highly complex solution for a vexing political problem, there was no single person who could articulate (or communicate) the overall structure and objectives of the project. (Bourne and Walker, 2005, p. 170)*

PORTFOLIOS AND PROGRAMMES

The sources of complexity that affect small projects tend to be associated with either technical challenges or directional issues (inability to come to agreement about goals, sub-goals and goal-paths) (Remington and Pollack, 2007). Directional sources of complexity can continuously cycle back to affect communication and trust, if technical or environmental challenges persist. Directional sources of complexity, which result in unshared goals or misunderstandings, can derive from cultural differences (communication, work practices, organisational norms and national differences) or they can derive from deliberate obfuscation by people with hidden agendas. Because of their much longer durations, programmes are more likely to be affected by temporal sources of complexity, as the following comment about a rail upgrade programme illustrates:

> *The programme itself is 33 years in duration – individual projects within the program have much shorter durations – there are so many events that can affect the programme over such a long period and most of them are totally outside our sphere of control. Interview 31 PM*

The twin terms, programme and project, have different meanings in different settings, as do the terms programme and portfolio. Recognising organisational differences in nomenclature is vital. For our purpose, a project will be taken to mean an enterprise of shorter duration than a programme, and a programme can be taken to mean a group of interrelated projects that, together, deliver a business outcome or set of outcomes, usually as part of a business portfolio.

Portfolio management has been defined as the co-ordinated management of a collection of projects that may be related or independent of each other (Martinsuo and Dietrich 2002) or as the process of analysing and allocating organisational resources to programmes and projects across the organisation on an ongoing basis to achieve corporate objectives and maximise value for the stakeholders (Thiry, 2004). The latter definition is the one used in this book because it includes organisational processes as well as collections of projects (programmes) and individual projects.

CURRENT PRACTICE

Most executive leaders interviewed routinely conceptualised organisational strategy as programmes managed as part of a business portfolio. However, the literature reveals (Ashurst et al., 2008) that portfolio management is generally not rigorously linked with benefits realisation:

> You need valid portfolio management reporting to the top level leaders on how the portfolio is tracking and when re-enforcement of the vision is required ... [large organisations] often have no idea about how many projects they are running, how these projects align to strategy and whether they have any chance of delivering on their goals. If there was a simple portfolio management tool that tracked simple and key metrics of a projects performance and rolled this up to executive management then projects that are floundering in their own directionless mud pool could be resurrected or put out of their misery significantly quicker than they do now with millions of dollars saved and made through the resulting benefits realisation when the course of a project is corrected. Interview 52 C.

If sound portfolio and programme management is not always in place, as the plea above from a senior consultant suggests, the established link between benefits realisation and integrated management of this kind is a good argument in favour of so doing (OGS, 2006; Jamieson and Morris, 2004; Reddington et al., 2004). Providing the reporting tools are up to the job, managing projects as part of a programme and/or portfolio allows executive leaders to have quick overviews of how projects are tracking in relation to one another, which projects need support and which are no longer relevant.

ADVANTAGES OF A HIGH LEVEL APPROACH

Conceptualising the projects in terms of a co-ordinated collection of projects that, together with other business processes, deliver strategy against an emergent environment (internal as well as external) has a number of advantages. It is as relevant in healthcare (see for example Sapountzis, et al., 2008) as it is in the commercial sector (see for example, Kooyman and Steel, 2009; Thiry and Deguire, 2007). The portfolio can change and emerge in response to changes in the environment, adding programmes and projects or deleting them in response to environmental impact. Implementation approaches can be tailored to suit the volatility of the environment. It makes it easier to bridge the communication gap between strategy and implementation More effective deployment of resources can be achieved across portfolio and programmes. Knowledge management is facilitated.

COMMUNICATION GAP

Reiss et al., (2006) argue that in unsuccessful programmes, definition of benefits is often characterised by vagueness. This vagueness in translation is a major contributor to complexity in individual programmes and projects. Whatever the motivation for imprecise definition by the Executive Board, the consequences are serious in terms of waste of resources and failed programmes and projects. For some time management writers have observed that there is a lack of communication between the strategic and tactical levels of management (Hatch, 1997; Neal, 1995; Pelligrinelli and Bowman, 1994; Thomas et al., 2000). Kooyman and Steel (2009) describe this communications abyss as a *strategic implementation gap*. They argue that very few projects move seamlessly from strategy to successful operation and they cite a lack of integration between business and project management as a major causal factor. Part of this disintegration is due to focus and part of this is communication.

EVALUATION AND MEASUREMENT

One dominant idea in the management literature argues that a clear boundary between the project and the business domains can and should be maintained, as exemplified by this quote:

> *Responsibility for the actual realisation of benefits will fall to the business managers in the relevant areas [...]. The achievement of benefits should be assessed independently from the process of delivery (that is the programme) (CCTA, 2000, Sect. 5.9).*

Although it is not the purpose of this book to explore evaluation methodologies, it goes without saying that how we measure the benefits accrued resulting from delivered objectives is one important way of monitoring the organisation's responses to environmental changes – a major source programme and project complexity. The processes are inextricably linked (see for example Caldeira and Dhillon, 2010; Remenyi and Sherwood-Smith, 1998).

ORGANISATIONAL CHANGE AS PROGRAMMES

Although awareness of the role of projects in organisational change has increased in recent years, in some organisations there remains a very significant gap between specifying the desired strategic outcomes of an internal organisational development project, in financial terms, and ultimately fully realising the benefits to the organisation. For over 20 years researchers have been arguing the importance conceptualising internal development programmes in terms of organisational change. As Strassman 1990; p. 519 reflects on IT projects:

> *Computers add value only if surrounded by appropriate policy, strategy, methods for monitoring results, talented and committed people, sound relationships and well designed information systems.*

Melville et al., (2004) also comments that:

> *Improvements in process and organisational performance are conditional upon appropriate complementary investments in workplace practices and structures.*

Consequently, a fundamental purpose of any investment appraisal must be to explicitly establish the scope and implications of the associated organisational change (Lubbe and Remenyi, 1999).

Some authors continue to argue that a key causal factor preventing project outcomes from translating into actual benefits is that project teams typically fail to recognise the critical role of organisational change. However, this argument might also be turned around to place the responsibility for recognising the organisational change function on the executive leaders who are responsible for the business portfolio. Whilst there is a strong recognition amongst researchers, and perhaps practitioners also, that effective benefits delivery is predicated on well focused organisational change, it is possible for this aspect to be overlooked if projects are conceptualised independently – as if they exist and deliver benefits in a way which is independent of the rest of the organisation. Understanding projects as one form of contribution to changes necessary for the organisation to evolve and maintain relevance, places projects with a combination of implementation efforts that deliver strategy.

Part 3: Tailored Implementation Strategies

FLEXIBILITY AND EMERGENCE

Controlling a short term project in a prevailing climate of change and uncertainty is within the realms of possibility. Controlling a long term project in terms of originally conceptualised budget, scope, quality and schedule parameters is much, much more difficult. The number of factors that come to be out of the control of the project leader increases exponentially as duration increases. Changes in executive sponsor or project board, resignations, removals and acquisition of team members, changes in key external stakeholders, changes in client or client organisation, budget restrictions that don't reflect scope and quality changes and new regulatory requirements, are some examples of changing constraints that increase in number as time progresses.

Conceptualisation of strategy as an integrated collection of programmes, projects and other supporting activities, allows leadership to tailor the implementation strategies to suit the complexity. In a volatile environment the business needs as much flexibility as possible to emerge and change with the environment in order to survive. This applies as much to the public sector as it does to the commercial sector. The nonlinear effects of such pressures result in emergence and adaptation, but the focus is on expected benefits and the process can 'display consistent patterns of actions over time' (Mintzberg and Waters, 1985, p. 257).

The level of complexity (simple to very complex) and type (structural, technical, directional, temporal) of complexity can be predicted with greater accuracy for a small, short term project than is possible for a programme as a whole. Also, if projects within a larger programme are conceptualised as short, well defined undertakings, losses can be minimised when a project needs to be terminated due to a change in strategic direction forced by environmental turbulence. Technological complexity can also be packaged into small 'test parcels' making it easier to separate out those parts of the programme that are technically complex from other easily manageable parts.

PROCUREMENT AND TEMPORAL COMPLEXITY

Because of their typically long duration, programmes are very exposed to temporal forms of complexity, complexity induced as a result of changes to the external environment – market, economical, regulatory, and/or technical

– and the internal business environment – structural organisational changes, leadership changes and so on. In conditions of high temporal complexity, which affects all businesses operating today, it is important not to be locked into long projects that are so big that they are difficult to stop or change without incurring major losses to the business. Procurement strategies for projects within programmes need to be flexible enough to allow exit without major loss.

COMMUNICATION GAPS

As discussed in Chapter 2, how people and teams communicate relates also to discipline area and educational focus. Strategic teams and project teams can have very different communication styles. Project teams use charts and diagrams and speak in terms of concrete deliverables and specifics. Project teams may also use technical jargon which further complicates communication for non-technically trained people. Strategic teams tend to use language politically because of a necessary focus on the organisation and its environment. Hence, strategic teams use metaphorical language and speak in terms of strategic vision and direction.

The communications gap between strategic leadership teams and project teams is real and contributes to the complexity as experienced by both levels. In order to address this gap, Kooyman and Steel (2009) propose the establishment of a *strategic implementation team* which they describe as a small team empowered to direct and realign projects throughout their implementation phase but also to be held accountable for realisation of business benefits. This approach has been used with great effect on government large infrastructure projects, such as the Sydney airport.

FLEXIBLE DEPLOYMENT OF RESOURCES

> *Not all parts of a large initiative are complex you know – in air traffic control systems – we have about 42 large programmes about half of which can be called complex. Interview 47 GM.*

Most programmes and many projects are orderly and chaotic at the same time. Some parts will be very complex and other parts will be relatively simple. The term *chaordic systems thinking* has emerged from complexity theory to describe that which encompasses both order and chaos (van Eijnatten, 2004; Stogatz, 2003). Chaordic systems-thinking shares with sensemaking (Weick, 1995; Backström, 2004; Jensen, 2004), the idea that effective leadership is more about orienteering and path-finding than control against pre-established rules and regulations.

Defining short term projects, managed as part of a larger programme, also makes more effective use of project team members who have other functional roles. They can be assigned to short term assignments giving them dedicated project time with the opportunity to return to their functional roles with less disruption. This might be preferable to expecting staff to manage functional and project roles simultaneously, where divided loyalties can create personal stress and inefficiencies. One example is a major police initiative. The sponsor, the police commissioner conceptualised the organisational changes needed as a programme in which she was fully engaged and responsible.

> *The eighty projects, when people came back with their assessments after three months, I was the only person in charge who sat down and listened to them all. They didn't all get up of course but they knew I made a promise, I made the commitment, and you had the consistency of leadership and feedback. I think that respectfulness for the people you work with is very important. So we did sexual assault, family violence, stolen motor vehicles, robberies, family violence, all of those things. Interview 70 CEO.*

Some of these projects would have been enormously complex, others complicated but still manageable. Conceptualising the projects as a programme allowed the sponsor to select.

NATURE OF COMPLEXITY WITHIN THE PROGRAMME

Apart from level of complexity, decisions about how best to implement the projects within the programme should also relate specifically to the nature of the complexity expected. For example, a programme which involves design and implementation of a new IT inventory and warehousing function that has never been implemented in this kind of setting before may exhibit aspects of many types of complexity: *technical* (or design), *structural* (or organisational) and *directional* complexity. Technical complexity might come from challenges in designing the code and the hardware to support the new processes. Structural (organisational) complexity can be one associate of technical complexity. How much time do we allow in the schedule for design and development of new components and how will those bottlenecks impact on commitments to key stakeholders and budget? How do we decide when the design is 'good enough'? How do we organise procurement which will also allow us to take advantage of emergent characteristics commonly found during the design phase? Directional complexity, about goals and goal-paths, may become apparent when obtaining agreement on objectives and sharing understanding about what the final deliverable will actually deliver. In a project of this nature directional complexity is ideally dealt with at project conception, however, it often reappears when technical problems are not resolved satisfactorily, resulting in spiralling project costs. People affected might question how they are expected to adapt to the new system and, faced by opposition, key stakeholders might begin to lose faith in the original idea. The longer the time span of the project the more likely it is to encounter temporal complexity as the environment moves on.

How do we manage stakeholders, risk, finance and procurement in such circumstances? Conceptualising the project as a programme does not remove complexity but it does allow for some breaking down of the project into sensible bits so that executive leaders can make more effective strategic decisions about the viability of the project.

SELECTING KEY PERSONNEL

People and skills can be deployed more effectively if the leader takes a global view of the organisation. By recognising which projects within a programme are likely to be complex and which are not, leaders can assign experienced project personnel to the complex projects, while utilising the more straightforward projects as a training ground for less experienced project personnel. Also, by monitoring the level of project complexity the people with more expertise can be incorporated if the project becomes more complex (Bourne and Walker, 2005). Leaders can also help to establish career pathways by allowing less experienced people to shadow and assist more experienced personnel. As discussed in Chapter 3, selecting the right people for the project is critical to the success of any complex project. If the project is important then the last place to cut costs should be in the area of personnel. Lack of appropriate resources and people who are overly stressed come from a lack of integrated planning at the business level that can be addressed through programme and portfolio management.

MATCHING PEOPLE TO COMPLEXITY

Finding appropriate personnel that work effectively with the types of complexity identified is also important. Not everyone is comfortable with uncertain and ambiguous environments. Not everyone has the intellectual acuity to maintain a detailed knowledge of the status of hundreds of activities and multiple contracts, and interdependencies, to ensure quality delivery to strict deadlines. Not everyone is able to sensitively manage political struggles and obtain agreement from a disparate group of stakeholders. Not everyone is able to motivate designers and technical experts to deliver within a time-frame. Therefore, it is very helpful to be able to identify the types of complexity and divide the programme into projects accordingly with appropriate personnel to manage each type of complexity. Too often projects are simply assigned to the departments within the functional area of the project owner or end user. It is possible that personnel with the capabilities needed to manage the particular type of complexity may be found in other departments or elsewhere.

Part 4: Projects, Programmes and Organisational Knowledge Management

Kerzner (2000, p. 13) argues that project management works '... because a successful project is as much an organization of learning by its participants as a way of doing work'. In spite of this assertion, the project by itself has proved to be an inefficient mechanism for transfer of learning. Individuals may learn but the organisation rarely benefits from their learning (Haunschild and Sullivan, 2002). One view is that mature organisations need to adopt integrative approaches that will enable consistent structures and effective knowledge management. However, even project-based organisations are struggling to integrate knowledge and structures and projects are often viewed as 'singular ventures' (Thiry and Deguire, 2007). Organisational learning stems from the real-time action learning by individuals and teams (Cavaleri and Fearon, 2000). In very complex projects new knowledge is constantly being created as teams find innovative solutions to technical and organisational obstacles (McKenna, 1999; March and Olsen, 1988). This learning needs to be captured and transferred more effectively. It is at the portfolio or programme level that learning can be captured; where results can be regularly appraised against benefits during implementation, changes managed and benefits redefined if necessary against an emerging landscape.

FACTORS AFFECTING LEARNING DIFFER WITH INDIVIDUAL LEARNING STYLES

It appears that generalists and specialists learn in different ways. Specialists appear to learn from differences detected in prior incidents. Generalists, in contrast, appear to learn less from differentiated prior experience. They appear to learn more from their own accumulated general experience, including outside factors, such as technological improvements learned by the industry as a whole (Haunschild and Sullivan, 2002). The fact that individuals learn differently has important implications for learning in a project environment. It would be expected that the focus of people at project, programme and portfolio levels of the organisation might be different with more specialists employed at the project level and more generalists to be found at strategic levels. Obviously, the wider the 'learning net' the more likely that lessons will be captured at all levels of experience and be richer as a result.

ORGANISATION-WIDE KNOWLEDGE MANAGEMENT

Whereas projects are discreet entities, a portfolio or programme of projects provides a more viable base for learning. The iterative process of building experiences and capacities for effective actions requires an infrastructure where the organisation as a whole gains wisdom from participation in projects. Project reviews constitute one major way an organisation can learn from its past, however there needs to be an organisation-based management framework for this to happen (Kulunga and Kuotcha, 2008).

Knowledge management also implies knowledge preservation. Another key element of knowledge management is the ability to share knowledge with those you want to and refrain from sharing with others. Organisations, '... along with providing transfusions of knowledge, are wary of knowledge haemorrhage' (Szymczak and Walker, 2003, p. 135). There must be layers of security and procedures to safeguard information and knowledge. This is also best achieved at the organisational level.

In Summary

Conceptualising large projects as programmes of smaller, preferably short term, projects assists in managing complexity, particularly through the provision of increased flexibility and access to a wider range of responses:

- Ashby's law of Requisite Variety states that the greater the number of parts the greater the variety of responses needed to control the system.

- Organisational benefits are more effectively delivered and measured through a systemic approach involving portfolio and programme management.

- The degree (simple to very complex) and type (structural, technical, directional, temporal) of complexity can be estimated with much greater accuracy for small, short term projects than for a programme as a whole.

- Appropriately skilled project personnel can be assigned to each project within the programme so that under-skilled personnel are not exposed to situations where they cannot cope and highly skilled personnel are reserved for the very complex projects and for mentoring roles.

- Project skill shortages are easily detected and addressed.

- Procurement strategies can be tailored to match the needs of each project according to the level of uncertainty expected.

- Reporting and decision-making processes can be tailored to match the needs of each project.

- Sponsors can be selected who are able to provide appropriate support to each project.

- Mentors with appropriate experience can be sourced for those projects that are likely to be affected by complexity.

Conceptualising programmes and projects, along with other organisational processes, as part of a business portfolio means that:

- Important processes, such as change management, are integrated to help deliver benefits.

- Learning, which is unlikely to be efficiently captured at the project level, can be captured at the organisational level.

- The gap between strategy and implementation can be addressed (provided it is acknowledged and resourced appropriately) meaning that the programme can continue to deliver appropriate benefits, given the emergent nature of the environment.

- Complex adaptation to environmental change is possible at the strategic level. Programmes and projects deliver strategy but if the strategy changes then so must the programme and project respond, either by being redefined, adjusted or eliminated. This must be effected quickly in order to optimise use of resources.

Project specific knowledge is not effectively captured at project level. In order for it to be of use to the organisation in the future it needs to be managed on an enterprise-wide basis.

References and further reading

APM (2007) Introduction to Programme Management, Bedforshire, UK: APM Publishing (available from http://www.apm.org.uk/IntroductiontoProgrammeMangement.asp).

Ashby, W.R. (1957) An Introduction to Cybernetics, 2nd Imp. London, UK: Chapman and Hall.

Ashurst, C., Doherty, N.F. and Peppard, J. (2008) Improving the Impact of IT Development Projects: The Benefits Realization Capability Model. European Journal of Information Systems, 17, pp. 352–370.

Backstrom, T. (2004) Collective Learning: A Way Over the Ridge to a New Organizational Attractor. The Learning Organization, 11(6), pp. 466–77.

Bradley, G. (2006) Benefit Realisation Management. A Practical Guide to Achieving Benefits Through Change. Farnham, Surrey: Gower Publishing.

Caldeira, M. and Dhillon, G. (2010) Are We really Competent? Assessing Organizational Ability in Delivering IT Benefits. Business Process Management, 16(1), pp. 5–28.

Cavaleri, S.A. and Fearon, D.S. (2000) Integrating Organizational Learning and Business Praxis: A Case for Intelligent Project Management. The Learning Organization, 7(5), pp. 251–258.

CCTA (2000) Managing successful programmes. London, UK: Central computer and telecommunications agency (now called OGC-Office of government communications) CD Rom Version, Sec. 5.9.

Fonseca, J. (2002) *Complexity and Innovation in Organizations*. London: Routledge.

Hatch M.J. (1997) *Organization theory*. Oxford, UK: Oxford University Press.

Haunschild, P.R. and Sullivan, B.N. (2002) Learning from Complexity: Effects of Prior Accidents on Airlines Learning. *Administrative Quarterly*, 47, pp. 609–643.

Hodgson, D.E. (2002) Disciplining the Professional: The Case of Project Management. *Journal of Management Studies*, pp. 37–9.

Jamieson, A. and Morris PW. (2004) *Moving from Corporate Strategy to Project Strategy. The Wiley Guide to Managing Projects*. Hoboken, NJ: John Wiley and Sons; 2004.

Jensen, J.A. (2004) An Inquiry into the Foundations of Organizational Learning and the Learning Organization. *Learning Organization*, 11(6), pp. 478–86.

Kooyman, B. and Steel, J. (2009) Integration of Project Outcomes with Strategic Policy, Paper presented at UTS Seminar, August, 2009: Tracey Brunstrom and Hammond Pty. Ltd.

Kulunga, G.K. and Kuotcha, W.S. (2008) Measuring Organisational Learning Through Project Reviews. *Construction and Architectural Management*, 15(6), pp. 580–595.

Lubbe, S. and Remenyi, D. (1999) Management of Information Technology Evaluation – the Development of a Managerial Thesis. *Logistics Information Management*, 12(1/2), pp. 145–156.

March, J.G. and Olsen, J.P. (1988) The Uncertainty of the Past: Organizational Learning Under Ambiguity. In: March, J.G. (ed.), *Decisions and Organizations*, pp. 335–358. Oxford, UK: Basil Blackwell.

Martinsuo, M. and Dietrich, P. (2002) Public Sector Requirements Towards Project Portfolio Management. In: Proceedings of PMI Research Conference, July; 2002, Seattle, Newtown Square, PA: Project Management Institute.

McKenna, S. (1999) Learning Through Complexity. *Management Learning*, 30(3), pp. 301–320.

Melville, N., Kraemer, K. and Gurbaxani, V. (2004) Information Technology and Organisational Performance: An Integrative Model of Business Value. *MIS Quarterly*, 28(4), pp. 283–322.

Mintzberg, H. and Waters, J.A. (1985) Of Strategies, Deliberate and Emergent. *Strategic Management Journal*, 6(3), pp. 257–72.

Neal R.A. (1995) Project Definition: The Soft Systems Approach. *International Journal of Project Management*, 13(1), pp. 5–9.

Office of Government Commerce (OGC) (2006) Managing Business Benefits: Key Principles, Office of Government Commerce, London, The Stationary Office; available at: www.ogc.gov.uk (accessed 14/3/2009).

Office of Government Commerce (OGC) (2007) Managing Successful Programmes. UK: The Stationery Office; available at http://www.best-management-practice.com/Online-Bookshop/Programme-Management-MSP/Managing-Successful-Programmes-2007-Edition.

Pellegrinelli, S. and Bowman, C. (1994) Implementing Strategy Through Projects. *Long Range Planning*, 27(4), pp. 125–32.

Project Management Institute (PMI) (2008) The Standard for Program Management, 2nd Ed. Newtown Square, PA: Project Management Institute.

Reddington, M., Withers, M. and Williamson, M. (2004) Realising the Benefits. *Personnel Today,* April 6, p. 22.

Reiss, G., Chapman, J., Leigh, G., Pine, A. and Rayners, P. (2006) *Gower Handbook of Programme Management.* Aldershot, UK: Gower Publishing.

Remenyi, D. and Sherwood-Smith, M. (1998) Business Benefits from Information Systems Through an Active Benefits Realisation Programme. *International Journal of Project Management*, 16(2), pp. 81–98.

Sapountzis, S., Yates, K. and Kagioglu, M. (2008) Realising Benefits in Primary Healthcare Infrastructures. *Facilities*, 27(3/4), pp. 74–87.

Strassman, P. (1990) *The Business Value of Computers.* Connecticut, USA: The Information Economics Press.

Strogatz, S.H. (2003) *Sync: The Emerging Science of Spontaneous Order.* New York, NY: THEIA Hyperion Books.

Szymczak, C.C. and Walker, D.H.T. (2003) Boeing – A Case Study Example of Enterprise Project Management from a Learning Organisation Perspective. *The Learning Organization*, 19(2/3), pp. 125–137.

Thiry, M. (2006) Managing Portfolios of Projects. In: Turner J.R, editor. *Gower handbook of project management.* Aldershot, UK: Gower Publishing; Chapter 4.

Thiry, M. (2002) The Development of a Strategic Decision Management Model: An Analytic Induction Research Process Based on the Combination of Project and Value Management. In: Frontiers of Project Management Research and Application: Proceedings of PMI Research Conference 2002 (Seattle, July 2002). Newton Square, PA: Project Management Institute. pp. 482–92.

Thiry, M. and Deguire, M. (2007) Recent Developments in Project-based Organisations. *International Journal of Project Management*, 25(7), pp. 649–658.

Thomas, J., Delisle, C., Jugdev, K. and Buckle, P. (2000) Selling Project Management to Senior Executives: What's the Hook? In: Project Management Research at the Turn of the Millennium: Proceedings of PMI Research Conference 2000. Sylva, NC: Project Management Institute.

Van Eijnatten, F.M. (2004) Chaordic Systems Thinking: Some Suggestions for a Complexity Framework to Inform a Learning Organization. *The Learning Organization*, 11(6), pp. 430–449.

Weick, K.E. (1996) *Sensemaking in Organizations*. Thousand Oaks, CA: Sage.

Wieck, K.E. (1987) Organisational Culture as a Source of High Reliability. *California Management Review*, Winter, pp. 112–127.

5

Challenge Through Innovation

Innovation is not the product of logical thought, although the result is tied to logical structure.

Albert Einstein, (1879 – 1955).

Innovative thinking is one important key to managing complexity. Project leaders are responsible for creative problem-solving in many ways. Simon's (2006) study of project manager behaviour in R&D projects supports those of our earlier studies (2004, 2005) where we found that senior project managers used a diverse range of behaviours, that could only be labelled creative, which helped them to manage very challenging situations. This is entirely consistent with research data on creativity and leadership in the general management literature (Christensen et al., 1978).

Key Points in This Chapter:

- Unstructured or 'wicked' problems.

- How project leaders use innovative thinking.

- Using the right tools.

- Effects of time pressure on innovative thinking.

Part 1: Unstructured or 'Wicked' Problems

As early as 1973 Horst Rittel and Melvin Webber observed that there were types of problems that cannot be resolved with traditional analytical approaches. They labelled these problems 'wicked problems'. Problems of this kind are also termed *ill-defined* or *nonprogammed* (Simon, 1957), *complex* (Dearborn and Simon, 1958; Dorner, 1983), *ill-structured* (Ungson et al., 1981) *unstructured or ill-behaved* (Mason and Mitroff, 1972, 1981), *unstructured strategic* (Mintzberg et al., 1976) or *messy* (Ackoff, 1979). In complex situations 'wicked' problems are commonplace. They usually go beyond the capacity of one person, one group or even one organisation to understand or solve. There will be disagreement about the causes of the problems and the best way to tackle them. Design problems are typically 'wicked' and may also require creative management responses.

> *Sydney Airport – we won that in joint venture with a big firm of engineers, a tender for the newly formed Federal Airports Corporation. We were contracted from procurement to completion. The design phase was the most complex because of so many conflicting requirements, for instance security. Security and Immigration Departments like to close doors and corral people into areas, which in this case, was against the principles of fire safety. Those were issues to be fought through, and because the project was so big in scale, none of the current bylaws had a hope of coping with it. So we had to develop a totally new concept of fire engineering to deal with the scope and take into account how humans react to crises. We effectively rewrote the codes. Interview 64 PM.*

Other typical projects that are plagued by 'wicked problems' include large-scale organisational changes, organisational mergers, projects in the public domain that attract high levels of public scrutiny and new product development, particularly if market forces are unpredictable. For successful delivery, project leadership teams must effectively negotiate the many problem challenges involved. In 1976, Mintzberg and others argued that complex problems involve '... decision processes that have not been encountered in quite the same form and for which no predetermined and explicit set of ordered responses exist in the organization' (p. 246).

Ungson et al., (1981) considered problems to be ill-structured due to 'the ambiguity and incompleteness of problem related information, the extent to which problems are continually defined and redefined by managers, the lack of a programme for the desired outcomes, the possibility of influences from many people or groups, and the extended period in which a decision is made' (p. 121). However, many processes for addressing these problems '... are based only on a rational extension of the basic ideas of routine problem solving' (VanLehn, 1989 p. 549). It could be argued that this is still predominantly the case in business and project management practice. Problem solving methods suitable for complicated problems are being applied to complex problems where they are inappropriate (Snowdon, 2002).

In project management the prevailing method is to apply a linear kind of logic, which reduces problem-solving to a sequence of predictable steps. Decomposition techniques, like work or organisational breakdown structures, are examples of this kind of logic. These approaches are effective if the problem is well-structured, where the initial and final states of the problem are clearly defined, where there exists a number of discreet steps which lead to the final state and where there are ways of ascertaining if the final solution is the desired end state (Newell and Simon, 1972). The underpinning assumption is that the whole complex problem may be broken down and then reconstructed as a meaningful whole once again. This works for projects that lie closer to the control end of the spectrum. At the other end of the spectrum, at the complex end projects can defy linear approaches to problem-solving.

CREATIVE PROBLEM SOLVING

Most complex projects require creative or nonlinear approaches to problem-solving. While creative thinking is part of decision-making and problem-structuring, it is much more. Innovation involves creating something new or original. It involves the skills of flexibility, adaptability, originality, fluency, elaboration, modification, imagery, associative thinking, attribute listing, metaphorical thinking and creating unexpected relationships. Innovative, or creative, thinking promotes divergence. Critical thinking promotes convergence. Both are essential to solving problems but they involve different cognitive processes. Much of the thinking taught in formal professional education emphasises the skills of analysis –understanding claims, following or creating a logical argument, figuring out the answer by deduction, eliminating incorrect paths and focussing on the correct one, etc. Creative or innovative thinking explores ideas, generates possibilities and looks for many right answers rather than just one. Critical thinking might be differentiated from creative or innovative thinking as follows:

Table 5.1   Differences between critical thinking and creative or innovative thinking (adapted from Harris, 1998)

Critical thinking	Creative, or innovative, thinking
Analytic	Generative
Convergent	Divergent
Vertical	Lateral
Probability	Possibility
Judgment	Suspended judgment
Focused	Diffuse
Objective	Subjective
The answer	Many answers
Left brain	Right brain
Verbal	Visual
Linear logic	Associative, or nonlinear, thinking
Reasoning	Richness, novelty
Yes but	Yes and

The process moves from awareness of a problem or a 'mess', through data collection, problem definition (problem statement) to idea generation, to solution finding, to evaluation (Isaksen and Treffinger, 1985). Schon (1990) describes a contingent relationship between variables in the 'problem space', in which variation of one element will cause a change in related variables forming unpredictable and emergent patterns. A model of the interactions during the initiation and design phases of a project to design and construct two low-energy vehicles illustrates this process. The process is not linear, it is iterative, with a great deal of backtracking, as ideas are trialled and found to be lacking in some aspect (see Figure 5.1).

> The programme included two projects to design and manufacture two different light-weight energy efficient vehicles for a low-energy vehicle race. Separate industrial design teams were responsible for the design of the body, driver ergonomics and safety compliance. Graphic design teams were responsible for the marketing and advertising elements, including logos and decals, and other design teams were responsible for the engine components and the chassis. The goal, to win the race, appeared to be straightforward, however once the design teams started to explore their separate problem areas the actual problem expanded as

interdependencies were revealed, risks triggered and new opportunities arose. Decisions made along the way by each separate team impacted on those made by other teams in significant ways. For example, an unexpected opportunity relating to design of the fuel system in one vehicle required a slight change in the engine configuration which in turn forced a complete redesign of the chassis and redesign of the seating configuration and windscreen. The resulting change in the body design also meant that the graphic design team had to rework the decals. The new ideas also impacted the other vehicle design team forcing them to rethink some of their initial assumptions. And so it went on. Interview 43 PD.

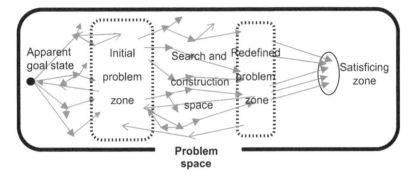

Figure 5.1   **Model of the interactions during the early phases of a low energy car project (Remington, 2005, after Newell and Simon, 1972 and Middleton, 1998)**

THE 'SATISFICING ZONE'

Eventually, after many compromises due to time and cost constraints, skills shortages and technological assumptions that proved to be inaccurate, the vehicle design teams reached 'satisficing' solutions. The term 'satisfice' was coined by Herbert Simon to describe the the process of seeking solutions or accepting choices or judgments that are 'good enough' for their purposes (Simon, 1957, cited in Kunda, 1999). It is a good term to describe the kind of accommodated decisions that project leaders regularly have to achieve in order to move forward.

The 'satisificing' zone in design problems is also complex because it is also ill-defined when precise goal criteria are still unknown (Simon, 1981). For example, a project to design a car to suit a newly identified market is complex because the criteria that define success may only be fully determined after the product has reached the market. In addition, the 'satisficing' zone for a design problem is complex because the goal criteria can be linked and may also be contradictory.

Design thinking, such as described above, can be applied to other complex projects where there are 'wicked problems' with contradictory goals or changing requirements. In an organisational change project, for example, the vision espoused by senior leaders of creating a more collaborative culture might require more effective cross-functional teamwork. At the same time pressure to increase production might have resulted in a culture that singles out individuals or winning teams for special rewards. These aims are contradictory and if not addressed in a systemic way, if one goal is treated in isolation from the larger system or broader context, the dominant existing culture might subvert the achievement of the current goal.

Part 2: How Project Leaders Use Innovative Thinking

HOW SENIOR PM'S RATE CREATIVE THINKING

When senior project managers were asked to nominate the personal attributes that they most valued when working on high risk and complex projects, creative thinking was high on the list (reported in Kokotovich and Remington, 2007). The five top attributes mentioned, were: communication skills, relationship management, creative thinking, flexibility and negotiation skills. Although some of these skills reinforce each other we presented them separately them because they were mentioned as discreet skill sets. As might be expected, attributes such as communication and relationship management skills scored very high. Creative thinking ability was cited next, often expressed as the ability to 'think out of the box' and 'find new ways of achieving objectives'. Flexibility also scored very high; sometimes described by interviewees as adaptability, flexibility is an attribute that appears to be associated with creativity.

We added the sixth category as a reliability check. 'Knowledge of PM principles and processes' was not actually mentioned by any of the interviewees when initially asked 'which personal attributes do you value most as a PM?'. We

Mean ratings on a scale of 1–7

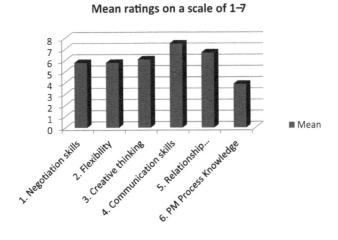

Figure 5.2   Thirty senior project managers rated their skill sets. Themes
               1–5 emerged as the most behaviours they used and valued
               most

added this theme to the questionnaire to provide a point of comparison. It might be that knowledge of the standard PM processes was assumed by the participants, that it was considered to be a basic requirement and therefore not worth mentioning, or that it is significantly less important than the other attributes when dealing with complex projects (Kokotovich and Remington, 2007).

Our studies revealed that project leaders consciously use innovation, and encourage others to think creatively, in order to:

- Overcome management barriers and challenges; being adaptable.

- Recognise when old ways of working are no longer effective and invent others.

- Negotiate political mazes.

- Assist key stakeholders to find agreed solutions and paths to get there.

- Work with teams to develop appropriate technical and design solutions.

- Manage conflicted stakeholder groups.

- Motivate teams during tough times.

- Increase product quality through creation of work-related meaning.

- Stimulate learning and knowledge creation.

- Mitigate risks.

OVERCOMING MANAGEMENT BARRIERS AND CHALLENGES

Complex projects are often highly constrained in terms of time to delivery. Project leaders need to be able to 'think outside the square' and find different ways of working with key stakeholders to manage around obstacles and find more effective solutions to management challenges.

> *Absolute determination has forced us into creative thinking – a number of builders' contract dates were up – so we aligned all the building contracts to make sure that we were three months ahead – could have had a large number of builders going into liquidated damages – we could have proceeded with the liquidated damages which would have delayed progress considerably – we would have found ourselves stifled by red tape – agreed with builders that if they carried on they would get an offset against the liquidated damages – offered them an incentive to carry on – giving up was never a possibility for us so we had to think 'what can we do'. Interview 48 PD.*

This major construction project was procured using traditional procurement systems but that did not prevent the project director and his team from using a partnering philosophy in order to avoid an administrative nightmare that would have slowed the project down significantly.

The following project, a merger between two large financial entities, was a high risk, 'knotty' sort of a project that involved extensive reporting, due to the [financial regulator] 'looking over our shoulder, as they should', the joint venture partner and the firm's other partner, all taking a keen interest in what was taking place. The project incurred very high risks because failure to meet the deadline would have involved several millions of dollars in penalties. Adaptability requires an ability to think 'outside the box'.

... you have to be adaptable. Because it was highly controversial and litigious and all that sort of thing, we found ourselves in fairly murky water on this project and you really just had to adapt to the circumstances. Everybody in the project has to be adaptable to react to changing circumstances all the way, it's not all nice and neatly laid out where you can just go down that path very smoothly. Inevitably the outside influences come in to bear on the path you are taking, and while you try to minimise deviations because you've got this goal you're trying to hit down here, you must accept that there will be deviations from the straight and narrow path. So I think adaptability is essential for everyone on the project, but certainly those who are running it, the project manager, the development manager, the testing manager ... Interview 26 Deputy CEO.

Recognising when old ways of working are no longer effective and invent others.

One of the challenges can be convincing senior leaders that things need to be done differently, particularly in organisations that have entrenched ways of working. The project manager working on an international project, involving seven countries, and as many agencies in each country, reported that:

One of the hardest challenges was getting acceptance of new and innovative ways of doing work. Doing things differently – attempting to sway senior leaders' views of how work can be undertaken – trying to be more open to new and innovative ways of doing work rather than 'we've done it this way for the past x years and we should keep doing it this way. People in the project need to be willing to try new things.' Interview 50 PM.

The project manager leading this project realised that existing ways of working would not achieve the goals. He set about gradually changing the way that the project was managed until the agencies started to work together successfully. This involved not only creative thinking but tenacity.

ASSISTING KEY STAKEHOLDERS TO FIND MORE EFFECTIVE SOLUTIONS

Both the pressure of time and the kind of analytical thinking training that most people receive in their education may discourage people from fully exploring all the dimensions of a problem (Simon, 1973). Also, people have a tendency towards premature solution finding. We tend to hang on to early solutions once they have been developed and then go to enormous lengths to justify those solutions (Mathias, 1993).

Project leaders are frequently presented with preconceived solutions which may not be sufficiently thought through and are unlikely to deliver the stakeholders' needs. Therefore, it may fall to the project leader to work through problem definition and resolution with the client or key decision-makers until a solution is obtained which delivers the best value, within the budget and time constraints.

Alternatively, the goal of the project may be understood at a high level by some, while other key stakeholders can leave briefings with different and conflicting notions of the goal state; an aspect of the type of complexity that we refer to as *directional complexity*. Complexity resulting from confusion about the pathway to achieve the goal was reported more than once by project managers in large defence projects.

> *Some stakeholders don't seem to appreciate the complexity. There is a long period of real confusion about how we can achieve the goal – and, in various forms, uncertainty about how to achieve the goal, or if we can achieve it at all, returns again and again as new problems arise. Interview 37 PM.*

Any of these situations means that leadership teams should be able to think creatively, to assist stakeholders to arrive at an agreed solution or way of achieving the goal at the beginning and frequently during the project life cycle as the surrounding landscape changes.

NEGOTIATING POLITICAL MAZES

In complex projects that are characterised by ambiguity and unclear or unshared goals, experienced project leaders use creative problem-solving skills to find new and innovative ways to negotiate the political mazes which often characterise these project contexts.

> *Sometimes it takes a good deal of creative thinking to find your way around the politics – finding how you can influence so and so, when you don't even get to see him, except at the very rare board meeting*

when he is sitting in the chair and you are invited in for a 5 minute update – or, alternatively, finding a work around a bit of 'red tape' that you know is only being exercised to delay the project because one person doesn't want to shift his position- you have to find ways of making sure that person comes around and doesn't lose face. Interview 44 PD.

Exercising political astuteness not only requires high levels of empathy but also creative thinking and adaptability. Thinking up several alternative ways to move, when boxed into a corner, is a creative activity.

ASSISTING TEAMS TO DEVELOP APPROPRIATE TECHNICAL AND DESIGN SOLUTIONS

Technical and design challenges require creative ability on the part of the designers but also the project leaders play an important integrating role, facilitating others to arrive at satisfactory solutions that can be implemented; so-called 'satisficing' solutions. As Simon argues (1973), it is often rational to seek to 'satisfice' because looking for the very best solutions expends too many resources. A better solution would thus have to justify the extra costs incurred in finding it. Alternatively, a solution might be valid and well-tested but with daunting technical design challenges, requiring the project leader to work with the design teams and support their search for alternative solutions. The low energy vehicles example illustrates this important role:

Four main design teams were involved in each project. Initially a relatively inexperienced project manager was appointed to oversee the projects however he ran into trouble when it was quite apparent that none of the teams seemed at all interested in adhering to his schedules and they were definitely not interested in filling out forms. It was immediately obvious that all the teams were very dedicated to the design problems at hand but the atmosphere was competitive, particularly between the different disciplines; mechanical engineering, software engineering, industrial design, graphic design. The challenge was how to motivate the teams to work together and deliver on time. At this stage we had to work with what we had so we had to 'think outside of the box' to be able to help the project manager to integrate the teams and their output. The project manager was coached to lead in a different way, deciding eventually to take all the 'nasty' reporting responsibilities away from the design teams and assuming responsibility for that work, which was achieved mainly through observation, questioning and listening. The project management role changed to information source and knowledge integrator, keeping each team fully informed about what the other teams were doing and bringing everyone together periodically to share information. The PM came to be seen as the design teams' friend and helper rather than a monitor-controller, the enemy, as had been the case earlier. The atmosphere improved measurably. They got to the deadline with two fully functioning, innovative vehicles! Interview 43 PD.

MANAGING CONFLICTED STAKEHOLDER GROUPS

Complex projects also require creative ways of managing stakeholder groups. The large urban bio-remediation projects at Homebush Bay for the 2000 Sydney Olympics are good examples.

Technologically the solutions were exciting for the time – using enzymes and bugs– nature to clean up the site. However the major challenges to the project team came from environmental lobbies like Greenpeace, the local council that had lost control of the Homebush Bay area, now under the control of the OCA [Olympic Coordination Authority], the Homebush Bay Residents Action Group who were concerned about the future of their children's health and the press, looking for any opportunities to criticise. We had to think 'outside the box'. Interview 46 GM.

In order to engage potential detractors and reassure those who were concerned about the environment, the project team initiated community meetings once a month, and special tours of the site every three months, with barbeques, that became major community events. Education packs for school children were developed and children were involved in watching the sea eagles coming back to breed after three years' absence; there were fish monitoring programmes and the local children were involved in tree planting.

Children started to educate their parents about the environment. After the first six monthly meetings Greenpeace rarely attended. The press disappeared when they saw there was nothing in it. The project value was eleven million dollars – we gave the OCA back half a million dollars in change. Interview 46 GM.

STIMULATING LEARNING AND KNOWLEDGE CREATION

Creative thinking has long been linked to learning and there is a great deal of evidence linking learning with emergence and nonlinear thinking. Because complex projects are often undertaken in uncertain situations, Holmquist (2007) argues that project leaders who adopt a rational-oriented strategy tend to face difficulties in adapting and adjusting to changes that occur during the project. Finding different ways of managing through learning seems to be fundamental to leading a complex project. Creative learning opens up possibilities for transforming processes as ways of developing and improving project delivery. Argyris and Schön's (1978) double loop learning, March's (1991) explorative learning, Senge's (1990) generative learning and Engeström's (1987) expansive learning are all examples of creative learning.

Senior project managers also frequently report that they liked to be challenged by project executive leaders. Challenging in order to encourage creative thinking was particularly successful when executive leaders adopted a partnering approach with project personnel. As indicated earlier, in Chapter 2, micromanagement was never appreciated. The following excerpt referred to a construction company with global projects. The project manager is referring to his boss:

> She was very clear in the way she communicated. She was very focused. Extremely motivated. And she challenged you. I like to be challenged, doing the same thing, day in day out, I get bored. She challenged me to think outside the box, made me consider other things. You couldn't just throw something onto the table unless you could justify it and back it up. She wasn't a yes person and I think that's great. She pushed you and expected you to push back. If she said something she expected you to challenge her as well. Interview 2 PM.

MOTIVATING TEAMS DURING TOUGH TIMES

There are many ways to motivate teams when times are tough and people are exhausted. Encouraging creative thinking achieves a number of things. Creativity is closely linked with fun, and laughter is a great antidote to despair when problems look as if they are insurmountable.

> I knew a wonderful project manager in the public sector in New Zealand, an English guy with a zany sense of humour. He and his

team were struggling with some really tough environmental projects. In spite of all the difficulties he managed to keep the team laughing. One of his mad ideas was to have a team theme each week. Each week everyone in the team was expected to bring something in to 'decorate' the office in line with the theme. When I visited them one week the theme was 'all those dreadful presents that you can't get rid of'. On another occasion it was inflatable things! The office was littered with extraordinary floating coloured plastic objects ... the atmosphere in the team was always positive, even when things were very grim and the press were having a field day – and they got things done, often against all odds – it was almost as if the humour flowed over into the project and no barriers were too great for them. Interview 43 PD.

INCREASING PRODUCT QUALITY THROUGH CREATION OF WORK-RELATED MEANING

In his research into projects Simon (2006) found that creative project leaders were providing both individuals and the team with meaning, knowledge-sharing spaces, and a balance of challenges and support, acting as context builders as opposed to planning and control managers (see also Picq, 1999). In line with other recent works on middle-management (Van Der Weide and Wilderom, 2004; Nguyen, 2001), Simon (2006) argues that project leaders play a determining role in structuring and integrating the group, the individual and the organizational context (Agrell and Gustafson, 1996). In performing this structuring and integrating function, project leaders play a major role with respect to product quality, internal efficiency, internal politics and stakeholder relationships. This contributes to the argument that project leaders need to possess skill sets that allow them to help others and groups to creatively solve problems.

MITIGATING RISKS USING CREATIVE THINKING

Creative thinking is involved in good risk mitigation because it involves 'thinking outside the box' in order to find better ways to avoid serious risks and risk patterns. Innovative thinking is involved in several stages of risk management. Creative thinking is essential to risk identification, which requires 'thinking the unthinkable, not being constrained by "the Plan"' (Hillson, 2009, p. 10). Potential threats and unexpected benefits can be indentified using a range of creative thinking techniques, such as brainstorming, assumptions-busting, root-cause analysis, visualisation, scenario planning and futures thinking. Similar creative thinking tools need to be applied to risk response development. As Hillson argues '... risk management without innovation merely rehearses and records the inevitable ... the risk process must embody innovative and creative thinking in both risk identification and response development, proactively seeking potentially significant uncertainties and addressing them appropriately.' (2009; p. 10).

Part 3: Using the Right Tools and Approaches

Tailor the process and tailor the tools to the problem context . Interview 47 GM.

It is so clear from our research over the past few years that experienced project leaders use multiple methodologies. They are not wedded to one particular methodology but have access to a broad range of tools, methods and approaches from which they can draw to construct the methodology needed for each particular project context.

To enable project leaders to deal creatively with dynamic, complex and interrelated issues, project leaders need access to a range of different methods to help them structure these complex problems. Further, if, as a profession, we are to help less experienced leaders' transition to expertise it is important to look for new methodologies beyond those traditionally associated with project management. The companion book to this one, *Tools for Complex Projects*, presents a range of tools used by senior project leaders to deal with different aspects of complex projects.

PROBLEM STRUCTURING TOOLS

Creative problem-solving requires that the problem be understood in as much of its complexity as is humanly possible. Problem structuring tools help the project leader draw widely upon knowledge and information flows systemically. Complexity implies interconnectedness and nonlinearity. Many of the tools that emphasise linear rational thinking are unable to capture complex interrelationships. Special problem structuring tools and methods are needed to structure and map the salient issues, thoughts, and ideas relevant to the problem. Problem structuring requires the leader to draw upon knowledge and information flows and diagrammatically map the information/issues in order to move towards and develop solution/solutions.

LEARNING ABOUT CREATIVE PROBLEM-SOLVING FROM THE DESIGN INDUSTRY

Creative problem-solving is a core activity of the design process. Much can be learnt from studies of the design process, especially those involving both experienced with novice designers. In a study of how exceptional engineers and product designers worked, Cross (2003) revealed three common design process aspects:

- Experts take a broad 'systems approach' to the problem as opposed to merely accepting narrow problem criteria.

- Experts frame the problem in a distinctive and personal manner.

- Experts design from 'first principles'.

These findings are consistent with others (Restrepo and Christiaans, 2003; Ho, 2001; Mathias, 1993) who also found in the process of developing abstract concepts, a great number of dynamically interrelated issues were raised and explored by expert designers prior to developing a solution. Overlooking the many intricate and dynamic relationships narrows the search space, limiting creative solution finding. In the process of rushing to a solution, a less experienced project leader might tackle situations with only a narrow understanding of the problems and relationships.

STANDING BACK

Mathias (1993) found that novice designers tended to rush to solutions rather than 'stepping back from the brief'. In so doing, they tended not to separate ideas from the development of those ideas, resulting in less creative and more pedestrian solutions. Introducing problem structuring tools enables leaders to help the group to forestall solution development and focus first on the complex issues surrounding a given problem. This results in more considered responses. It was found that by introducing problem structuring strategies/tools it was possible to move the thinking framework of young designers closer to the framework of experts.

> Often better to take a breath and stand back. 'We'll move when we are ready to move and we've got it right'. Interview 46 GM.

Standing back is important especially when there is pressure to move quickly. Christiaans (1992) reported that the more time a subject spent in the process of defining and understanding the problem, the more likely a creative result was achieved. Matthias (1993) also found that expert designers utilised an enriched problem-solving process/framework compared with novice designers. Ho (2001) found that expert designers tend to establish the problem structure at the beginning of the design process and then step back from the initial problem that has been outlined in the brief, in order to contextualise the problem.

Creative problem-solving seems to involve a continuous iteration of analysis, synthesis and evaluation, all happening coincidently as both the problem and ideas for a solution are formulated (Dorst, 2001; Maher et al., 1996; Cross and Clayburn, 1998). Schön (1983) refers to this as 'problem-framing' ability which is crucial to high-level performance in creative design.

USEFUL APPROACHES

The following suggestions have been derived from observations of both novice designers and non-designers when solving complex problems (Kokotovich, 2002):

- Use a variety of problem structuring tools, not just one, to help extend the problem-framing process. Significantly more creative responses were achieved when the problem-solvers were forced to develop ideas mentally and forestall resolution of the problem. Problem structuring tools help to achieve this.

- Sketches and notes applied in rapid and unformed ways seem to be useful as an aid to long term memory.

- During early periods of problem definition, tools and approaches which encourage mental conceptualising and reasoning should take precedence over tools and approaches which might force premature containment of the problem space.

- Highly structured approaches, such as checklists which force analytical thinking, should be avoided in the early stages of problem-solving. In preference, tools that encourage freer problem exploration are important so that ideas can be generated for later evaluation.

Part 4: Effects of Time Pressure on Innovation

Time is a constraint in many complex projects. Leaders need to be aware that that time pressure can have positive as well as negative effects on innovation (Unsworth, 2004). Some studies suggest that time pressure can be a motivating element (Bunce and West, 1996). Amabile and Gryskiewicz (1987) also found that urgency due to time was cited as leading to innovation in twenty-two per cent of respondents in their study. Other researchers argue that time pressure leads to a reduction in innovation (Farr and Ford, 1990). Ganesan and Subramanian (1982) report that time pressure increased anxiety levels experienced by agricultural scientists and this was associated with decreased levels of innovation. Being creative takes time and it is possible that under pressure there will be inadequate time to work through all the options (Koestler, 1964). Time is needed for the associations to take place between disparate concepts (Mednick, 1962). In another study engineers and R&D scientists reported that having the time is important to be able to develop creative options (Hards, 1999; Amabile and Gryskiewicz, 1987). The important questions for project leaders are, when is time pressure motivating and when does it affect the quality of the outcomes?

More recent research has attempted to resolve these apparent contradictions. Some very interesting conclusions for project leadership emerged from a study of 177 employees by Annabile et al., (2002). Their findings, combined with those of Unsworth's (2004) study of the defence and aerospace industries can be summarised as follows.

Time pressure is *less* likely to help creativity and more likely to be a barrier if people:

- Are distracted when working on something.

- Do not feel the work is important.

- Work in groups rather than alone, or in small groups of two.

- Experience a lot of last minute changes.

- Think that innovation is a low priority.

- Need a broader focus (as in the project definition stage).

Time pressure is *more* likely to help creativity if people:

- Can work undisturbed.

- Are doing challenging work.

- Know the work is important.

- Understand that innovation is a high priority.

- Need a narrow focus, such as during detailed design.

TIME PRESSURE AND RISK

Regardless of other conditions, Unsworth (2004) found that time pressure increases risk aversion during implementation and evaluation stages. High time pressure encourages people to prioritise tasks, including innovation. Time pressure also encourages people to discard a wider systemic focus in favour of a narrower focus. As 'firefighting' is a common form of management when time is a constraint it is important to consider what might happen if a narrow focus is developed in response to time-related stress. The non-linear, emergent nature of any complex adaptive system means that fighting 'spot fires' will almost certainly impact other parts of the system in unanticipated ways. As Williams (2004) points out, the tendency for project managers to take immediate action to attend to a local 'fire' can have serious effects on other parts of the network.

Although much more research is needed these are important considerations for project leadership.

In Summary

Innovative or creative thinking is an important key to managing complexity because problems in complex projects are not routine, they are usually unstructured or 'wicked'. Finding 'satisficing' solutions to these kinds of problem requires both critical and creative thinking processes. Experienced project leaders use creative thinking in many ways in order to:

- Assist key stakeholders to find agreed solutions and paths to get there.

- Overcome management barriers and challenges.

- Negotiate political mazes.

- Recognise when old ways of working are no longer effective and invent others.

- Work with teams to develop appropriate technical and design solutions.

- Manage conflicted stakeholder groups.

- Motivate teams during tough times.

- Mitigate risks.

- Enhance learning.

Senior project managers surveyed in our original study (2004, 2005) valued creativity or 'thinking outside the box' as one of their most important skill sets.

'Wicked' problems require project leaders to make use of problem structuring tools in order to understand the problem from as many perspectives as possible. Research into how designers deal with 'wicked' problems provides some insights for project leaders. Effective solution finding involves standing back and forestalling solution development as long as possible. Solution finding is a continuous iteration of analysis, synthesis and evaluation processes; refining them together, involving coincidently the formulation of a problem and ideas for a solution, as occurs in proto-typing or testing.

Finally, leaders should consider the effect of time pressure on creative solution finding. More research is needed, however, there are some indicators that might assist leaders when time related pressure is a factor. When innovation is a high priority and when a narrow focus is appropriate, such as during detailed design, time pressure may help, but when innovation is not seen as a high priority or when a broader focus is appropriate, such as during problem definition, time pressure might be a barrier to creativity.

References and Further Reading

Ackerman, F. and Eden, C. (2001) SODA – Journey Making and Mapping in Practice. In: Rosenhead, J. and Mingers, J. (eds), *Rational Analysis for a Problematic World Revisited*. (Chichester: John Wiley and Sons), pp. 43–60.

Ackoff, R. (1979) The Future of Operational Research is Past. *Journal of Operational Research Society*, (30), pp. 93–104.

Agrell, A. and Gustafson, R. (1996) Innovation and Creativity in Work Groups. In: West, M.A. (ed.), *Handbook of Work Group Psychology*. Chichester, UK: Wiley, pp. 317–343.

Amabile, T.M. (ed.) (1996) *Creativity in Context*. Boulder, USA: Westview Press.

Amabile, T.M. (1988) A Model of Creativity and Innovation in Organizations. In: Staw, B.M. and Cummings, L.L. (eds), *Research in Organizational Behavior*. Greenwich, CT: JAI Press, pp. 123–167.

Amabile, T.M. (1982) Social Psychology of Creativity: A Consensual Assessment Technique. *Journal of Personality and Social Psychology*, 43, pp. 997–1013.

Amabile, T.M. and Gryskiewicz, S.S. (1987) Creativity in the R&D Laboratory, (Technical Report No. 30). Greensboro: Center for Creative Leadership.

Argyris, C. and Schön, D. (1978) *Organizational Learning: A Theory-in-action Perspective*. Reading, MA: Addison-Wesley.

Blankevoort, P.J. (1983) Management of Creativity. *International Journal of Project Management*, 1, pp. 1–33.

Broadbent, J. and Remington, K. (2005) Managing Creativity: Observations on Ecodesign Projects, (2004 and 2005) Working paper series, Colloquium, Sydney: Univeristy of Technology Sydney.

Bunce, D. and West, M.A. (1996) Stress Management and Innovation at Work. *Human Relations*, 49, pp. 209–232.

Buzan, T. (1995) *The Mind Map Book*. London, UK: BBC Books.

Christensen, C.R., Andrews, K.R. and Bower, J.L. (1978) *Business Policy: Test and Cases*, 4th ed. Homewood, IL.: Richard D. Irwin, Inc.

Christiaans, H. (1992) Creativity in Design, PhD Thesis, (Delft, The Netherlands: Delft University of Technology).

Cross, N. and Clayburn Cross, A. (1998) Expert Designers. In: Frankenburger, E., Badke-Schaub, H. and Birkhofer, H. (eds) *Designers – The Key to Successful Product Development*. London, UK: Springer Verlag.

Cross, N. (2003) The Expertise of Exceptional Designers. In: Proceedings of the 6th Design Thinking Research Symposium: Expertise in Design, in: Cross, N. and Edmonds, E. (eds) University of Technology, Sydney, Australia, 17–19 November, pp. 23–35.

Dearborn, D.C. and Simon H.A. (1958) Selective Perception: A Note on the Departmental Identification of Executives. *Sociometry*, June, pp. 140–148.

Deci, E.L. and Ryan, R.M. (1985) *Intrinsic Motivation and Self-determination in Human Behavior*. New York: Plenum.

Dewett, T. (2004) Creativity and Strategic Management: Individual and Group Considerations Concerning Decision Alternative in Top Management Teams. *Journal of Managerial Psychology*, 19(1/2), pp. 305–319.

Dewett, T. (2007) Linking Intrinsic Motivation, Risk Taking, and Employee Creativity in an R&D Environment. *R&D Management*, 37(3), pp. 197–208.

Dorner, D. (1983) Heuristics and Cognition in Complex Systems. In: Groner, R., Groner, M. and Bischof W.F. (eds), *Methods of Heuristics*. New Jersey: Lawrence Erlbaum.

Dorst, K. (2001) Creativity in the Design Process: Co-evolution of Problem-solution. *Design Studies*, 22, 425–437.

Eden, C. (2004) Analyzing Cognitive Maps to Help Structure Issues or Problems, European. *Journal of Operational Research*, 159, pp. 673–686.

Engeström, Y. (1987) Learning by Expanding: An Activity-theoretical Approach to Developmental Research. Retrieved 12/2/2005, http://lchc.ucsd.edu/MCA/Paper/Engestrom/expanding/toc.htm.

Farr, J.L. and Ford, C.M. (1990) Individual Innovation. In: West, M.A. and Farr, J.L. (eds), *Innovation and Creativity at Work*, pp. 63–80. Chicester. John Wiley and Sons.

Ferris, G.R., King, T.R., Judge, T.A. and Kacmar, K.M. (1991) The Management of Shared Meaning in Organizations. In: Giacalone, R.A. and Rosenfeld, P. (eds), *Applied Impression Management: How Image Making Affects Managerial Decisions*. Sage, Newbury Park, CA, pp. 41–64.

Feurer, R. Chaharbaghi, K and Wargin, J. (1996) Developing Creative Teams for Operational Excellence. *International Journal of Operations & Productions Management*, 16(1), pp. 305–310.

Frooman, J. (1999) Stakeholder Influence Strategies. *Academy of Management Review*, Vol. 24, pp. 191–205.

Ganesan, V. and Subramanian, S. (1982) Creativity, Anxiety, Time Pressure and Innovativeness Among Agricultural Scientists. *Managerial Psychology*, 3(1), pp. 40–48.

George, J.M. and Zhou, J. (2001) When Openness to Experience and Conscientiousness are Related to Creative Behavior: an Interactional Approach. *Journal of Applied Psychology*, 86, pp. 513–524.

Gist, M.E. (1989) The Influence of Training Method on Self-efficacy and Idea Generation Among Managers. *Personnel Psychology*, 42, pp. 787–805.

Griffin, M. and McDermott, M.R. (1998) Exploring a Tripartite Relationship Between Rebelliousness, Openness to Experience and Creativity. *Social Behavior and Personality*, 26, pp. 347–356.

Hards, R. (1999) An Investigation of Barriers to Creativity in Engineering Design: A Progress Report. Plymouth: School of Comuting, University of Plymouth.

Harris, R. (1998) Introduction to Creative Thinking. http://www.virtualsalt.com/crebook1.htm; accessed 20/2/11.

Helm, J. and Remington, K. (2005a) Adaptive Habitus – Project Managers' Perceptions of the Role of the Project Sponsor, Proceedings of EURAM Conference, May, Munich: TUT University.

Helm, J. and Remington, K. (2005b) Effective Sponsorship, Project Managers Perceptions of the Role of the Project Sponsor. *Project Management Journal*, 36(3), pp. 51–62.

Hillson, D. (2009) Innovative Risk Management. *Project Manager Today*, April, p. 10.

Ho, C. (2001) Some Phenomena of Problem Decomposition in Strategy for Design Thinking. *Design Studies*, 22, pp. 27–45.

Holmquist, M. (2007) Managing Project Transformation in a Complex Context. *Creativity and Innovation Management*, 16(1), pp. 46–52.

Isaksen, S. and Treffinger, D. (1985) *Creative Problem Solving: The Basic Course.* Buffalo, NY: Bearly Limited.

Kim, S.H. (1990) *Essence of Creativity – A Guide to Tackling Difficult Problems,* New York, NY: Oxford University Press.

Koestler, A. (1964) *The Act of Creation.* New York, NY: MacMillan.

Kokotovich, V. (2002) Creative Mental Synthesis in Designers and Non-designers: Experimental Examinations, Thesis (PhD), University of Sydney, Sydney, Australia.

Kokotovich, V. and Remington, K. (2007) Enhancing Innovative Capabilities: Developing Creative Thinking Approaches with Tomorrow's Project Managers, IRNOP VIII, Brighton, UK, Conference Proceedings.

Kokotovich, V. and Purcell, T. (2001) Ideas, the Embodiment of Ideas and Drawing: An Experimental Investigation of Inventing, Proceedings of 2nd International conference on visual and spatial reasoning in Design, in: Gero, J., Tversky, B., Purcell, T. (eds), Bellagio Conference Center, Bellagio Italy, 17–19 July, pp. 283–298.

Kunda, Z. (1999) *Social Cognition: Making Sense of People.* Cambridge, MA: MIT Press.

Lewis, C. (2004) Being Creative in the Workplace. *The British Journal of Administrative Management*, Oct/Nov, pp. 24–26.

Maher, M.J., Poon, J. and Boulanger, S. (1996) Formalising Design Exploration As Co-evolution: A Combined Gene Approach. In: Gero, J.S. and Sudweeks, F. (eds), *Advances in Formal Design Methods for CAD*. London, UK: Chapman and Hall.

March, J.G. (1991) Exploration and Exploitation in Organizational Learning. *Organization Science*, 2(1), pp. 71–87.

Mason, R.O. and Mitroff, I.I. (1981) *Challenging Strategic Planning Assumptions*. New York: John Wiley and Sons.

Mathias, J.R. (1993) A Study of the Problem Solving Strategies used by Expert and Novice Designers, PhD Thesis University of Aston, Birmingham, UK.

Mednick, S.A. (1962) The Associative Basis of the Creative Process. *Psychological Review*, 69(3), pp. 220–232.

Middleton, E. (1998) The Role of Visual Mental Imagery in Solving Complex Problems in Design, PhD Thesis, Griffith University, Queensland, Australia.

Mintzberg, H. (1975) The Manager's Job: Folklore and Facts. *Harvard Business Review*, July–August, pp. 49–61.

Mintzberg, H., Raisinghani, R. and Theoret, A. (1976) The Structure of Unstructured Decision Processes. *Administrative Science Quarterly*, 21, pp. 246–275.

Mumford, M.D., Scott, G.M., Gaddis, B. and Strange, J.M. (2002) Leading Creative People: Orchestrating Expertise and Relationships. *Leadership Quarterly*, 13(6).

Mumford, M.D. and Gustafson, S.B. (1988) Creativity Syndrome: Integration, Application, and Innovation. *Psychological Bulletin*, 103, pp. 27–43.

Narayanan, V.K. and Fahey, L. (1982) The Micro-politics of Strategy Formulation. *Academy of Management Review*, 7(1), pp. 25–34.

Newell, A. and Simon, H.A. (1972) *Human Problem Solving*. Englewood Cliffs, New Jersey: Prentice-Hall.

Nguyen, H.Q. (2001) In Praise of Middle Managers. *Harvard Business Review*, 79(8), pp. 72–80.

Oldham, G.R. and Cummings, A. (1996) Employee Creativity: Personal and Contextual Factors at Work. *Academy of Management Journal*, 39, pp. 607–34.

Parnes, S. (1967) *Creative Behavior Guidebook*. New York, NY: Scribner's.

Picq, T. (1999) *Manager une équipe de projet: Pilotage, Enjeux, Performance*, Dunod, Paris.

Poon, J.M.L. (2002) Situational Antecedents and Outcomes of Organizational Politics Perceptions. *Journal of Managerial Psychology*, 18(2), pp. 138–55.

Prince, G.M. (1992) The Practices of Creativity. In: Thorne, P. (ed.), *Organizing Genius*. Blackwell Business Publishers, Oxford.

Redmond, M.R., Mumford, M.D. and Teach, R. (1993) Putting Creativity to Work: Effects of Leader Behavior on Subordinate Creativity. *Organizational Behavior and Human Decision Processes*, 55, pp. 120–151.

Restrepo, J. and Christiaans, H. (2003) Problem Structuring and Information Access in Design. In: Proceedings of the 6th Design Thinking Research Symposium: Expertise in Design, in: Cross, N. and Edmonds, E. (eds), University of Technology, Sydney, Australia, 17–19 November, pp. 149–162.

Rittel, H. and Webber, M. (1973) Dilemmas in a General Theory of Planning. *Policy Sciences*, 4, pp. 155–169.

Schön, D.A. (1990) The Design Process. In: Howard, V.A. (ed.) *Varieties of Thinking: Essays of Harvard's Philosophy of Education Research Center*. New York: Routledge.

Schön. D.A. (1983) *The Reflective Practitioner: How Professionals Think in Action*. NY: Basic Books.

Senge, P. (1990) *The Fifth Discipline: The Art and Practice of the Learning Organization*. New York, NY: Doubleday/Currency.

Shalley, C.E. and Gilson, L.L. (2004) What Leaders Need to Know: A Review of Social and Contextual Factors that can Foster or Hinder Creativity. *Leadership Quarterly*, 15, pp. 33–53.

Shalley, C.E. (1991) Effects of Productivity Goals, Creativity Goals, and Personal Discretion on Individual Creativity. *Journal of Applied Psychology*, 76, pp. 179–185.

Simon, H.A. (1973) The Structure of Ill-structured Problems. *Artificial Intelligence*, 4, pp. 181–201.

Simon, H.A. (1957) A Behavioral Model of Rational Choice. In: Simon, H.A. *Models of Man*, Wiley, pp. 241–260.

Simon, L. (2006) Managing Creative Projects: An Empirical Synthesis of Activities. *International Journal of Project Management*, 24(2), pp. 116–126.

Snowden, D. (2002) Complex Acts of Knowing: Paradox and Descriptive Self-awareness. *Journal of Knowledge Management*, 6(2).

Sternberg, R.J. and Lubart, T.I. (1991) An Investment Theory of Creativity and its Development. *Human Development*, 34, pp. 1–31.

Sutton, M.J. (2003) Problem Representation, Understanding, and Learning Transfer Implications for Technology Education. *Journal of Industrial Teacher Education*, 40, 4.

Ungson, G.R., Braunstein, D.N. and Hall, P.D. (1981) Managerial Information Processing: A Research Review. *Administrative Science Quarterly*, 26, pp. 116–134.

Unsworth, K.L. (2004) Firefighting: The Effects of Time Pressure on Employee Innovation, Proceedings of the 18th Annual Conference of the Australian and New Zealand Academy of Management, 8–11 December, Dunedin, New Zealand. Available http://eprints.qut.edu.au/3031/1/Time_pressure_&_innov_ANZAM.pdf; accessed 21/2/11.

Van Der Weide, J.G. and Wilderom, C. (2004) Deromancing Leadership: What are the Behaviours of Highly Effective Middle Managers? *International Journal of Management Practice*, 1(1), pp. 3–20.

VanLehn, K. (1989) Problem Solving and Cognitive Skill. In: Posner, M.I. (ed.) *Foundations of Cognitive Science*. Cambridge, Mass: MIT Press.

Williams, T. (2004) Why Monte Carlo Simulations of Project Networks can Mislead. *Project Management Journal*, 25(3), pp. 53–61.

Woodman, R.W., Sawyer, J.E. and Griffin, R.W. (1993) Toward a Theory of Organizational Creativity. *Academy of Management Review*, 18, pp. 293–321.

Zhou, J. and George, J.M. (2001) When Job Dissatisfaction Leads to Creativity: Encouraging the Expression of Voice. *Academy of Management Journal*, 44(4), pp. 682–696.

Yin, Y., Vanides, J., Ruiz-Primo, M.R., Ayala, C.C. and Shavelson, R.J. (2005) Comparison of Two Concept-mapping Techniques: Implications for Scoring, Interpretation, and Use. *Journal of Research in Science Teaching*, 42(2), pp. 166–184.

6

Think About Thinking

To manage in a complex environment you need to be able to adapt what you do to deal with emergent situations, to do this you need to step back and be conscious of how you are thinking in the situation; notice when your approach is not gelling with the environment; when your approach isn't achieving the results you want; you need to think about thinking itself.

Interview 31 PM.

One of the lasting impressions from the interviews was that the majority of senior leaders interviewed in our sample were reflective. They think about how they made decisions and they 'think about thinking'. Decision-making under conditions of uncertainty is fraught with difficulty. Although research in this field has developed considerably there is a great deal yet to understand. The following chapter summarises some of the current thinking and alerts project leaders to some of the issues about reliability of information.

Key Points in This Chapter:

- How we make complex decisions.

- The reliability of information during uncertainty.

Part 1: How We Make Complex Decisions

RATIONAL DECISION-MAKING

Our ability to make rational decisions has long been thought to distinguish human beings from other creatures. Decision-making theory based on the idea of rational causality has dominated management science and project management theory. Nevertheless, a number of people have questioned how humans actually come to make decisions. Herbert Simon's (1976, 1990) theory of decision-making under *bounded rationality* offers the notion that in decision-making, or rationality, is limited or bound by the information available, the cognitive limitations of our minds and the finite amount of time we have to make decisions. The theory challenges the idea of decision-making as a fully rational process of making optimal choices given the information available. Simon (1976, 1990) argued that decision-makers lack the ability and resources to arrive at the optimal solution; they instead apply their rationality only after having greatly simplified the choices available.

Opposition to classical decision theory also comes from experimental psychologists who have shown that the basic assumptions of decision theory, for example, choosing from among alternatives in order to get the optimum outcome, so-called transitive thinking processes, (if A is preferred to B, and B is preferred to C, then A is preferred to C) is often violated by people when making decisions (Tversky and Kahneman, 1981; Kahneman and Tversky, 1979). How emotions influence our decision-making has been of particular interest. Recent developments in neuroscience have generated much greater understanding of how human cognition works and how we make decisions under conditions of uncertainty. The brain can be seen as comprising interconnected neural nets with an enormous amount of redundancy in pathways. Of particular importance to project leadership is the brain's ability to recognise patterns. (Churchland, 2002, 2007; Clark, 1997; Clark and Eliasmith, 2002).

Enhanced ability to integrate complex information and find meaningful patterns would appear to be vital for project leaders, particularly when the project is complex. *Cognitive complexity* is the label given to the study of how people process complex information. *Cognitive differentiation* represents an individual's ability to dissect information into smaller units. *Cognitive integration* is the ability of an individual to combine smaller units of information into a whole unit, or the capacity to form conceptual frameworks that organise complex situations. The ability to integrate information is often deemed as the more important component of cognitive complexity (Stabell, 1978). Research suggests that there are differences in individuals' ability to differentiate and integrate information (Schroder, et al., 1967). Clift and Vandenbosch (1999) note that for complex projects in particular, project leaders must be able to coordinate disparate groups and use high levels of improvisation. They also must be able to integrate many types of information. Saarinen (1990) found that in instances where stakeholder assessments of project success were low, internal integration was also found to be low. Hauschildt et al., (2000), as part of a survey of 58 organisations, found that 'integrative thinking', which they defined as the ability to think analytically while bringing together many different ideas, was a key attribute of successful project leaders. The most successful project leaders, scored higher in integrative thinking than other, less successful project leaders. Yiu and Saner (2000) found that cognitively complex thinking was required in order for managers to be effective in global efforts. More recently, Green (2004) found that, in general, project leaders displaying higher levels of integrative complexity performed better in project definition tasks than those with lower integrative complexity scores.

FALLING SHORT OF RATIONALITY

Human behaviour falls short of rationality in the following ways:

- Rationality requires complete knowledge and anticipation of the consequences that will follow each choice.

- Knowledge of consequences is always fragmentary. Since these consequences lie in the future, imagination must substitute for the lack of experience when attaching values to them, but values can be only imperfectly anticipated.

- Rationality implies a choice among all possible alternative behaviours. In actual behaviour only a very few of all these possible alternatives ever come to mind (Simon, 1976, p. 81).

Thagard and Millgram (1997) argue that in most situations humans have multiple interrelated goals that determine which actions are preferred. The following story illustrates:

> *[...] an eminent philosopher of science once encountered a noted decision theorist in a hallway at their university. The decision theorist was pacing up and down, muttering, 'What shall I do? What shall I do?'*
>
> *'What's the matter, Howard?' Asked the philosopher.*
>
> *Replied the decision theorist: 'It's horrible, Ernest – I've got an offer from Harvard and I don't know whether to accept it.'*
>
> *'Why Howard,' reacted the philosopher, 'you're one of the world's great experts on decision making. Why don't you just work out the decision tree, calculate the probabilities and expected outcomes, and determine which choice maximizes your expected utility?' With annoyance, the other replied: 'Come on, Ernest. This is serious.' (cited in Thagard and Millgram, 1997).*

Whereas earlier theory explained preferences on the basis of a single alternative, decision-making under uncertainty involves multiple interrelated goals. Moreover, when people are expected to choose between multiple attributes, the goals and sub-goals do not remain static; they are often adjusted during the decision-making process (Thagard and Millgram, 1997). Goals are not fixed in a person's mind; they become more or less important to us over time. We hold views on many issues and we tend to change our minds from time to time as we discover new information (Carpenter, 1989). This suggests that the decision process is a much more fluid activity. Also, at any one time we have multiple goals, some of them consonant with each other but others that are mutually contrary or discordant (Kolnai, 1978).

As decision-makers, in addition to deciding on actions to accomplish our initial goals, in the process of exploring or achieving initial goals we find other goals to be achieved. For example, a runner who likes to run every day may adopt the goal of running in a marathon. Running every day facilitates running the marathon, not the other way around, but in this case the goal is adopted to fit the means for accomplishing it. People have a deep need to adopt goals that provide them with a sense of purpose and unity to their lives and therefore those goals my attract preference over others that do not provide a sense of purpose (Frankfurt, 1992; Harman, 1976).

EMOTIONS AND DECISION-MAKING

Emotions play a vital part in decision-making. The idea that emotion and cognition are two separate systems that interact only occasionally is no longer accepted scientifically. In fact, it is now understood that interaction between emotion and cognition is essential for adaptive human functioning (Ochsner and Phelps, 2007). As Dolan (2002, p. 1191) notes, emotions '... are less susceptible to our intentions than other psychological states insofar as they are often triggered unawares; ... and most importantly, they are less encapsulated than other psychological states as evident in their global effects on virtually all aspects of cognition.'

Emotion can interfere with values by making us behave inconsistently. For example, people can value impartiality when evaluating alternatives but at the same time can find themselves wanting to favour some alternatives in comparison with others, which they might find repugnant, even if others in the group do not express a similar negative emotional response. Also, we frequently present decision alternatives in ways that take advantage of emotional responses to sway decision-making. Because we are prone to evaluate equal situations differently when they are described differently, an entrepreneur recognises that those providing the funding for a project would prefer to think of the project having an eight-five per cent chance of success than a fifteen per cent chance of failure, even though the two are equivalent in actuarial terms (Dolan, 2002).

EMOTIONS AND STRESS

More often than not, when a project is complex, decision-making involves multiple parties and also occurs under stress. It is important to recognise that emotion, rather than strict logic, informs many decisions under these circumstances. R&D projects in the pharmaceutical industry are good examples of projects that are characterised by genuine uncertainty. Usually, decision-makers need to take account of many regulatory demands, financial concerns in terms of clinical trials being costly, accounting for a very high proportion of the entire new drug development costs and they need to respond to organisational ambiguities in terms of more than one governing body within the organisation.

As Styhre et al., (2010) found, in their study of pharmaceutical development projects, project management processes that prescribe the range of decisions the teams and team leaders are entitled to make are not adhered to. When stakes are high it is important to understand that people will not behave in a linear rational manner. Decisions are made on the basis of emotion rather than evidence and previously careful decisions based on evidence are overturned in an apparently arbitrary manner. For example, high levels of anxiety due to diminishing returns on investment in R&D resulted in members of the project executive boards overturning earlier decisions. In this case, fear was an overriding emotion that contributed to what seemed like erratic decision-making to the researchers.

UNCERTAINTY CAN RESULT IN DELAYS IN DECISION-MAKING

Returning to the previous example of R&D in the pharmaceutical industry, Styhre et al., (2010) found that decision-making was far from linear in practice. Several committees had a say in the design. The clinical project teams would have to lobby for their decisions in each of these committees. Serving as an intermediary level between the strategic decision-making in the executive tiers of the organisation and the operative functions of the firm, the clinical trial teams had to buffer the tension between the decision-making anxiety at the top of the organisation and the need for 'go/no go decisions' regarding the trials. At times, the inability to make decisions higher up in the organisation delayed the progress in such a way that processes were rendered obsolete by the time decisions were made. Other procedures, such as occasional migration of quite minor decision-making up the hierarchy also slowed progress, leaving the clinical team leaders at the lowest levels without guidance on how to proceed, increasing the stress at the level of the clinical project teams at the intermediary level and eliminating the more strategic focus at the more executive levels (Styhre et al., 2010).

DECISION-MAKING IS NONLINEAR DURING UNCERTAINTY

Under circumstances like the above some might suggest that strictly following prescribed project management models would eliminate much of the confusion and nonlinearity regarding decision-making. Rather than operating as smoothly as prescribed in the formal project management models promoted by the organisation, the decision-making process was described by the researchers as 'a form of a garbage-can decision-making' (Styhre et al., p. 141) in which decisions were overturned, choices were made in an apparently erratic manner, decision-makers came and went and problem definition and solution finding was reversed Similar studies of R&D teams suggests that decision-making under uncertainty and under the pressure to perform financially is characterised by nonlinearity (Cohen et al., 1972; March and Olsen, 1976).

INTUITION, HUNCHES OR 'GUT FEEL'

Instead of ignoring emotions we need to recognise that emotions are instrumental in developing tacit or implicit knowledge through experience and our experience is a critical input to decision-making. 'As practicing managers or administrators, we learn that when faced with an array of – possibly conflicting and ill-defined choices – our "hunches" or "gut-feels", our sweaty palms or increased heart rates, are to be taken note of as indications of non-conscious decision processes our brains and bodies generate from past experience.' (Lakomsky and Evers, 2009, p. 440). As opposed to logically weighing options and alternatives in a kind of cost-benefit analysis, as rational theories of choice suggest (Clore and Huntsinger, 2007), what most of us knew all along has now been demonstrated scientifically. We frequently make decisions at 'gut' or emotional level (Bechara, 2004; Bechara et al., 2000; Damasio, 1996).

For example, as project leaders we may have a negative 'gut' reaction about a course of action that appears, on the basis of rational analysis, to be the best course. The somatic marker, or 'gut' feeling, might cause us to reflect further on our decision. Most of us recognise this as a kind of early warning system. According to Damasio et al., (1991), the reaction serves to help us narrow down the pool of available options for selection. In this manner, somatic markers help to make decision-making more accurate and efficient. Specifically, '… somatic markers are a special instance of feelings generated from secondary emotions. Those emotions and feelings have been connected, by learning, to predicted future outcomes of certain scenarios' (Damasio, 1996, p. 174). A negative somatic marker functions like an alarm bell while a positive somatic experience serves as an incentive; this accumulated experience, expressed through our emotions, or 'gut feel', is what we know as intuition.

INFORMED INTUITION

However, there are dangers if our emotions reflect values that are inappropriate for the situation. Racist feelings are examples of deeply ingrained emotional responses that can colour decision-making. Gender preferences are usually similarly driven by emotional responses. Rather than dismiss the positive aspects of intuition during important decisions, rather than leaping to an immediate intuitive choice, leaders might consider using a process like the following (adapted and modified from Thargard (2001):

- Set up the problem space carefully.

- Identify the initial goals to be accomplished by your decision.

- Specify the broad range of possible actions that might accomplish those goals.

- Reflect on the importance of the different goals.

- Reflection should be more emotional and intuitive rather than just putting a numerical weight on them, but should help you to be more aware of what you care about in the current decision situation.

- Identify goals whose importance may be exaggerated because of any emotional distortions.

- Identify if new goals emerge in the process.

- Reflect on whether these new goals contribute to or are contradictory to original goals.

- Examine beliefs about the extent to which various actions would facilitate the different goals.

- Are these beliefs based on good evidence?

- Are they driven by deeply held values that are inappropriate?

- If they are, revisit them.

- Make an intuitive judgment about the best action to perform, monitoring your emotional reaction to different options.

- Test your decision.

- Run your decision past other people to see if it seems reasonable to them.

- Test it using economic models if appropriate.

This process alters normal decision-making, which either tends to get bogged down in analysis, evidence which is then overturned on the basis of emotional responses like fear, or which involves predetermined decisions, which decision-makers may then seek to justify by selecting and manipulating evidence to support.

Part 2: Reliability of Information During Uncertainty

The old adage 'garbage in – garbage out' springs to mind because sound decision-making still relies on the reliability of the information on which decisions are based – so-called evidence-based decision-making. However, conditions of uncertainty tend to interfere with the quality of information available.

ENVIRONMENTAL SCANNING IN UNCERTAINTY.

Vital to decision-making for project leaders is the ability to scan the environment. This is the only way that temporal sources of complexity, those related to changes in the environment, can be detected. Miller (1993) observed that over time and with experience, most managers tend to become more narrow and 'simplistic' in their thinking. Although executive leaders are not the only sources of environmental information, they do play a significant role in gathering external intelligence. Research has shown that executives can spend as much as one quarter of their time monitoring the environment (Hambrick, 1981; Kefalas and Schoderbek, 1973). And yet, environments can be diffuse, complex, dynamic and elusive. The magnitude of the scanning task can be daunting to any individual's information processing capabilities. Boyd and Fulk (1996) argue that whilst scanning may well provide useful information, when the environment is not predictable or difficult to analyse (perceived complexity), external information search is less beneficial. Amount of scanning will vary depending on perceived variability, complexity and perceived relevance. An important issue, for example, may receive only limited scanning if it is thought to be too complex to yield any valuable strategic information.

As would be expected scanning for important events tends to be stepped-up when threats are anticipated. If, on the other hand, an event is not sufficiently important to rate regular monitoring, even high levels of threat do not cause monitoring levels to be increased (Boyd and Fulk, 1996). Of even greater concern is the finding that an increase in perceived complexity acts as a significant disincentive to executives to continue scanning the environment. These results support earlier findings (Fredrickson, 1984; Fredrickson and Mitchell, 1984) that comprehensive information search and decision-making is more likely to occur in stable environments as opposed to unstable environments. As organisations mainly get to know their environments through their leaders' perceptions (Weick, 1969), unnoticed events do not affect organisational decisions and actions and are not responded to (Miles et al., 1974).

The implications of these results should be of concern to project leaders. Project leaders depend on executive leaders for timely warning about changes in the external environment that could impact the project. Under conditions of volatility and uncertainty, project leaders might expect that environmental information will be incomplete at best and inaccurate at worst. In order to reduce potential sources of error due to inadequate or inappropriate information, project executive leaders at executive level need to take special precautions to step up scanning during turbulent times, involving as many people inside and outside the project to increase the richness of the information. As discussed in Chapter 5, standing back to take in as much environmental information as possible is a vital first step.

> *Always take the highest possible perspective. You can't get high enough.*
> *Interview 54 PD.*

INFORMATION OVERLOAD AND STRESS

Information is gathered and used because it helps to make choices. Continuous information collecting can also be symptomatic of decision paralysis. Also, information overload increases the risk of being unable to comprehend the information or use it effectively in a decision. As Feldman and March (1981) note, a common organisational response is to keep on collecting information, resulting in users becoming overloaded and the quality of decisions and organisational knowledge becoming impaired, contributing to a further increase in perceptions of uncertainty. It is a vicious cycle. When organisations lack the right mechanisms for information processing, information gathering alone is not sufficient for reducing uncertainty. Without appropriate processing mechanisms gathering more and more information, things might actually get worse (Ellis and Shpielberg, 2003). It is important that leaders ensure that information collected can be utilised appropriately and that information collecting is not continuing for its own sake.

INFORMATION FOR RISK MANAGEMENT IN UNCERTAIN ENVIRONMENTS

Organisations operating in uncertain environments use fewer formal learning procedures than those in certain environments (Ellis and Shpielberg, 2003; Hovarth et al., 1981). This has important implications for the role of information in decision-making processes under conditions of uncertainty. Information becomes meaningful as a consequence of how it is filtered, interpreted, shared and ultimately used (Heath, 1994). This is often referred to as the organisation's absorptive capacity (Cohen and Levinthal, 1990; Zahra and George, 2002). Without ways of absorbing the information, organisations and programmes or projects, which depend upon their sponsoring organisations for intelligence, may not be able to access the knowledge needed to manage the risks. Harnessing informal channels in problem structuring might provide more relevant information than relying exclusively on existing channels. Decision-making relies on processes such as sensemaking and situational awareness– which emerge in natural settings and take forms that are not easily replicated using formal channels.

MODELLING OTHERS – A COMMON RESPONSE IN UNCERTAINTY

Under conditions of uncertainty, it is natural that leaders look for models that might show them the way. During environmental uncertainty organisations imitate one another, looking for answers to their uncertainty by modelling how other organisations in their field have faced similar uncertainties. Organisations tend to adopt the structure and managerial techniques that are used by the other organisations with which they interact (DiMaggio and Powell, 1983). However, under conditions of complexity, collecting information about how another organisation or project managed in the past is likely to provide information that is only partially relevant.

Innovative approaches will be needed. 'Thinking outside the box' using problem structuring and creative thinking tools and involving as many relevant people in providing and structuring rich information will be more likely to achieve a sustainable way forward (see Chapter 5). Relying on existing experts is risky because existing experts will continue to apply the pattern of their previous knowledge. As Snowdon (2002) argues, when the whole knowledge base is changing the very least leaders should do is bring in competing expertise and not think that what worked in the past will work in the future. Drawing from complexity theory, he suggests leaders use catalytic probes, actions or ideas that stimulate a pattern of activity called an *attractor*. If it is a beneficial attractor the idea is to stabilise it, or amplify it – if it is a negative attractor the response is to dampen it or destroy it very quickly. In complexity theory an attractor is something that becomes a focus for activity and information.

In one project, through which some of my colleagues were trying to radically change work practices, a smart new process was created, but instead of insisting everyone use it the project leader made it available only to an exclusive few. Gradually more and more people in the organisation got to know about it and wanted it. The new process became an attractor which resulted in the change rolling out throughout the organisation with almost no opposition. During times of uncertainty copying what worked in the past or is working for others will rarely produce a useful way forward. Experimentation through innovative thinking is needed both in terms of the new processes and new ways of gaining acceptance.

'SATISFICING' DECISION-MAKING UNDER UNCERTAINTY

Decision-making under uncertainty is unlikely ever to be perfect. It is more likely to be 'satisficing', the best decision at the time, taking into account as much relevant information as possible. In large infrastructure projects, there is always a balance between how much information can be obtained and the need to make a decision in time as an exerpt from an interview with a project leader working in the water management sector demonstrates:

> You need to be consultative, and not have just one view and that's all there is. By consultative I mean recognising a timeframe when you need to make a decision by and try and work with that, allowing other views to be put, massaging as you go where it is appropriate. The other thing is to be decisive, to actually make the decision and not let things procrastinate. There's a balance, sometimes you have to make very quick decisions where you don't get much opportunity. You try to engage with the appropriate people to allow that process to happen while recognising when you need to make decisions. Interview 65 PM.

Decision-making under uncertainty requires project leaders to have a number of skills. They include the ability to:

- Collect and sort rich information and continue to do so as the project unfolds.

- Monitor and work with organisational politics to expedite higher level decision-making.

- Protect specialist teams from organisational politics so that they can get on with their work.

- Pay attention to as many stakeholders as possible and maintain a broad focus to make sure that changing requirements are monitored.

- Stand back and reflect.

- Use informed intuition.

- Develop innovative solutions (see Chapter 5).

- Model emotional resilience to cope with disruptions (see Chapter 2).

- Communicate appropriately (see Chapter 2).

This is a tall list. When facing the kinds of turbulent environments that characterise complex projects, there is a strong argument for responsibility being taken by leadership teams, rather than individual leaders being expected to shoulder the whole burden. At the start of this chapter it was noted that the majority of leaders interviewed were reflective. Our assessment was that they spent time thinking about how they made decisions. An ability to reflect is probably one of the key survival characteristics for decision-makers in these kinds of projects. Rarely can a decision made under turbulent conditions be perfect. Self-awareness and the ability to reflect will reduce mistakes, even if they can't be eliminated. The last say should be given to one of the leaders interviewed:

> *Any behaviour that doesn't encourage honest self appraisal and dialogue is undermining. Interview 54 PD.*

In Summary

Research into how we make decisions now recognises that linear rationality is more often the exception rather than the rule:

- Enhanced ability to integrate complex information and find meaningful patterns would appear to be a vital characteristic for project leaders.

- Personal values, beliefs and emotions influence apparently rational decision processes.

- Emotions are important. Emotional reactions can impair decision-making and also enhance intuitive responses, due to the role of emotions in tacit learning.

- Under conditions of uncertaintyinformation gathering is often impaired. During periods of uncertainty leaders make decisions with less reliable information that might be at their fingertips during more stable times. This fact alone should ring alarm bells for project leaders.

- An ability to reflect is probably one of the key survival characteristics for decision-makers in conditions of uncertainty and turbulence.

References and Further Reading

Bartunek, J., Gordon, J. and Weathersby, R. (1983) Developing a 'Complicated' Understanding in Administrators. *Academy of Management Review*, 8, pp. 273–284.

Bechara, A. (2004) The Role of Emotion in Decision-making: Evidence from Neurological Patients with Orbitofrontal Damage. *Brain and Cognition*, 55, pp. 30–40.

Bechara, A. and Damasio, A.R. (2005) The Somatic Marker Hypothesis: A Neural Theory of Economic Decision. *Games and Economic Behavior*, 52, pp. 336–372.

Bechara, A., Damasio, H. and Damasio, A.R. (2000) Emotion, Decision-making and the Orbitofrontal Cortex. *Cerebral Cortex*, 10, pp. 295–307.

Boyd, B.K. and Fulk, J. (1996) Executive Scanning and Perceived Uncertainty: A Multidimensional Model. *Journal of Management*, 22(1), pp. 1–21.

Carpenter, G.A. (1989) Neural Network Models for Pattern Recognition and Associative Memory. *Neural Networks*, 2, pp. 243–57.

Churchland, P.M. (2007) *Neurophilosophy at Work*. Cambridge, MA: Cambridge University Press.

Churchland, P.S. (2002) *Brain-wise*. Cambridge, MA: MIT Press.

Clark, A. (1997) *Being There: Putting Brain, Body, and World Together Again*, Cambridge, MA: MIT Press.

Clark, A. and Eliasmith, C. (2002) Philosophical Issues in Brain Theory and Connectionism. In: M.A. Arbib (ed.), *The Handbook of Brain Theory and Neural Networks*, 2nd. Ed. MIT Press.

Clift, T. and Vandenbosch, M. (1999) Project Complexity and Efforts to Reduce Product Development Cycle Time. *Journal of Business Research*, 45, pp. 187–198.

Clore, G.L. and Huntsinger, J.R. (2007) How Emotions Inform Judgment and Regulate Thought. *Trends in Cognitive Sciences*, 11(9), pp. 393–9.

Cohen, M.D., March, J.G. and Olsen, J.P. (1972) A Garbage Can Model of Organizational Choice. *Administrative Science Quarterly*, 17, pp. 1–25.

Cohen, W.M. and Levinthal, D.A. (1990) Absorptive Capacity: A New Perspective on Learning and Innovation. *Administrative Science Quarterly*, 35, pp. 128–152.

Daft, R.L. and Weick, K.E. (1984) Toward a Model of Organizations as Interpretation Systems. *Academy of Management Review*, 1984, 9, pp. 284–295.

Damasio, A.R. (2003) *Looking for Spinoza*. New York, NY: Harcourt.

Damasio, A.R. (1999) *The Feeling of What Happens*. New York, NY: Harcourt.

Damasio, A.R. (1996) *Descartes' Error*. London, UK: Macmillan.

Damasio, A.R., Tranel, D. and Damasio, H. (1991) Somatic Markers and the Guidance of Behavior: Theory and Preliminary Testing. In: Levin, H.S., Eisenberg, H.M. and Benton, A.L. (eds), *Frontal Lobe Function and Dysfunction*. New York, NY: Oxford University Press.

DiMaggio, P. and Powell, W.W. (1983) The Iron Cage Revisited: Institutional Isomorphism and Collective Rationality in Organizational Fields. *American Sociological Review*, 48, pp. 147–160.

Dolan, R.J. (2002) Emotion, Cognition and Behavior. *Science*, 298(5596), pp. 1191–1194.

Ellis, S. and Shpielberg, N. (2003) Organizational Learning Mechanisms and Managers' Perceived Uncertainty. *Human Relations*. 56(10), pp. 1233–1254.

Frankfurt, H. (1992) On the Usefulness of Final Ends. *Lyyun: The Jerusalem Philosophical Quarterly*, 41, pp. 3–19.

Feldman, M.S. and March, J.G. (1981) Information in Organizations as Signal and Symbol. *Administrative Science Quarterly*, 26, pp. 171–186.

Fredrickson, J.W. (1984) The Comprehensiveness of Strategic Decision Processes: Extension, Observations, and Future Directions. *Academy of Management Journal*, 27, pp. 445–466.

Fredrickson, J.W. and Mitchell, T.R. (1984) Strategic Decision Processes: Comprehensiveness and Performance in an Industry with an Unstable Environment. *Academy of Management Journal*, 27, pp. 399–423.

Green, G.C. (2004) The Impact of Cognitive Complexity on Project Leadership Performance. *Information and Software Technology*, 46, pp. 165–172.

Hambrick, D.C. (1981) Specialization of Environmental Scanning Activities Among Upper Level Executives. *Journal of Management Studies*, 18, pp. 299–320.

Harman, G. (1976) Practical Reasoning. *Review of Metaphysics*, 29, pp. 431–463.

Hauschildt, J., Keim, G. and Medeof, J. (2000) Realistic Criteria for Project Management Selection and Development. *Project Management Journal*, 31(3), pp. 23–32.

Heath, R.L. (1994) *The Management of Corporate Communication*. Hillsdale, NJ: Erlbaum.

Hovarth, D., Macmillan, C.J., Azumi, K. and Hickson, D.J. (1981) The Cultural Context of Organization Control: An International Comparison. In: D.J. Hickson and C.J. Macmillan (eds), *Organization and Nation: The Aston Program*, IV. Aldershot: Gower, pp. 173–183.

Howard, R. A. (1966) Decision Analysis: Applied Decision Theory. Proceedings of the 4th International Conference on Operational Research. pp. 55–77, http:// decision.stanford.edu/library/ronald-a.-howard/Decision%20Analysis-%20 Applied%20Decision%20Theory.pdf/view; accessed 17/2/11.

Kahneman, D. and Snell, J. (1990) Predicting Utility. In: Hogarth, R.M. (ed.), *Insights in Decision-making*, pp. 295–310. Chicago: University of Chicago Press.

Kahneman, D. and Tversky, A. (1979) Prospect Theory: An Analysis of Decision Under Risk. *Econometrica*, 47, pp. 263–291.

Kefalas, A. and Schoderbek, P. (1973) Scanning the Business Environment: Some Empirical Results. *Decision Sciences*, 4, pp. 63–74.

Khalil, D. and Clark, J. (1989) The Influence of Programmers' Cognitive Complexity on Program Comprehension and Modification. *International Journal of Man–machine Studies*, 31, pp. 219–236.

Kolnai, A. (1978) Deliberation is of Ends. In: Kolnai, A. *Ethics, Value, and Reality. Selected Papers of Aurel, Kolnai*, pp. 44–62. Indianapolis, USA: Hackett.

Lakomski, G. and Evers, CW. (2009) Passionate Rationalism: The Role of Emotion in Decision-making. *Journal of Educational Administration*, 48(4), pp. 438–450.

March, J.G. and Olsen, J. (1976) *Ambiguity and Choice in Organizations*. Oslo, Norway: Universitetsforlaget.

Miles, R.E., Snow, C.C. and Pfeffer, J. (1974) Organization-environment: Concepts and Issues. *Industrial Relations*, 13(3), pp. 244–264.

Miller, D. (1993) The Architecture of Simplicity. *Academy of Management Review*, 18(1), pp.116–138.

Oschner, K.N. and Phelps, E. (2007) Emerging Perspectives on Emotion – Cognition Interactions. *TRENDS in Cognitive Science*, 11(8), pp. 377–378.

Porter, S. and Inks, L. (2000) Cognitive Complexity and Salesperson Adaptability: An Exploratory Investigation. *The Journal of Personal Selling and Sales Management*, 20(1), pp. 15–21.

Saarinen, T. (1990) Systems Development Methodology and Project Success: An Assessment of Situational Approaches. *Information and Management*, 19(3), pp. 183–193.

Schroder, H., Driver, M. and Streufert, S. (1967) *Human Information Processing: Individuals and Groups Functioning in: Complex Social Situations*. New York: Holt, Rinehart and Winston.

Simon, A. (1990) Invariants of Human Behavior. *Annual Review of Psychology*, 41, pp. 1–19.

Simon, A. (1976) *Administrative Behavior*, 3rd ed. New York, NY: The Free Press.

Snowden, D. (2002) Complex Acts of Knowing: Paradox and Descriptive Self-awareness. *Journal of Knowledge Management*, 6(2).

Stabell, C. (1978) Integrative Complexity of Information Environment Perception and Information Use: An Empirical Investigation. *Organization Behavior and Human Performance*, (22), pp. 116–142.

Styhre, A., Wikmalm, L. Olilla, S. and Roth, J. (2010) Garbage-can Decision-making and the Accommodation of Uncertainty in New Drug Development Work. *Creativity and Innovation Management*, 19(2), pp. 134–146.

Thagard, P. (2006) Evaluating Explanations in Law, Science, and Everyday Life. *Current Directions in Psychological Science*, 15(3), pp. 141–145.

Thagard, P. (2001) How to Make Decisions: Coherence, Emotion, and Practical Inference. In: Millgram, E. (ed.), *Varieties of Practical Inference*. Cambridge, MA: MIT Press, pp. 355–371.

Thagard, P. and Millgram, E. (1997) Inference to the Best Plan: A Coherence Theory of Decision, available at: http://cogsci.uwaterloo.ca/Articles/Pages?Inference.Plan.html; accessed 24/1/11.

Tushman, M. (1977) Communication Across Organizational Boundaries: Special Boundary Roles in the Innovation Process. *Administrative Science Quarterly*, 22, pp. 587–605.

Tversky, A. and Kahneman, D. (1981) The Framing of Decisions and the Psychology of Choice. *Science*, 211, pp. 453–458.

Walsh, J. (1995) Managerial and Organizational Cognition: Notes from a Trip Down Memory Lane. *Organization Science*, 6(3), pp. 280–321.

Weick, K.E. (1969) Laboratory Organizations and Unnoticed Causes. *Administrative Science Quarterly*, 14(2), pp. 294–311.

Yiu, L. and Saner, R. (2000) Determining the Impact of Cognitive Styles on the Effectiveness of Global Managers: Propositions for Further Research. *Human Resource Development Quarterly*, 11(3), pp. 319–324.

Zahra, S.G. and George, G. (2002) Absorptive Capacity: A Review, Reconceptualization and Extension. *Academy of Management Review*, 27(2), pp. 185–221.

7

Consider Culture

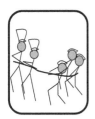 *Those other people are human beings, like us, doing what they need to do to preserve their self-respect; their humanity. They might speak differently or dress differently or have different ways of working; reminding oneself that they are also human helps us to find ways of working together.*

Interview 43 PD.

Cultural differences and misunderstandings contribute to project complexity. As many complex projects involve multiple organisations and/or are conducted internationally, this chapter summarises what project leaders should consider when programmes and projects cross cultural boundaries.

> *At the project management level, simply understanding the cultural issues within his team would have resolved many of the issues that lead to higher than optimum team turnover. The Germans especially found his leadership style difficult to work with. Interview 49 PD.*

Key Points in This Chapter:

- Organisational cultures.

- Project cultures.

- Organisational and project cultural boundaries.

- International projects.

- Generational culture.

Cultural differences are always there, national, organisational, generational, but, at the same time, if strong relationships are built from the beginning problems associated with cultural differences tend to dissolve. Mutual respect nearly always overrides cultural differences. People are people after all, and basically they have the same needs, at all levels of Maslow's hierarchy (1943). What gets in the way of strong relationships between cultures are often surface issues, ways of doing things, ways of saying things – habits.

Nevertheless, it is very easy to make *faux pas* when moving from one culture to another. If getting things right is important then one should study the new culture assiduously before entering it. If enjoying the experience and building good long term relationships is the goal then being willing to ask questions of your hosts about what is appropriate and being ready to laugh at your mistakes with your hosts will probably win more friends than being perfect. Indeed, one effect of categorising people into cultures is that of stereotyping, as Billikopf (2009) states: 'How anyone can try to make generalizations about an entire continent of people ... is beyond me.'

Part 1: Organisational Cultures

Some authors distinguish between 'culture' and 'climate' in an organisation; *culture* being a shared set of understandings, whereas *climate* being more to do with people's perceptions about the extent to which the organisation is currently living up to its espoused values – 'the routines of the organization and the behaviors that get rewarded, supported and expected ...' (Schneider and Rentsch, 1987, p. 7). Culture is moderated by history, norms and values that people believe underpin 'why we do things around here', whereas climate is more about 'what happens around here.' (Deshpande and Webster Jr., 1989, p. 4) According to Schein (1984), culture is the most difficult organisational attribute to change, outlasting organisational products, services, founders and leadership and all other physical attributes of the organisation. However, cultures are created by people and serve people's needs, even in ways that might appear to be destructive to outsiders.

UNIVERSAL HUMAN NEEDS

Still the most widely used model of its kind, Maslow's (1943, 1954) model (see Figure 7.1) describes stages of psychological growth in terms of needs. Maslow's theory suggests that the most basic level of needs must be met before

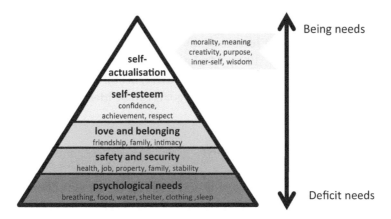

Figure 7.1   A representation of Maslow's Hierarchy of Needs

the individual will strongly desire (or focus motivation upon) higher level needs. Maslow also coined the term *metamotivation* to describe the motivation of people who go beyond the scope of the basic needs and strive for constant betterment. Metamotivated people are driven by 'being needs', such as self-esteem and self-actualisation, instead of deficiency needs. Maslow argues that the only reason people might not move in direction of self-actualisation is because of hindrances placed in their way by society (Maslow, 1998). However the path is not necessarily uni-directional, upwards. It varies with time and circumstances.

Most people have a need for self-respect and self-esteem. Maslow noted two versions of esteem needs, a lower one and a higher one. The lower one is a need for the respect of others, the need for status, recognition, fame, prestige, and attention. The higher one is the need for self-respect, the need for strength, competence, mastery, self-confidence, independence and freedom. The latter one ranks higher because it relies more on inner competence won through experience. Maslow argues that these are not strict, separate levels but closely related to others (Maslow, 1954). This level of need, described by Maslow as *self-actualization* is related to realising potential. Maslow describes this desire as the desire to become everything that one is capable of becoming. In order to reach a clear understanding of this level of need one must first not only achieve the previous needs, physiological, safety, love, and esteem, but master these needs. Maslow later added *self-transcendence*, related to spiritual needs, which Frankl (1946) describes as a search for meaning, seeking a time when organisations are managed by self-actualising people along lines which would encourage the self-actualisation of people from all levels of the organisation. Maslow's vision was that this would lead to really effective organisations and a much improved society (Maslow, 1998). Maslow's theory has also been extended to planning financial investments (De De Brouwer, 2009). For each need level in Maslow's hierarchy of needs, investment goals can be identified, and those are the constituents of the overall portfolio.

A USEFUL CULTURAL INVENTORY

Numerous books and articles have been written about organisational culture and its ramifications (see for example, Cameron et al., 2005; Black, 2003; Kotter, 1992; Handy, 1985; Deal and Kennedy, 1982).

One useful approach, informed by Maslow's thinking and similar behavioural models, is a cultural inventory developed by Cooke (1993). It defines organisational culture as the behaviours that members believe are required for them to be accepted and meet expectations of their organisations. Providing a way of understanding cultural behaviour, Cooke's Organizational Culture Inventory measures twelve behavioural norms that are grouped into three general types of cultures: *constructive cultures, passive-defensive cultures and aggressive-defensive cultures.*

Constructive cultures (Cooke, 1993) encourage members to interact with people and approach tasks in ways that help them meet Maslow's higher level needs. Organisations with constructive cultures allow members to work to their full potential, resulting in high levels of motivation, satisfaction, teamwork, service quality, and innovation. Quality is often valued over quantity, creativity is valued over conformity, co-operation is believed to lead to better results than competition, and effectiveness is judged at the level of the larger system level rather than locally or by product. Cooke's four cultural norms in this cluster are:

- Achievement

- Self-actualizing

- Humanistic-encouraging

- Affiliative.

Passive/defensive cultures (Cooke, 1993) respond to Maslow's lower level needs, such as safety and security. In these cultures members might interact with people in ways that will not threaten their own security. In organisations with passive/defensive cultures, members might be conscious of behaving the way they think they should in order to be effective. People are expected to please others (particularly superiors) and avoid interpersonal conflict. Rules, procedures, and orders are often more important than personal beliefs, ideas, and judgment. Passive/defensive organisations can experience lot of unresolved conflict and staff turnover, and organisational members often report lower levels of motivation and satisfaction. The four cultural norms in this cluster are:

- Approval

- Conventional

- Dependence

- Avoidance.

Aggressive/defensive cultures (Cooke, 1993) are also driven by Maslow's lower level needs, such as safety and security, but express those needs in a more aggressive manner. Self-esteem, or status, is protected by members in order to appear competent, controlled, and superior. In such cultures members who seek assistance, admit shortcomings, or concede their position can be viewed as incompetent or weak. These organisations emphasise finding errors, eliminating mistakes, and often encourage members to compete against each other rather than collaborate. If team work is encouraged it is more likely to be competitive. Cooke (1993) argues that short term gains associated with these strategies are often at the expense of long term growth. The four cultural norms in this cluster are:

- Oppositional

- Power

- Competitive

- Perfectionistic.

As many complex projects are conducted within large organisations and project teams routinely engage with other organisations, it is important for leaders to be aware of the culture of their own organisation and the culture of the other organisations with which they must interact in order to identify cultural mismatches that might be problematic in future.

Project Cultures

Extrapolating from the idea of organisational culture, some authors (see for example Gareis, 2004) advocate developing a project culture. A constructed project culture is believed to increase competitive advantage for the project through the establishment of clear boundaries between the project and other projects, through securing recognition for the project and through team members identifying with the project. The project culture contributes to the development of the team spirit within the project and it provides orientation to the team members. Artefacts of the project culture, such as the project name, a project logo, project slogans, and so on also form the basis for professional project marketing. Some also recommend devloping a project vision and mission statements.

As long as there is some continuity of leadership and key team members, a project of long duration will develop its own culture, particularly those programmes and projects that continue long enough to be considered temporary organisations (Lundin and Söderholm, 1995), such as large infrastructure projects like rail upgrades or Olympic facilities. However, projects rarely have the long histories that some organisations can boast and therefore any project culture will be relatively ephemeral by comparison. This has advantages as well disadvantages. Compared with organisations, unproductive project cultures are much easier to shift. Frequent changes in teams or at executive sponsorship level can also make it difficult to achieve a productive climate.

Whilst the artefacts suggested by Gareis (2004) and others are useful symbols they do not actually create a culture. It is probably more accurate to say that they help define the 'climate' of the project rather than its 'culture' in the sense that culture is related to history; the reasons 'why we do things', the values that direct our behaviour, rather than what we do. The artefacts only become symbols in the real sense if they reflect the behaviour and values communicated by the project leaders. A positive project culture will only remain strong if the underpinning values are espoused consistently and reinforced through action.

Productive team cultures or 'climates' can be useful to help project team members to cope with the pressures and also to help buffer against leadership changes at the top which introduce temporal sources of complexity. However, suitable project climates must be developed rapidly and nurtured carefully throughout the project life cycle.

Although there are some obvious advantages in attending to the project 'culture' or 'climate', it is also important to be aware that boundaries can create a 'club' environment. In one sense a 'project club' can serve to support and nurture team members, but in another sense the same club atmosphere can mitigate against establishing and maintaining good relationships with others outside the club. One outcome might be to effectively separate or distance members of the project club from others in the organisation on whom they depend for co-operation and information. Imposed cultural artefacts may encourage a positive team self-image and even a sense of invincibility, very helpful to help the team get through tough times.The same sense of invincibility can also encourage 'group think', where the team becomes deaf to dissenting opinions from within the team or, insularity, where the team refuses to take account of external criticism.

Part 2: Organisational and Project Cultural Boundaries

One of the first questions to ask is whether or not the cultures of the organisations with which the project is interfacing will support the project. According to Michael Stanleigh, a business consultant, 60 per cent of the Project Management Offices (PMO) they have surveyed say that the organisational culture is not supportive of the PMO. If the project is being conducted in-house it might be helpful to try to align corporate cultural artefacts with those needed to conduct the project. If the project team is contracted this often involves alignment of more than one organisation, each with their own culture and own artefacts, 'ways of doing things'. As evidence from the number of failed company mergers suggests, combining cultures is immensely challenging. It is particularly challenging because of the weight of history. Practices and customs that take years to establish are difficult to shift.

CULTURAL AUDIT

Using Cooke's (1993) 12 norms as a basis, it is relatively simple to identify potential mismatches. The following example is a snapshot but demonstrates how Cooke's inventory might be adapted to the project context.

A check on cultural fit at the beginning of the programme or project should indicate where potential difficulties might occur; which organisations should work together well and which organisations will have cultural misalignments. It will also help to highlight where leaders need to spend most of their effort in helping the project team to align with the organisation. As an external stakeholder in relation to the other organisations it is only possible to guess the answers, however, it is amazing how much information can be obtained from a few casual conversations with others who have worked there.

Table 7.1   **Cultural audit example based on Cooke's (1993) Organisation Culture Inventory**

Attribute (derived from Cook, 1993)		Your team	Organisation 1 (Constructive culture)	Organisation 2 (Passive-defensive culture)	Organisation 3 (Aggressive-defensive culture)
Constructive culture	Achievement (focus on quality rather than quantity of output)	H	H	L	H
	Self-actualising (supports individual growth)	M	M	L	M
	Humanistic (encouraging of others)	H	H	L	L
	Affilliative (team-oriented)	H	H	L	L
Passive-defensive culture	Approval (not encouraged to work independently)	L	H	H	M
	Conventional (prefers tried and true to new)	L	H	H	H
	Dependent (direction expected from leaders)	L	H	M	M
	Avoidance (tension below the radar)	L	H	H	L
Aggressive-defensive culture	Oppositional (win-lose attitude encouraged to appear in control)	L	L	L	H
	Power (status and security favoured)	L	L	M	H
	Competitive (encouraged rather than co-operation)	H	L	L	H
	Perfectionistic (mistakes and weakness not tolerated)	M	L	M	H

Team members can also anonymously answer similar questions on behalf of their own team or organisation. Such an audit can be used to highlight aspects of the team culture that need addressing.

WORKING WITH CULTURAL MISALIGNMENTS

Several things can be done if cultural misfits are detected at the beginning of a project. It is important to find out whether the leaders are part of the problem or whether they want and would support a change in their own culture. Where leaders are involved in promulgating a counter-productive culture project success might require that this be addressed through the highest possible level of leadership of each participating organisation. If the project outcomes are important to the participating organisations, the project leaders need top level support to reduce or remove barriers. On the other hand, as has often occurred, the project might provide leaders with welcome opportunities to make desirable adjustments to work practices in their own organisations using the project to model more productive behaviour. Sub-texts of this kind must be revealed and articulated because the project teams will need exceptional support from leaders. The project teams will almost certainly experience organisational resistance and the project will become decidedly more complex as a result. Reiterating Schein's (1984) statement, culture is the most difficult organisational attribute to change, outlasting products and services.

At the level of the executive leadership teams in all participating organisations, it is important to clarify behaviour and work practices required for project success. Executive leaders will need to be engaged in making sure that the right people are on the teams in each of the partnering organisations, project sponsors are up to the challenge, department heads are willing to co-operate, decision-making processes are suitable and any other processes that need to be aligned are aligned. This is all part of project governance (see Chapter 10). It is important to stress that these kinds of negotiations must be done at appropriate levels of leadership in the partnering organisations. Leaving it to the teams to muddle through is *not* an option!

Because the project is temporary and the organisations with which it interfaces are not, a line of least resistance is probably the best one. Otherwise it is like David taking on Goliath with a faulty sling-shot. Project leadership teams need to look for those artefacts (processes, procedures, attitudes) that are essential to the project and work towards a compromise in order to ensure project success. A question to ask is what can the project teams live with and what would be fundamentally damaging to the project's success? It is important to realise, however, that what is being changed is not the organisation culture but the artefacts – those practices that are exposed and visible at the surface – not the underlying organisational values. Some of the challenges that have been reported include:

PROJECTS MANAGED IN-HOUSE

- Organisational performance management systems do not take into account new reporting structures, such as matrix management. The result is that employees identify time spent on projects as an intrusion to their daily job.

- Reporting standards, including status and exception reporting of risks are inconsistent across the organisation, making it difficult for executive leaders to quickly assess issues and make timely decisions. Project language (tools, jargon, and so on) is quite different from corporate language. Reporting standards should reflect the needs of those who are making the decisions at the executive level.

- Project success measures are not clearly defined at an organisation-wide level and used consistently from one project to another. As a result it is difficult for executive leaders to quickly assess success and for the organisation to capture and retain project knowledge.

- Climates of micromanagement exist in some departments, requiring project teams to spend most of their time reporting rather than getting on with the project (see Chapter 3). Micromanagement, if it exists, can be a product of the organisational culture.

EXTERNALLY MANAGED PROJECTS

Projects managed by external contractors have an even greater challenge because the project leaders and teams have to interface with the client organisation(s) and other project organisations, each one having its own culture and practices associated with that culture.

Time is the issue that most emphasises cultural differences and produces frustration for project teams when working with other organisational cultures. This is simply because projects are time driven and complex projects often operate under extreme time constraints. However many different perceptions of time exist in organisations, both cyclical and emergent (Mintzberg and Waters, 1985; Midgley, 2008). Organisational cultures can range from results-oriented cultures to cultures that favour work-life balance. Also, any enterprise will involve people who have very different personal constructs of time (Remington and Söderholm, 2009, 2011).

Cultural practices around time and decision-making are very important when a project is complex. A senior project manager from the head contracting firm working on an 11 year rail project had this to say about the government authority on which the project team depended for approvals:

> We are always waiting until the end of the financial year for major milestone payments – sometimes hundreds of millions. The approval processes in the contract meant that the client could always find a reason to postpone until it was convenient for them. We couldn't do anything about it. They are one of the few clients in a small pool. This is a big project impacting on the whole of the organisation. You can just imagine the financial strain that places on our company. Interview 31 PM.

The culture in the government department did not demand timely decision-making from its senior project officers. A pattern of low level or diffuse accountability had become entrenched in the culture. The same interviewee complained that:

> They would not sign-off on the drawings. They would only acknowledge that they had no further comments at this stage. PM Interview 31.

This also fits with a culture that Cooke (1993) would describe as 'passive-defensive' – rule bound with low levels of personal responsibility and high levels of avoidance. It also indicates that the executive leadership either does not understand the implications of allowing this kind of cultural practice to affect the project, are not aware that it was going on, or are themselves products of the culture.

CULTURAL DIFFERENCES WITHIN ORGANISATIONS

Even within one organisation different departments may have different cultural habits. A complete breakdown of respect and, eventually, communication occurred on a large infrastructure project at a university. By the end of the project the property development and management department (PDM) were barely communicating with the Information Systems (IS) and Audio Visual (AV) departments. The PDM department was driving the project and were responsible for project management of the physical infrastructure and the building refurbishment, the IS department was responsible for all the computer and telecommunications infrastructure and the AV department was responsible for all electronic teaching infrastructure, such as video, audio and data projection screens and consoles.

> *Part of the issue really boiled down to perception -the project managers from PDM came into work at about 7.30am. They were all engineers and builders – up with the birds. They usually left about 5pm each day. They complained that they could never meet with the IS and AV people who were 'real slackers' as they were never there! In fact they used to wander in to work at about midday. However they generally stayed at work until midnight – night owls – and worked just as hard if not harder than the PDM guys. It was just a perception but it was not identified early enough – it was the tip of the iceberg and the 'blame game' started – relations just went downhill from there. Interview 43 PD.*

There are some fundamental questions that should be asked at the beginning of any project to identify differences between the artefacts – the culturally defined and supported processes – that might hamper the progress of the project, so that agreement and support can be obtained at the highest level to remove barriers. Once again, overcoming culturally prescribed barriers can rarely be achieved at the team level. Executive leadership support is critical.

The following set of questions (Table 7.2) is offered as a start for leaders when assessing work practices that might be culturally misaligned between their own project organisation and the other organisations with which they must interface. Once identified, senior leadership teams need to get together to address the misalignments. Although it is advised that this assessment be done for any project, it is critical if the project is likely to be complex.

Table 7.2   Organisational cultural artefacts questionnaire

Question	Org. A	Org. B	Org. C	Org. D
Time:				
• Has each party shared their expectations in terms of timely responses?	☐	☐	☐	☐
• Will the culture support the timely responses needed for this project?	☐	☐	☐	☐
• Is project team's perception of time and that of the other organisations involved aligned (for example some organisations place much stronger values on work-life balance than others that are more strongly results driven)?	☐	☐	☐	☐
• Are the expected protocols for attendance at meetings, document response, RFQ, and so on agreed?	☐	☐	☐	☐
Reporting:				
• Are reporting requirements aligned and agreed?	☐	☐	☐	☐
• Have potential differences about the reporting standards been aligned?	☐	☐	☐	☐
• Is the level of reporting appropriate to the needs of the stakeholders (compared with a culture of micromanagement in which project teams be held up through over-reporting or the reverse)?	☐	☐	☐	☐
Decision-making:				
• Is the decision-making structure clear and robust (rather than circuitous or ill-defined)?	☐	☐	☐	☐
• Are designated decision-makers available to make decisions at short notice?	☐	☐	☐	☐
• Are executive decision-makers assigned to this project able and willing to make decisions (rather than a culture of diffuse accountability or avoidance)?	☐	☐	☐	☐
• Are the people who are responsible for signing off parts of the project able to make timely decisions (rather than to hold up the project due to prevarication or for other personal or political reasons)?	☐	☐	☐	☐
Budget:				
• Are the organisation's financial controllers aware and willing to work with the project team to make sure that funding is available according to the project requirements?	☐	☐	☐	☐
• Are the organisation's auditors able and willing to support the selected procurement methods (such as cost-plus or alliance partnerships)?	☐	☐	☐	☐
Procurement:				
• Are the legal and procurement officers willing and able to adjust processes and systems to meet the schedule needs of the project?	☐	☐	☐	☐
• Are the legal and procurement departments able to deal with newer forms of procurement (or are contracts formats 'set in stone')?	☐	☐	☐	☐

Table 7.2   *Continued*

Question	Org. A	Org. B	Org. C	Org. D
Internal alignment:				
• Is the organisation culturally homogeneous (or is it heterogeneous-many different cultures within the organisation)? Do we need to take this into account when agreeing on processes?	☐	☐	☐	☐
• Will the level of transparency required for the project be affected by existing organisational cultural norms (such as lack of accountability or political activity)?	☐	☐	☐	☐
• Are project team members likely to be supported by internal staff (or are they like to encounter other forms of resistance by organisation's permanent staff)?	☐	☐	☐	☐
• Is the organisation's senior leadership escalon willing and able to address potential staff resistance or process blockages within their own organisation?	☐	☐	☐	☐

PROTECTING CULTURAL NORMS – THE THREAT OF TRANSPARENCY

Sometimes apparently simple measures needed to correct misalignments such as these can threaten cultural norms in an organisation because they increase transparency. There may be little or no value to members of an organisation in increasing transparency if the culture firmly supports lack of accountability. Projects demand transparency and accountability and transparency and accountability are demanded of projects. Projects might be seen as threatening to organisational cultures if transparency is not a cultural norm in that organisation. Many organisations will go through intense 'growing pains' that either slow down or completely stop efforts to align practices with the needs of a project when cultural misalignments are allowed to go untreated. When project leaders start pushing more decisions onto the executive and more accountability onto the project team, it can be met with resistance if the culture does not support accountable decision-making. Even if senior project leaders have executive support, it is often at the project team level where resistance is felt. Senior project leaders should be very aware of organisational cultures which are misaligned with the needs of the project and be ready to support the project teams as soon as resistance is experienced. Often position power is the only way of making sure that the teams receive the assistance they need.

Part 3: International Projects

Many complex projects are complex because they cross national cultural boundaries. Leadership styles can reflect our national cultural backgrounds. Swedish culture tends to favour collaboration and Swedish project teams are known for taking a long time to reach agreed decisions. However,once they do agree they tend to move very quickly. Anyone who has worked in France will be aware of the need to include more social time in meetings, and the sacrosanct nature of the lunch hour and a half, not so important in Germany or even the UK. Those who have worked in the Middle East will know that the cultural perception of time in most Middle Eastern countries is very different, more organic and much more relaxed. It can be particularly infuriating to people from an Anglo-Saxon background who can be very conscious of deadlines and 'being on time'.

Issues to do with working in other countries can simply be due to unfair practices, driven by economics. As one project leader who worked on the Delhi International Airport observed:

> *From day one it was a shambles racing against time. And we were all being paid ten times the local guys, many of whom were very competent. There was some resentment there, and a reluctance to cooperate. Interview 64 PM.*

One of the best-known inventories of national cultural differences is that by Geert Hofstede, (1980; see his website for a more extensive description and national ratings on all the scales http://www.geert-hofstede.com; accessed 17/1/2011). Hofstede (1980, 2001) developed four main scales, dimensions of national culture, which he named: *power distance, uncertainty avoidance, individualism,* and *masculinity*. In addition to societies, organisation and project cultures can be classified and understood in a similar manner. Hofstede's four dimensions are defined as follows:

Power Distance (PD) is an indicator of how power is accepted by those in the society. It is a measure of deference. According to Hofstede's research the Power Distance (PDI) for Australia is relatively low, with an index of 36, compared to the world average of 55. This is indicative of greater equality between societal levels, including government, organisations, and even within families. ABC (national media) presenters frequently refer to senior government ministers, including the Prime Minister, using their first names, something that would be much less likely to occur in the UK or the USA, for example. It also suggests that interaction across power levels is expected to be co-operative. It would be expected to be more challenging for Australians to work in say China, India or the Arab world (which have higher PD ratings according to Hofstede's research), compared with the USA or UK that have similarly low PD ratings. However, to their credit project leaders do work in countries with very different PD ratings and often very successfully.

> *The implications for project delivery in a culture with high PD are that individual stakeholders in that culture may not be empowered to make decisions without consulting their superiors. Little individual autonomy in decision-making should be expected. Project leaders from a society with low PD might expect to have more individual autonomy in decision-making.*

Uncertainty Avoidance (UAI) is a measure of how well people in a society can accept, feel comfortable and work with uncertainty and ambiguity. Singapore has a very low level of UAI, United Kingdom has relatively low level UAI whereas Japan has the highest level. One would assume from this that in Japan requirements need to be very precisely defined whereas in Singapore there is room for ambiguity. This is particularly interesting given Singapore's rapid and highly successful infrastructure development over the past twenty years.

For project management, a culture with high UAI will require that issues be defined very precisely early in the project life cycle. In a culture with low UAI there will be tolerance of higher levels of uncertainty and fluidity in decision-making. This is very important for complex projects as complexity is often displayed as uncertainty.

Individualism (IDV) describes the ties between individuals in a society. In a society with high IDV everyone is expected to look after himself or herself and his or her immediate family. The opposite end of the spectrum applies to societies structured around groups or clans to which members are loyal. There are only seven (7) countries in the Hofstede research that have Individualism (IDV) as their highest Dimension: USA (91), Australia (90), United Kingdom (89), Netherlands and Canada (80), and Italy (76). The lowest IDV (according to Hofstede's research) is for the Arab World (38) and China might even be lower than this but data is not yet available.

Project managers from cultures that value individualism and autonomy (with high IDV) might find it challenging working in a culture with low IDV levels, where group decisions are most important, and the needs of the group are more important those of the individual. Cultures with low IDV might resist the idea of a single point of accountability, for example, if the matter affects the group.

Masculinity (MAS) for Hofstede is a quality that describes societies in which social gender roles are clearly defined (that is, men are supposed to be assertive, tough, and focused on material success whereas women are supposed to be more modest, tender, and concerned with the quality of life). In societies with low MAS, social gender roles overlap (that is, both men and women are supposed to be concerned with the quality of life and the welfare of others). The Netherlands has the lowest MAS score (according to Hofstede's research). The score for the Arab world (and probably also China) is lower than that for the UK and USA, with Japan showing the highest score.

For project management teams this aspect might also indicate how people prefer to work together. For example, in a workplace with lower MAS people will work together in teams more supportively (the people are important as well as the work). Workplaces with high MAS will tend to foster a competitive culture. People in societies with lower MAS might also value a broader range of cultural activities (for example. arts and music as well as sport).

Long Term Orientation (LTO) versus Short Term Orientation. This fifth dimension used a questionnaire designed by Chinese scholars (http://www. geert-hofstede.com; accessed 17/1/2011). It is a concept still in the process of development. Values associated with Long Term Orientation are thrift and perseverance; values associated with Short Term Orientation are respect for tradition, fulfilling social obligations, and 'saving face'.

ORGANISATIONAL AND NATIONAL CULTURE

Even more confusing is the overlay between organisational and national culture. For example, a person might be working in an organisation with an overriding 'passive-defensive' culture (Cooke, 1993) which does not value independent decision-making but the organisation exists in a national culture that values individualism.

For project teams this can be very confusing. The really important lesson is that cultural differences do exist and recognising and discussing them are important tasks for leadership teams.

PREPARING TEAMS FOR COMMUNICATION WITH INTERNATIONAL PARTNERS

As many complex projects involve international partners it is vital that this aspect be included in communications plans. Allowing the communication process to develop ad hoc is not an option! However, successful communication is as much to do with team members' attitudes and expectations as anything else. Leaders need to communicate positive attitudes to their teams about other national cultures. More effective communication behaviour will follow. These suggestions might help leaders to shift a team's perception from alien to partner:

- *Assume the best.* Your international partners will generally want the same overall outcome for your project as you do. They may express themselves differently, outwardly demonstrate different levels of emotion and commitment to you but those differences are more likely cultural than motivational. It is often easy to forget that the person on the other end of the telephone finds you as alien as you find them.

- *Be interested.* The more you understand about the country, history, language, values systems and culture the better you will understand the individual and the way those individuals behave and react in situations. Learning about an international partner, particularly their native language, communicates that you are interested in them and seeking a positive working relationship of equals. As English has now become the dominated global language, English speakers can communicate arrogance based on the expectation that everyone should speak their language. This implicit assumption can subtly colour communications and produce offence.

- *Assume differences not similarities.* It is always helpful to assume that there will be differences rather than be surprised or disgusted by them. Assuming that there will be differences helps us become alert to them.

- *Be patient.* If you have ever tried to communicate in a language other than your native language you will understand how difficult and how exhausting it can be.

- *Clarify misunderstandings.* A mutually agreed approach for clarifying misunderstandings can be very useful. In some cultures direct questioning to clarify issues might cause embarrassment. Particularly if the other party does not have the answer on the spot, it might even cause offence. An approach that allows everyone to save face might be to table questions for the next meeting. In other cultures it is acceptable and even expected to question anything you are unclear about in an open and direct manner.

- *Treat working with international partners like travel.* It broadens the mind and can be fun! Getting to really know and understand your international partners is a rare privilege afforded to only a few.

Working with other cultures requires respect. Respect requires leaders to go at least halfway. Making the effort to learn the local language speaks volumes! As a general manager in the chemical industry said about an earlier international project she was managing:

> *My French is OK and my Spanish is OK and if there was a problem I would go out to the site and talk to them. Technical jargon is the same but meanings of words differ. It definitely helped that I spoke the languages. I also spent years in the Middle East and I learnt Arabic. As English we tend to think that everyone else in the world should speak English. There is an old saying: Someone who speaks three languages is trilingual, someone who speaks two languages is bi-lingual and someone who speaks one language speaks English. Interview 67 GM.*

Part 4: Generational Culture

One other very important set of cultural differences transcends organisational and national boundaries and it relates to when people were born. Tensions can arise due to cultural differences based on generational norms. Leaders need to be extremely aware of differences and preferences so as not to disenfranchise one generation or another. Generational culture adds another dimension to interpersonal harmony and team productivity.

BABY BOOMERS

Born between 1946 and 1964, the so-called Baby Boomers generation is described as loyal, work-centric and cynical, who equate salaries and long hours with success and commitment to the workplace. They value face time in the office and may not welcome work flexibility or work-life balance trends. High levels of responsibility, perks, praise and challenges may motivate this generation (Strauss and Howe, 1992). This generation is ethnically less diverse than later generations.

GENERATION X

Members of Generation X, born between 1965 and 1980, (Shapira, 2008), on the whole are more ethnically diverse and are said to be more individualistic and independent, resourceful and self-sufficient. Generally, they value freedom and responsibility and many have a casual disdain for authority and structured work hours. They dislike being micromanaged and embrace a hands-off management philosophy. They tend to be more adept with technology than Baby Boomers. Many are less committed to one employer and more willing to change jobs to get ahead than previous generations. They adapt well to change and are tolerant of alternative lifestyles. Generation X is ambitious and eager to learn new skills but they usually want to accomplish things on their own terms. Work-life balance is important.

MILLENNIALS OR GENERATION Y

Generation Y (born mid 1980s onwards and also known as the Millennials) tend to seek out creative challenges, personal growth, meaningful careers, and supervisors and mentors who are highly engaged in their professional development. They can be excellent multi-taskers and prefer communications through e-mail and text messaging. Some argue that when working with or supervising Millenials, it is wise to impose some structure and stability and cultivate a team-oriented environment. Immediate feedback and praise will help motivate and reassure this younger generation. Frequent communication and reassurance will help keep them eager and involved (Shapira, 2008).

Many of the basic characteristics of this younger group cross national borders, having grown up with computers and the Internet and having been heavily influenced by the availability of information and entertainment from a wide variety of media. It may be that increasing globalisation through the

Internet will mean that national cultural morés become less important as time progresses. Increasing globalisation in projects might benefit from enhanced tolerance from growth in understanding of other cultures, through the Internet and from living in more culturally pluralistic societies. It is reasonable, therefore, to wonder whether Millennials will maintain the broad cultural themes of their countries of origin or whether other cultural themes found in music, sports, movies and fashion perpetrated through the Internet will dominate (Smith, 2002).

In Summary

Cultural differences exist between teams, departments, organisations, nations and generations. Culture develops over time and is particularly hard to dislodge or change. Its attributes or 'climate' expresses deeply held and shared values. When embarking on a new project involving other departments, organisations or nations, it is better to expect cultural differences rather than to assume that people will just work together. However, cultural tensions are significantly diminished if a leader approaches a new culture with an open mind and encourages teams to build strong trusting relationships from the very beginning:

- Culture is a deep concept and develops over a long period of time – it has history and it is underpinned by deeply held values (why we do things this way).

- The strong historical roots make cultural morés difficult, if not impossible, to change.

- Projects are relatively short term, often too short to be described as having a culture, but a 'climate' does develop, supported by artefacts (the way we do things).

- It is important that project leaders take account of potential cultural differences because inability to manage cultural interfaces can itself contribute to project complexity.

- National cultural influences will, in some cases, be moderated by organisational cultures and practices. This is becoming more and more apparent as nations become multi-cultural.

- At the very beginning of a complex programme or project, leaders need to assess potential cultural boundaries and differences between teams, between organisations and national boundaries, in order to make sure cultural barriers do not get in the way of progress and teams are supported throughout the project.

- Generational cultural differences can give rise to tensions in the short term if not addressed. Research indicates that different generations exhibit different motivations and values regarding work.

- Global projects might benefit in future from enhanced understanding of other cultures from living in increasingly pluralistic societies and also through globally accessible norms, spread by movies, music, sport and fashion, supplanting traditional national cultural morés.

References and Further Reading

Black, R. J. (2003) *Organizational Culture: Creating the Influence Needed for Strategic Success*. London, UK.

Cameron, K.S. and Quinn, R.E. (2005) Diagnosing and Changing Organizational Culture: Based on the Competing Values Framework. *The Jossey-Bass Business & Management Series*.

Cooke, R.A. (1993) Measuring Normative Beliefs and Shared Behavioral Expectations in Organizations: The Reliability and Validity of the Organizational Culture Inventory. *Psychological Reports*, 72(3), pp. 1299–1330.

Deal T.E. and Kennedy, A.A. (1982) *Corporate Cultures: The Rites and Rituals of Corporate Life*. Harmondsworth: Penguin Books.

De Brouwer, Ph. (2009) Maslowian Portfolio Theory: An Alternative Formulation of the Behavioural Portfolio Theory. *Journal of Asset Management*, 9(6), pp. 359–365.

Deshpande, R. and Webster Jr., F.E. (1989) Organizational Culture and Marketing: Defining the Research Agenda. *Journal of Marketing*, 53(1), pp. 3–15.

Frankl, V. (1946) *Man's Search for Meaning*. Boston: Beacon Press.

Gareis, R. (2004) Development of a Project-specific Culture: A Project Management Function. Conference paper. IPMA World Congress'04, Budapest.

Handy, C.B. (1985) *Understanding Organizations*, 3rd Edn., Harmondsworth: Penguin Books.

Hofstede, G. (2001) *Culture's Consequences: Comparing Values, Behaviors, Institutions and Organizations Across Nations*. Second Edition. Thousand Oaks, California: Sage Publications.

Hofstede, G. (1980) *Culture's Consequences: International Differences in Work Related Values*. Beverly Hills, CA, Sage Publications.

Hofstede, G., Geert Hofstede™ Cultural Dimensions. http://www.geert-hofstede.com; accessed 17/1/2011.

Kotter, J. (1992) *Corporate Culture and Performance*. Free Press.

Lundin, R. and Söderholm, A. (1995) A Theory of the Temporary Organization. Scandinavian. *Journal of Management*, 11(4), pp. 437–455.

Maslow, A.H. (1998) *Maslow on Management*. New York, NY: John Wiley and Sons, Inc.

Maslow, A.H. (1954, 1970) *Motivation and Personality*, 2nd. ed. NY: Harper and Row.

Maslow, A.H. (1943) A Theory of Human Motivation. *Psychological Review*, 50(4), pp. 370–96.

Midgley, G. (2008) Systems Thinking, Complexity and the Philosophy of Science. *Emergence: Complexity and Organization*, 10(4), pp. 55–74.

Mintzberg, H. and Waters, J.A. (1985) Of Strategies Deliberate and Emergent. Strategic. *Management Journal*, 6, pp. 257–272.

O'Donovan, G. (2006) *The Corporate Culture Handbook: How to Plan, Implement and Measure a Successful Culture Change Programme*. Dublin, UK: The Liffey Press.

Payne, R.L. (2000) Eupsychian Management and the Millenium. *Journal of Managerial Psychology*, 15(3), pp. 219–226.

Phegan, B. (1996, 2000) *Developing Your Company Culture, A Handbook for Leaders and Managers*. Context Press.

Remington, K. and Söderholm, A. (2011) Time: One Factor in the Project Management of Change. Special Issue of the *Journal of Project and Organization Management* (in press).

Remington, K. and Söderholm, A. (2009) Let's do the time warp again – the concept of time as a determining element in projects. IRNOP IX Conference, October, 2009, Berlin.

Schein, E.H. (2005) *Organizational Culture and Leadership*, 3rd Ed., Jossey-Bass.

Schein, E.H. (1984) Coming to a New Awareness of Organizational Culture. *Sloan Management Review*, 12 (Winter), pp. 3–6.

Schneider, B. and Retsch, J. (1987) Managing Climates and Cultures. A Futures Perspective. In: Hage J. *Futures of Organizations*. Lexington, MS\A: Lexington Books.

Shapira, I. (2008) What Comes Next After Generation X? Education (*The Washington Post*): http://www.washingtonpost.com/wp dyn/content/article/2008/07/05/AR2008070501599.html. Retrieved 2008–07–19.

Smith, P.B. (2002) Culture's Consequences: Something Old and Something New. *Human Relations*, 55(1), 119–135.

Stanleigh, M. *How to Establish and Organizational Culture that Supports Projects*. http://www.bia.ca/articles/HowToEstablishanOrgCultureThatSupportsProjs.htm; accessed 17/1/11.

Stoykov, L. (1995) *Corporate culture and communication*. Sofia: Stopanstvo.

Strauss, W. and Howe, N. (1992) *Generations: The History of America's Future, 1584 to 2069*. Perennial (Reprint), pp. 310, 327

8

Exercise Political Skill

All the ills of mankind, all the tragic misfortunes that fill the history books, all the political blunders, all the failures of the great leaders have arisen merely from a lack of skill at dancing.
Attributed to Molière, (1622–1673).

The most frequent references to the need to manage political activity in relation to projects came from the project managers in our sample, several regretting not having been more alert to the politics surrounding their projects. As the famous French playwright so cleverly observed, managing the politics is like dancing; learning to weave around the other dancers who are all dancing to their own tunes, at their own paces, and avoiding them so that you don't make a fool of yourself by tripping over.

> *Got to keep an eye on the political game internally – need to develop the internal relationships rather than focus completely on the project – you need to be managing at a higher level that allows you to manage the relationships that will give you support. Interview 45 PM.*

Key Points in This Chapter:

- Political influence and project leadership.

- Successful leaders use political activity positively.

- Building political influence skills.

- Dealing with negative political activity.

Uncertainty associated with complexity breeds distrust, lack of faith, reduction in confidence of self and others to deal with the problems (Geraldi, 2008; Geraldi and Adlbrecht, 2007). These conditions can result in a great deal of political activity as people defend their turf. Mostly we notice political behaviour when it becomes destructive. One survey concluded that 44 per cent of full-time employees and 60 per cent of independent contractors listed 'freedom from office politics' as extremely important to their job satisfaction (cited in Kreitner, 2007, p. 147). It is possible that some of what is referred to as office politics is confused with interpersonal conflict, adding to the bad press that political behaviour in general attracts, confusing the undesirable with the useful.

> *On the positive side organizational politics involves wielding influence for the greater good ... From a negative view-point, organizational politics are perceived as a group of influence tactics used to serve self-interest. (DuBrin, 2009, p. 5)*

The reality is that engaging in organisational politics takes up a substantial amount of a leader's time. One argument in favour of understanding organisational politics is that if leaders do not engage they are likely to be overrun by others who may not have everyone's best interests at heart. The reality is that a project leader must be astute and alert to organisational politics and be able to skilfully engage in order to survive and to obtain the best outcomes for the project in relation to other competing agendas.

Part 1: Political Influence and Project Leadership

There is a fine line between relationship building and political influencing. While both activities involve many of the same skills, political activity is undertaken with the clear intention of influencing the other part to perform some action. It is useful to think of political acumen as a set of skills that project leaders need to develop so that they can positively influence the organisations impacting the project and to use power effectivly and in an ethical manner to achieve agreed outcomes (Kurchner-Hawkins and Miller, 2006).

POLITICS AND THE PROJECT LEADER

As a project leader the question is not whether to indulge in political activity, but how much political activity should be undertaken and what kind of activity is appropriate. The answer depends a great deal on the project leader's assessment of the political culture of the organisations with which s/he is dealing and his/her assessment of the personalities involved. Understanding as much as possible about the way politics are played out is a necessary input into the stakeholder analysis for a project.

Within any organisation there are people who use their political influencing skills negatively, predominantly for self-interest, and those who are excellent politicians and predominantly use their political power for the good of the organisation and others. It is useful to identify those who are skilled in political influence and observe how they use their power within each particular organisational context. Project leaders need to be able to influence the full range of personalities in partner organisations and be very aware of the activity of those who should not be trusted. As one senior project manager discovered after he became ill and the project suffered during his absence:

> *Appointments were based on nepotism and protection of individuals ... My budget was 32–42 mill and the sponsor would be managing a budget of about $1–2 mil and six staff members – they [executive management] had no idea of the magnitude of skill and effort required – I had up to 130 people on site and 12 different contractors – huge amount of coordination, huge budget and huge amount of risk to manage and keeping track of cost blow outs – and senior management did not have an understanding of what that takes – when I had my accident they appointed one of their mates to my job and things started to go really wrong due to their poor understanding of the types of contract we were using (pure alliance) – they started to look for someone to blame and I wasn't there so I was the fall guy. When contractors sense weakness they will often exploit the situation, particularly in times of financial difficulty (post GFC) further inflating any cost blow-out. In basic terms 'the wolves came in to feed' when the defences were down. Interview 45 PM.*

This describes a culture in which executive leaders, having insufficient experience with projects of this size, acted politically to shift blame and save their reputations rather than address the issues and save the project - a cautionary tale for project leaders. Working in a negative political culture can have a significant effect on a project leader's reputation. A project leader needs to be able read the signs. It is easy, in the excitement of project start-up, to overlook early warning signs. Early warning signs might have included: unwillingness by the sponsor to engage collaboratively with the project manager to address risks, or unwillingness to allocate appropriate personnel to the project when requested and so on.

In this case political activity was a masking activity, intended to cover up incompetence or lack of experience on the part of the project sponsor. Lack of sponsor experience with a project of this complexity is a strong warning signal that should alert a project manager to potential problems ahead. To be fair, the project manager quoted above did not know that he would become ill and the project might have carried on without major issues if he had been able to remain on duty.

However, it does pay to be fully aware of the political culture and the past political activity of key players within the organisation, and take steps to address them early. The discovery might reveal that the problem is outside of the project leader's sphere of influence to address. If that is the case, if the project leader cannot find others who can influence the parties concerned, she or he needs to be politically astute enough to do his/her own personal risk assessment and decide whether it is worth his/her reputation to continue in the role. It might be less of a career risk to move on!

ORGANISATIONS ARE POLITICAL SOCIAL SYSTEMS

Organisations are complex social systems involving interactions and struggles between many individuals and groups. In that sense they are inherently political. DuBrin (2009, Ch. 1) cites the following reasons why organisations are politically active:

- Organisations, like people do not always perform rationality (see Chapter 6). Rational models of organisations with policies and processes based on fairness and merit do not take into account self-interest in decision-making.

- Work environments are inherently competitive. Employees compete for positions and scarce resources.

- Competition is exacerbated by hierarchical structures and downsizing.

- There are inherent conflicts of interests. For example, it has been demonstrated that internal audits are frequently morally compromised and fail to give truly independent assessments. People in organisations are often unaware of how morally compromised they can become because of conflicts of interest.

- Standards of performance are subjective and hence people may resort to politics because they do not believe that the organisation can objectively and fairly judge their performance.

- Environmental uncertainty and turbulence causes insecurity and people may believe that favouritism will help them survive organisational restructures and downsizing.

- Senior leaders behaving politically become role models for people they are leading. This can inculcate a negative culture of cronyism if senior leaders set a pattern by consistently promoting favourites.

- Senior leaders in some organisations have been known to encourage a culture of 'kissing up' rather than honest feedback.

WHY DON'T THEY ALL JUST GET ON WITH THE JOB?

This frequently heard catch-cry suggests that people who like working on projects tend to be task-oriented; more interested in solving technical problems and completing the job than being political for its own sake. In their experience, politics, particularly the negative kind, just get in the way of doing the job properly. Others in organisation may be motivated by different needs.

POLITICAL ACTIVITY SHOULD BE CONSIDERED AS PART OF THE RISK ASSESSMENT

Nothing can bring down a project more swiftly and more effectively than adverse political activity! Denying the realities of the political organisational world, means that politically induced dangers are not attended to and averted in time. Just as importantly, the higher level reinforcement that the project teams might need may not be forthcoming if a project leader fails to lobby to garner support. Assessing the political climate as part of the culture (see Chapter 7) should be part of the project risk assessment.

SOME INDIVIDUALS ARE INHERENTLY MORE POLITICALLY ACTIVE THAN OTHERS

Apart from recognising the need for leaders to influence others in organisations, project leaders should be aware of special personality characteristics that are associated with people who habitually use political means to achieve what they desire. DuBrin (2009, Ch.1) identifies the following personality traits that incline individuals to political behaviour in preference to more productive behaviours:

- *Self interest.* This might simply be the desire to be accepted or liked. On the other hand, if self-interest is placed before the interest of others and the organisation, such as a leader who bids for funds for a project only to expand his/her sphere of interest, a very negative effect on the culture of the organisation can result.

- *Personal need for power.* This is a personality trait that emphasises self-interest.

- *Machiavellian tendencies.* A belief that it is acceptable to treat people only as a means to an end (see also Biberman, 1985).

- *High levels of self-monitoring trait.* People with high levels of self-monitoring tend to fit the response to the situation and say what they think the other person would like to hear rather than offer an objective assessment of the situation (see also Day et al., 2002).

- *Emotional insecurity.* Can mean that people underrate their achievements and feel they need to resort to political activity to compensate.

- *Desire to avoid hard work.* In general, using political influencing skills to avoid work is associated with low motivation to work accompanied by a low need for power. The aim is to have an easy life at work through ingratiating tactics as opposed to just staying below the radar.

ORGANISATIONAL CULTURE AND NEGATIVE POLITICAL ACTIVITY

The nature of the political activity within an organisation is one clear indicator of the organisation's culture (see Chapter 7). Understanding an organisation's culture is an important starting point for a leader. How to work with the politics becomes even more complicated when the project leader is dealing with not one but several contributing organisations. As discussed in Chapter 7, each organisation will have a different culture and different types of political activity will be tolerated, or even endorsed. Negative political behaviour is much more likely when the following attributes are part of the culture (adapted from DeBrin, 2009, pp. 39–41):

- Leaders tend to promote people who agree with them.

- There is an closely guarded hierarchy and leaders are very conscious of their own status.

- Senior leaders have a 'private-club' mentality.

- There is little diversity in leadership and management teams – they all look and talk alike.

- Some people do not appear to have a clear role in the organisation.

- Expectations about roles and responsibilities are not clearly articulated.

- Who you know counts more that what you know.

- There appears to be entrenched bad-feeling or rivalry between teams or sections.

- Backstabbing is talked about in conversations.

- Micromanagement might also indicate political activity because it can be used to avoid and avert decision-making.

- Cliques exist that seem to be counter-productive, in terms of guarding information or patterns of co-operation with other cliques in the organisation.

- Most agreements are achieved through social interaction rather than through formal meetings.

Part 2: Successful Leaders Engage in Politics Positively

JOB PERFORMANCE

There are numerous reasons why political activity is linked with attaining and maintaining successful leadership. Leaders who are politically adept will, on average, show higher job performance characteristics (Lui et al., 2007). These results were validated with healthcare workers and again with business students in internship programmes. Political skill was found to be positively linked with reputation and a good reputation is positively linked with good job performance.

> *A project manager who uses political skill to convince executive leaders of the need for a change to the requirements specifications for a new vehicle so that it performs better and would therefore be better placed in the market, is more likely to have a higher job rating that another project manager who complains about the ineptitude of the specification writers but does not use political skill to influence for a change for the better. Interview 35 C.*

INGRATIATING BEHAVIOUR

A number of studies support the idea that being skilled at organisational politics facilitates career advancement – it is not just who you are and where you came from, but how successfully you can influence others. Westphal and Stern (2007), in their investigation of what it takes to rise to the executive board level of an organisation, found that ingratiating behaviour towards the power brokers in the organisation, such as the CEO, was often an effective method of promotion. They defined ingratiating behaviour as flattery, reinforcement of CEO's opinion and doing favours. In their research (a sample of 1,012 CEOs and senior mangers) they found that the ingratiating behaviour often resulted in the person being recommended for appointments at other firms where the CEO was also a director or at firms within the CEO's influence network.

Specifically, they found that over a 12-month period, challenging the CEO's opinion one less time, complimenting the CEO on his or her insight twice more than usual, and doing one personal favour increased chance of appointment to a board where the CEO was already a director by 64 per cent. They also found that managers who were not from an elite background (without social connections) or female managers must engage in a higher level of ingratiating behaviour in order to attain equal opportunity to board appointment (Westphal and Stern, 2007).

RECIPROCATION

It is easy to conclude from this that all executive leaders have obtained their position through political influence, as opposed to talent and experience. Although undoubtedly there are leaders who fit the former category, not all leaders are promoted on the basis of political influence alone. Nevertheless it helps, and the role of political influence cannot be ignored in relation to their progress. Partly this boils down to common sense. Leaders are unlikely to be promoted if they are not noticed and choose to remain 'below the radar'. Also, executive leaders are people like everyone else. As people they are vulnerable, often unsure of their decisions and from time to time they need backing up. They are also subject to flattery and, like most others, like to return a good deed. Often known as reciprocity (Cialdini, 1001; Cialdini et al., 2001), the human tendency to want to return a favour has been well researched and documented.

However, even though leaders are human and, like everyone else, are susceptible to occasional flattery, if 'kissing up' is the main way to influence a leader then it points to the fact that the leader him/herself is emotionally insecure. An emotionally secure and competent leader usually has a very active 'bullshit radar' and knows that 'yes people' are of little use in the long run.

Part 3: Building Political Influence Skills

LIKE EVERYTHING ELSE IT IS GOOD TO HAVE A PLAN OF ACTION

First it is important to know the people and the organisations with whom you are dealing and whom you might need to influence politically. All leaders need to build strong influence networks (Ibarra and Hunter, 2007). This is particularly important for leaders of complex projects. The simple questionnaire that follows has been designed as a checklist for those who are not naturally political animals but recognise the necessity to become a political player in order to realise the project. The check list has been constructed on the assumption that most complex projects involve many organisational interfaces – either within the organisation or between collaborating organisations.

POLITICAL ANALYSIS –WHO AM I DEALING WITH?

Answer yes, no, unsure or partly. (It goes without saying that the information obtained from such a survey is sensitive and should be destroyed immediately once the team has completed the exercise. An answer of 'no' or 'partly' means that you might encounter negative or destructive political activity when associating with leaders in that organisation.)

The answer 'unsure' means you need to find out more. Good sources of intelligence are required to answer these questions, and, in my experience that is usually not very hard to find. People love to gossip!

Table 8.1   A quick assessment of the type of political activity expected (positive or negative)

Assumption	Org. A	Org. B	Org. C	Org. D
ALL leaders have experience commensurate with project complexity. *If this is not the case some leaders might resort to underhanded means to divert attention from their lack of experience.*				
ALL leaders are emotionally mature and have demonstrated positive leadership styles in their organisations. *If this is not the case some leaders might resort to negative tactics, such as interpersonal conflict, depending on their personality deficits.*				
The organisation has a positive political culture. *Political activity, such as influencing key others, is used to solve problems and find creative ways forward through engagement of others with power.*				
The project is considered a high priority by ALL senior parties within each of partnering organisations. *If the project is not a high priority for all senior parties you might expect that there will be interpersonal struggles between key players during the project.*				
I (PM/PD) can expect high level support from ALL executive leaders if things get tough. *Without this support it will be very difficult to influence senior leaders from partnering organisations or units.*				

BEHAVIOURS SUCCESSFUL POLITICAL LEADERS EMPLOY

Effective political behaviour involves a vast range of experience skill and knowledge. Several studies have investigated which political tactics are most frequently used by leaders (Kipnis, et al., 1980; Schriesheim and Hinkin, 1990). Researchers list *influencing, social astuteness, network building* and *genuineness* as the key skills involved in political behaviour (Vigola-Gadot and Drory, 2006; Ferris et al., 2005).

Timing is critical. Socially skilled political individuals seem to be able to recognise exactly when they can use influencing tactics (Witt and Ferris, 2003). People who are socially skilled also seem to know how to improvise and use innovative thinking (see Chapter 5) when their planned impression tactic looks like failing. They seem to know when to remain silent and when to be assertive. In relation to political influencing, skills include the ability to observe, read and understand social situations and the ability to behave and capitalise on that insight in order to influence others.

According to research by Yukl and Tracey (1992) an effective tactic is one that leads to task commitment and they found that most effective political influence tactics used by leaders are:

- Rational persuasion.

- Consultation.

- Appeal to inspirational goals that capture people's imagination.

However, a vast range of others are used regularly with more or less success:

- Exchange of favours.

- Ingratiation (praise, flattery).

- Assertiveness and audacity.

- Negotiation.

- Being low key (as opposed to assertiveness) can be effective where people may distrust self-promoters.

- Being agreeable.

- Apologising when necessary can be very effective when building relations with clients and customers.

- Justifying your demands by explaining how your request will benefit others.

- Forming coalitions.

- Co-optation – forming an alliance with another party to influence a third party.

- Demonstrating expertise.

- Displaying charisma.

- Speaking in the native language of the other party – this has a positive influence on relationships.

- Thinking differently, be outspoken about radical ideas.

- Performing calmly under pressure.

- Using spin – emphasising the positive rather than the negative aspects of the situation.

TAKING ACTION

Project leaders may not realise they are dealing with inexperienced or emotionally immature leaders from other organisations until several meetings have occurred. By then it is almost too late. If you, as a leader, can gather intelligence beforehand, you may have a real chance of negotiating changes to senior representatives, project boards and steering committees while avoiding loss of face. Political activity is most effective if it is proactive.

Returning to the results of the previous questionnaire (Table 8.1), the following are suggestions for appropriate actions:

Table 8.2   **Some political management strategies**

If the answer to the question in Table 8.1 is	Action
Yes	The focus should be on relationship building.
	Building trusting partnerships based on agreed and documented guidelines will work in the majority of cases where leaders genuinely wish to work together to achieve the project.
Unsure	More intelligence is needed. Question others who have worked with the organisation. Have in-depth conversations with the people about whom you are unsure. If you do not have direct access to those people, speak to as many people as you can in the organisation and gradually build up a picture of the organisation and how it operates.
	This is challenging when working in another country, particularly if you have to rely on translators. It is very worthwhile to include a native speaker as part of your own team to attend meetings as an observer to help you to gauge the climate. In cultures with a high power distance (PDI) it is important to be aware that people might only translate what is considered to be polite in case they offend you.
Partly	More research is needed. The leader needs to be clear as to which sections/people from their own organisation or partnering organisations might use negative political means to undermine the project. Focus on building relationships with those who are amenable to trusting relationships and treat the others as described below.
	An agreed charter, outlining required levels of commitment and co-operation, is essential.
	It is also important to identify and co-opt any executive leaders who can exercise positive political power to sway or avert potentially negative political power by their colleagues.
No	Vigilance and care is needed in dealing with these people and their organisations.
	A leader needs to be careful about his/her own exposure to risk (for example, are these people likely to escape accountability by laying blame on others if things get tough?).
	A leader needs to be vigilant in monitoring commitment to the project (for example, are these people likely to 'drop' their support for the project if another, more personlly attractive option arises?).
	A leader needs to influence as many people as possible to make sure that people who are appointed to the project board, or to other executive and senior leadership positions, have the appropriate experience and emotional maturity needed to lead their part of the project. This begins with helping partner organisations to understand the level of complexity inherent in the project and the potential risks to their organisation(s). Once this is achieved the leader can help other senior leaders to appreciate what is expected from each role in a complex project of this nature (see Chapter 2).
	If the person cannot be replaced as a leader you might try to garner support from other influential leaders (champions) who are more emotionally mature and experienced who might be able to support or mentor the poorly performing leader. This is often a useful strategy when saving face is important for the other party.
	A leader needs to make sure that all project documentation, including definition of roles and responsibilities, is rigorous in case negatively influentila leaders deny changes and proceed to lay blame in the future.
	In avoidance culture, such as the 'non-sign-off' culture discussed in Chapter 7, it is important to ascertain at what level of the organisation this culture is being supported. Sometimes the culture exists at levels that are much lower than CEO and Board and bringing it to the attention of the CEO or executive leaders can be productive for all parties concerned.
	If the person who is engaged in negative political activity is immovable and there is no choice but to continue in your role, you might need to go down the path of influencing the person based on your assessment of their emotional needs and/or their experience. Note that this is a difficult and sometimes dangerous pathway. It is also likely that others have noticed the person's behaviour. Before taking this course of action seek out a high level mentor who can advise or, in cases where it is appropriate, obtain advice from a specialist psychologist about dealing with various forms of dysfunctional pathological behaviour.
	Above all assess the level of risk to you personally.

Part 3: Dealing with Negative Political Activity

For the purposes of this discussion it is useful to categorise negative political activity, or behaviour, as behaviour that appears to counter the agreed aims of the project. Negative political activity can be culturally determined or related to personal needs, like saving face or personal gain. Whether behaviour is seen as negative or unethical may also be influenced by your own perspective (your own cultural norms and your own reading of the situation).

CULTURE AND WORK PRACTICES

In some cases, what is read as negative political activity might be a product of cultural differences and work practices and a lack of understanding or confused expectations by the parties concerned; this can be due to insufficient research and risk management at the bid or feasibility stage. The following extract, from an interview with the project director for a very large programme of works in a foreign country, illustrates the effect of cultural differences. At the time of interview the parties in the following situation were at an impasse, with the contractor starting to experience serious cash flow problems:

> I took over this project half way through and by that time claims for variations were mounting but we kept going because the deadline was really tight – this was an important project for the firm – however we are not working to international legal standards here – they don't apply – the government is the law and decides – even now they [the client] have only paid about 15% of what our claims – this is disastrous for our bottom line – the claims are heard by panel set up by the government – the problem is the people advising the panel don't have the technical expertise – and they want to look good and look as if they are doing the best by their masters so they only approve a small percentage of each claim – the problem is I can't find who makes the final decisions! Interview 37 PD.

In this particular case the contractor tendered under the expectation that international legal standards would apply. It emerged that arbitration processes were autocratic, not subject to international standards, and, once claims started to arise, the officers appointed to advise the arbitration panel lacked the technical expertise to be able to make a qualified assessment of the claims. Using Hofstede's (2001) national cultures framework (see Chapter 7) the host country can also be described as have a culture characterised by high power distance

(PD). That is, functionaries are more likely to defer to superiors rather than take personal responsibility for decisions. Also, this culture can be described as having low level of individualism (IDV) which means that belonging to one's own group and pleasing superiors within the group overrides any loyalty to the project. In this kind of culture it would be reasonable to expect shared decision-making with diffuse levels of accountability. Saving face and maintaining status within the clan would be priorities for officials.

The negative political activity that emerged in this case is more likely to be driven by cultural differences and expectations. The tactics by individuals to save face and disguise their lack of experience exacerbated an already difficult situation. It illustrates how important it is for project leaders to gather intelligence about local procedures and customs as well as about the people who will be associated with the project, at the beginning of the project, at bid stage, and certainly before contracts have been signed. If the contracting firm had realised that the client and client advisors lacked so much experience in the field (technical and procedural) there might have been opportunities to work out ways in which the gaps might have been filled so that all parties would benefit in the long term. This might mean that the contracting firm takes on an educative role; partnering with the client to up-skill their representatives or partnering with the client in other ways to the immediate advantage of the contract and to forge relationships in the long term.

NEGATIVE POLITICAL BEHAVIOUR BY INDIVIDUALS

Self-serving political behaviour by individuals seems to fall into two categories:

Self-rescue: this includes tactics to avoid embarrassment or shifting blame to others in order to transfer accountability. Sometimes this kind of behaviour can be managed. Often it stems from 'being in over one's head' due to lack of experience. If as project leader you are able to gather enough intelligence early you may be able to take steps to address the person's shortcomings, such as suggest that the project is so complex that all senior leaders (including those on your side) should have independent mentors, or suggest an advisory panel, or set up a partnership so that the individuals can learn on the job, or get executive support to replace the leader.

In some projects we have set up the expectation from the beginning that senior project leaders might need to be changed periodically as the complexity in the project changes in nature (see Remington and Pollack, 2007). Different aspects of complexity require different skill sets, therefore, as the project emerges, different skills sets will be required (see Chapter 2). Setting up the expectation that leadership will change to reflect changing levels of complexity can make it easier to replace dysfunctional leaders down the track if need be.

It is very difficult for project leaders when the executive sponsor uses negative political behaviour. In our first set of interviews with senior project managers we found that many PMs managed 'around their sponsors' as this excerpt illustrates:

> *People in our general group are uncomfortable around him. He [the sponsor] is aloof. Walks into the room and does not even talk to people. Because it is customer service there is a lot of work to be done internally to promote staff confidence. Not a robust leader – does not champion the people in his team – doesn't like to talk to anyone. I manage communication with the sponsor via emails and reports but not via direct discussion. He will make judgments – he will just pull something out of the air – not consultative. Tend therefore to work through the sponsor surrogates. Have to get his PA to talk to him – one of the most significant projects in the change programme for the company – he should be initiating it but I have to initiate it – I send urgent memos to him by email and he doesn't respond – either his surrogates pick it up or he transfers it but no direct contact. I manage around him – I get the job done in spite of him. Interview 9 PM.*

It is likely, in this case, that the sponsor's dysfunctional behaviour was not deliberate. Coupled with his uncommunicative style, he might have had other issues that were more important to him at the time making it particularly challenging for the project manager to build any kind of relationship with him. This particular interviewee was highly experienced and very good at building relationships; however, in this situation he had to resort to political influencing behaviour in order to influence those he had identified as surrogates who might be able to get through to his executive leader.

Deliberate Aggressive Tactics: as discussed earlier in this chapter. Some people use political behaviour because that is the way they gratify personal need to dominate or to win every time. Behaviour can include favouritism and nepotism, bullying (Quinne, 1999), fixating on seeking revenge (McGregor, 2007), stealing ideas from others, luring team members from other leaders, backstabbing, eliminating perceived enemies, theft of ideas, creating a false impression, abusing contacts, misrepresentation of what people have said and corporate espionage.

There is no simple advice for dealing with these kinds of people. As much of the behaviour is pathological in nature such as narcissism (see Chapter 2), you need high level help, expert assistance or, in some cases, you need to find a way out and salvage what you can. An international negotiator described a situation where he was called in to save a merger project and the two associated companies from collapse because the CEO in one of the companies 'just liked to destroy other people':

> I got an urgent call from the States ... [Board members] called me in desperation offering to try and get him to come to see me but told them I would fly over. It sounded as if he was very unstable and I did not want to destabilise him further by taking him out of his comfort zone. It took me two weeks working with him intensively but in the end he 'decided' to leave the company. They achieved the merger and we saved the day but the problem is he will go away and acquire another company and proceed to destroy that one as well. Interview 38 C.

Some years ago, as a consultant on another international project, I discovered that many project team members were on the verge of walking out due to the behaviour of the project director. The teams comprised highly specialised people who would have been very difficult to replace. The project was in danger of losing European Union funding if something was not done very quickly. The problem was that the project director seemed to be unable to carry through a decision. He said 'yes' but nothing ever happened. As I was there and 'relatively neutral', in political terms, I suggested I have a go on behalf of the project teams. The director was in denial that there was anything going wrong with the project. He took a little convincing but when I explained that he might lose the project teams if we didn't do something, he agreed to allow me to facilitate a negotiation between himself and the project teams. In the meantime, the director acted politically in an attempt either to save face or demonstrate that he was being proactive, by notifying the higher project authorities that he had called me in specially to facilitate negotiations with the teams. It took some effort. It was one of the hardest negotiations I have ever done, but the project teams started to work again and we saved the funding. The team members indicated to me privately that they didn't believe the director when he promised to act and they were correct. However, in spite of his camouflage behaviour the higher authorities were not fooled and soon after the director was replaced.

If destructive political behaviour is detected, especially if it has a pathological origin, it is vital that responsibility is placed at the correct level of leadership. A project team leader, or project manager, can manage around ineffective sponsorship behaviour to some extent, but if the behaviour is malicious, unpredictable and destructive, it is important to raise this with those who have the power to take action. According to De Janasz et al., (2003) project leaders need mentors and mentor networks How well this works depends on the industry, the internal politics and culture of the organisation and the leader him or herself. As one interviewee from the defence industry put it:

> *Mentors – works for some individuals and some industries but not for others – in our industry if you have the courage to take one on of these kinds of projects you are a pretty determined and proud. Interview 47 GM.*

The same interviewee did recommend coaching by a professional coach, possibly because it could be a more confidential arrangement; preferable when internal organisational politics are combative or competitive.

> *Leading complex projects– no-one is perfect and when you find yourself in demanding situations – everyone goes through it but certain individuals get more –the role of coaching by professional coach is vital – for the project and the leader. Interview 47 GM.*

As a project leader it is important to develop strong, wide-reaching relationships with other senior leaders associated with the project and the participating organisations, relationships based on respect and trust; those relationships can be used to influence at high levels when the need arises. Sometimes we are overly politically correct to our detriment and the detriment of the project (Ely et al., 2006).

In Summary

Project leaders need to be able to use political influence skills at all levels – the Board, executive leaders, key stakeholders, colleagues, team members and so on. Political influencing skills are necessary to support the progress of the project:

- Emotionally mature and experienced leaders regularly use political influencing skills to obtain resources, facilitate approvals and help parties to reach negotiated agreements.

- Emotionally immature or inexperienced leaders may resort to political influencing skills to avoid decision-making, shift blame and save face.

- Some political activity is culturally specific. It is important to understand the cultural norms (national, organisational, departmental) of the partnering organisations to understand what kind of political activity is undertaken and what is expected of you.

- Some political activity is driven by personal pathological conditions, such as personal need for power, disdain for others' rights and needing to win at all costs. If you suspect that a person is exhibiting these kinds of traits, the best advice is to seek help from trained professionals and higher project authorities.

- Effective political influencing depends on preparation – gaining good intelligence. The earlier that intelligence can be obtained about the other organisations and the people who will represent them, the better. Intelligence about cultural, organisational and personal issues that will affect the project needs to be obtained at bid stage and definitely before contracts are signed.

- Obtain assistance and advice through mentoring or coaching.

- Ultimately the degree of support you can muster depends upon the 'bank' of positive political influencing (relationship building based on trust and respect) which you accumulated with key parties up to this point in time.

References and Further Reading

Biberman, G. (1985) Personality Characteristics and Work Attitudes of Persons with High, Moderate and Low Political Tendencies. *Psychological Reports*, 57, pp. 1303–1310.

Cialdini, R.B. (2001) *Influence: Science and Practice* (4th ed.). Boston: Allyn and Bacon.

Cialdini, R.B., Sagarin, B. J. and Rice, W.E. (2001) Training in Ethical Influence. In: Darley, J., Messick, D. and Tyler, T. (eds), *Social Influences on Ethical Behavior in Organizations*, pp. 137–153. Mahwah, NJ: Erlbaum.

Day, D.D., Schleicher, D.J., Unckless, A.L. and Hiller, N.J. (2002) Self-monitoring Personality at Work: A Meta-analytic Investigation of Construct Validity. *Journal of Applied Psychology*, April, 2002, pp. 390–401.

DuBrin, A. (2009) *Political Behavior in Organizations*. Thousand Oaks, CA: Sage Publications.

De Janasz, S.C., Sullivan, S.E. and Whiting, V. (2003) Mentor Networks and Career Success: Lessons for Turbulent Times. *Academy of Management Executive*, Nov, 2003, pp. 78–91.

Ely, R.J., Meyerson, D. and Davidson, M.N. (2006) Rethinking Political Correctness. *Harvard Business Review*, Sept. 2006, p. 80.

Ferris, G.R., Treadway, D.C., Kolodinsky, R.W., Hochwarter, W.A., Kacmar, C.J. and Douglas, C. (2005) Development and Validation of the Political Skill Inventory. *Journal of Management*, 31, pp. 126–153.

Geraldi, J. (2008) Patterns of Complexity: The Thermometer of Complexity. Project Perspectives 2008. *The Annual Publication of International Project Management Association*, pp. 4–9.

Geraldi, J. and Adlbrecht, G. (2007) On Faith, Fact and Interaction in Projects. *Project Management Journal*, 38(1), pp. 32–43.

Hanna, M. (2006) Ingratiation. The Other Pathway to the Boardroom. *Wharton Leadership Digest*, October, pp. 9–10.

Hofstede, G. (2001) *Culture's Consequences: Comparing Values, Behaviors, Institutions and Organizations Across Nations*, Second Edition. Thousand Oaks, California: SAGE Publications.

Ibarra, H. and Hunter, M. (2007) How Leaders Create and Use Networks. *Harvard Business Review*, Jan. 2007, pp. 40–47.

Kipnis, D., Schmidt, S. and Wilkinson, I. (1980) Intraorganizational Influence Tactics: Explorations in Getting One's Way. *Journal of Applied Psychology*, Dec., pp. 440–452.

Kreitner, R. (2007) *Management*, 11th ed. New York, NY: Houghton Mifflin Company.

Kurchner-Hawkins, R. and Miller, R. (2006) Organizational Politics: Building Positive Political Strategies in Turbulent Times. In: Vigoda-Gadot, P.E. and Drory, A. (eds), *Handbook of Organizational Politics*, pp. 328–352. Northampton, MA: Edward Elgar.

Lui, Y., Ferris, G., Perrewé, P., Zinko, R., Wietz, B. and Jun Xu (2007) Dispositional Antedcedents and Outcomes of Political Skill in Organizations: A Four Study Investigation with Convergence. *Journal of Vocational Behavior*. 71, pp. 146–165.

McGregor, J. (2007) Sweet Revenge: The Power of Retribution, Spite, and Loathing in the World of Business. *Business Week*. Jan. 2007, pp. 64–70.

Quinne, L. (1999) Workplace Bullying in the NHS Community Trust: Staff Questionnaire Survey. *British Medical Journal*, pp. 228–232.

Schriesheim, C.A. and Hinkin, T.R. (1990) Influence Tactics Used by Subordinates: A Theoretical and Empirical Analysis and Refinement of the Kipnis, Schmidt, and Wilkinson Subscales. *Journal of Applied Psychology*, Oct., pp. 246–257.

Vigoda-Gadot, E. and Drory, A. (eds) (2006) *Handbook of Organizational Politics*. Northampton, MA: Edward Elgar.

Westphal, J.D. and Stern, I. (2006) The Other Pathway to the Boardroom: How Interpersonal Behavior can Substitute for Elite Credential and Demographic Minority Status in Gaining Access to Board Appointments. *Administrative Science Quarterly*, June, pp. 169–204.

Witt, L.A. and Ferris, G.R. (2003) Social Skill as a Moderator of the Conscientiousness-performance Relationship: Convergent Results Across Four Studies. *Journal of Applied Psychology*, Oct., p. 811.

Yukl, G. and Tracey, J.B. (1992) Consequences of Influence Tactics used with Subordinates, Peers, and the Boss. *Journal of Applied Psychology*, August, pp. 525–535.

9

Pilot Projects Through Crises

In soloing—as in other activities—it is far easier to start something than it is to finish it.
Amelia Earhart, (1928). 20 Hours: 40 minutes.

Do not spin this aircraft. If the aircraft does enter a spin it will return to earth without further attention on the part of the aeronaut.
First handbook issued with the Curtis-Wright flyer.

Chaos differs from complexity because chaotic situations rapidly become turbulent, highly disordered and unmanageable (Gleick, 1987). Even though complex adaptive systems are hard to predict they do have structure. During chaos, such as a major risk event, structures collapse and normal ways of doing things don't apply. This is a world in which leaders need to act quickly in order to stabilise the situation, then take stock of their actions afterwards (Snowdon and Boone, 2007; Axelrod and Cohen, 2000). However, in order to act quickly leadership teams need as much information as can possibly be obtained in a very short space of time, and from many different perspectives.

Key Points in This Chapter:

- Taking different systemic perspectives.

- Learning from crisis management.

Part 1: Taking Different Systemic Perspectives

The leaders we interviewed have consciously, or intuitively, embraced a bottom-up style of leadership that suits complex adaptive systems, rejecting strictly hierarchical approaches which do not suit complexity. This applies even in industries that are traditionally rule-bound, like defence. During business-as-usual they 'lead' their complex projects similar to the way the Internet functions, as a decentralised multi-nodal information system, integrating rather than controlling, through information exchange. This usually involves establishing boundaries and attractors, such as sensible reporting pathways and clearly communicated targets, then letting people get on with it in their own way while facilitating 'rich' communication between all parties.

When things become chaotic, such as during a crisis or major risk event, the leaders interviewed also seem to be able to switch to a top-down, directive form of leadership.

John Snow (1813–1858), an English physician, is considered to be one of the founders of epidemiology, because of his work in tracing the source of a cholera outbreak in London. The genius of Dr. John Snow's 1854 proof that cholera was spread by contaminated water was in relating the deaths to geography. If he hadn't investigated potential anomalies – like isolated cholera deaths occurring further away and two significant communities (a brewery and workhouse, each with their own well) that were unaffected – then he would have had less proof of a cause and effect relationship. If he had displayed the data differently on his map, he might have never noticed the concentration was greatest near the Broad Street pump. There are ways of grouping and reviewing the graphical data that completely obscure the link. He chose the right one and changed the course of medical history.

This true story illustrates how taking another perspective to assess a crisis situation systemically and from different perspectives can pay.

TAKE THE WIDEST POSSIBLE VIEW AND THEN ACT VERY QUICKLY

The paradox for leadership is that it is necessary to take the widest possible view and, at the same time act quickly. One action seems to contrdict the other. Whoever takes charge must be able to make, think and act quickly to try to stabilise the situation, be courageous enough to own those decisions, communicate clear and directly, and from the top down. Crises exhibit the same kind of emergent patterns that we see in any complex adaptive system, but they escalate very quickly and have much wider ramifications. As we have seen in weather patterns, causing cyclones and floods, the consequences for the communities affected can be grave. A crisis is qualitatively different from an incident. During a crisis there is a need to analyse things in real time – what is going on now. At the same time leaders need to find people who can give advice on what might happen in a day, a week's time, a month's time. Practice will be completely novel. In chaotic situations there are few, if any, precedents. Because of the rapidity that nonlinear patterns escalate it is impossible to predict outcomes based on prior knowledge (Snowdon, 2000, 2002).

Also, patterns of events may not be immediately comprehensible. Therefore, taking time to discover patterns might not be an option. The best response seems to be for the leadership to gather as much information as quickly as possible, choose a pathway and act very quickly, then monitor the effects of the action and respond to those effects. Although leadership's immediate job is to 'staunch the bleeding' (Snowdon and Boone, 2007, p. 74), leaders must be aware that the vicious cycles of events can escalate so rapidly that almost any local, non-systemic intervention has just as much chance of exacerbating the situation as fixing it (Williams, 2004). Close collaboration between key players is vital (see Chapter 12) as this project leader reports about the way his sponsor performed during a critical period:

> Yes, but she was a keen participant ... because she's that kind of a person, having a sponsor in the organisation to be there and be seen there, actively involved in communicating the messages instead of a message from on high when you never see the person. If we didn't have an answer we'd work out how to manage the issues. That in itself creates an environment for the likelihood of a successful project that could be at risk. Interview 65 PM.

Part 2: Learning from Crisis Management

Some of the leadership capabilities identified (adapted from James, 2007 and 2008) include:

- Identifying obvious and obscure vulnerabilities.

- Building an environment of trust.

- Changing the mindset of key stakeholders.

- Making wise and rapid decisions.

- Taking courageous action.

- Learning from crises.

Stated in a list like this, these statements are simply platitudes. In a crisis, as we have seen in recent flood and earthquake events, leaders who are remembered are those who can state issues in clear, plain language, who have the courage to make decisions quickly and who own the consequences. As explained in Chapter 2, clarity wins over direction during uncertainty. Frontline leadership is vital at these critical moments; however, leadership action in crisis reflects the competency of the organisation, or community, as a whole.

A CRISIS TESTS THE ROBUSTNESS OF THE ORGANISATION AS WELL AS THE LEADER

The test in a crisis is the robustness of the organisation's, or the community's, leadership structure – how well it serves common goals (James, 2007, 2008). Learning plays a vital role. During the devastating floods that hit Queensland, Australia in 2011, the Premier, Anna Bligh, noted that the leadership could not have responded as rapidly as it did if the relevant government departments and authorities in Queensland had not learned from New Orleans.

CRISIS MANAGEMENT RESEARCH MIGHT APPLY TO PROJECTS APPROACHING CHAOS

There has been very little research on how leaders and teams manage these kinds of emergent risk patterns in complex projects. The most relevant information comes from the growing field of crisis management. Writers on crisis management argue that effective crisis management involves some or all of the following activities.

Although these activities are usually presented in a linear order, to suggest that these activities follow a particular pattern would be incorrect. They happen iteratively and interactively. Decision-making can't take place without innovating, which feeds back into sense-making activities, and so on. Effective crisis management is 'rich' communication in action. It includes:

- *Signal detecting* – being alert to signals that indicate a crisis is imminent.

- *Sense-making* – diagnosing the problem from as many perspectives as possible.

- *Decision-making* – choosing a direction based on the evidence.

- *Innovating* – finding new ways to address problems.

- *Co-ordinating* – aligning all the key players in a co-ordinated effort.

- *Meaning-making* –persuading key players about the course of action.

- *Preparing* – setting the ground so that teams are prepared for action.

- *Implementing* – planning and delivering the action needed to address the situation.

- *Monitoring* – checking to see if it is working and making adjustments as needed.

- *Learning* – sharing and understanding.

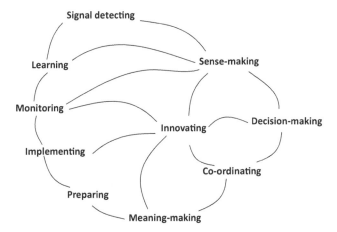

Figure 9.1   **The crisis management mess (deliberately simplified to prevent all the words from being completely obscured by connecting lines)**

Adding to the complexity, all this will be happening at once! Therefore, the thinking styles that are most useful during these events are nonlinear, interconnected, interdependent and 'rich'. Nevertheless, for the sake of clarity, and because a book page is not a multi-dimensional medium, the activities that seem to contribute to effective crisis management will be discussed as if they exist separately – which they do not!

SIGNAL DETECTING

Being aware of the signals that something is not as it should be depends on the leader's ability to scan the environment, listen and observe. These are often referred to by complexity theorists as 'weak signals'. However, it is important to maintain a healthy distrust for the efficacy of any information received. As discussed in Chapter 6, although executives spend a substantial amount of their time monitoring the environment, the magnitude of the scanning task can be daunting to any individual's information processing capabilities (Hambrick, 1981; Kefalas and Schoderbek, 1973), especially when environments are diffuse, complex, dynamic and elusive. Boyd and Fulk (1996) also argue that while scanning may well provide useful information, if the environment is not predictable or there is perceived complexity, external information search is less effective. As a result some situations may receive only limited scanning if they are perceived as too complex to be understood.

We also have selective attention. We tend to focus on things we know about. As the project director of this multi-national environmental clean-up exercise observed of his technically trained teams:

> Technical risks were generally well handled as the safety critical nature
> of the project attracted specialists who understood the risk situation
> clearly. Political and emotional risks were invariably identified late and
> then were poorly handled because they were dealt with inappropriately.
> Interview 49 PD.

One of the most interesting aspects associated with emergent risk patterns in complex projects is that the accumulation of often quite small issues ('weak signals' in complexity theory) can rapidly escalate in a nonlinear manner to cause a crisis. This is known in complexity theory as the *edge of chaos*, and in the popular press as the *tipping point* (Gladwell, 2000. p. 12). A *tipping point* is described as '...the moment of critical mass, the threshold, the boiling point.' Often the triggers are small events. In society this can be an idea that behaves like a virus, sometimes referred to as a *meme* that moves rapidly through the population. An example is the informal communication networks, via mobile phone, using Facebook and other social networking sites that triggered and sustained protests in early 2011 in several Middle Eastern countries, such as Egypt and Libya.

Remington and Pollack, (2007, p. 162) illustrate a cognitive diagnostic map of a construction project that a series of emergent risk patterns, resulting in eventual termination of the contracts and massive losses to most parties involved. The tipping point occurred when the head contractor filed for bankruptcy but causes could be traced back to a collection of small events that hardly hit the risk register. At the tipping point everything associated with the project, including formerly civil relationships, changed. On analysis it was a series of temporally related conditions and minor risks that compounded, forming nonlinear reinforcing loops that caused a rapid collapse of the project. Complexity theorists refer to this kind of collapse as a phase change, a term that describes an apparently sudden change in state. The substance is the same but its state is different – like a local increase in temperature causing lower layers of ice to melt causing the snow and ice on top to start to slip down the mountain, collecting more snow and ice as it moves down, rapidly gaining momentum and causing an avalanche. A number of the senior leaders interviewed stressed the importance of being alert to and attending to little things. A regional general manager in the defence industry stressed:

> *A lot of people tend to look for the one or two big things that are wrong – usually it's a long list of small items rather than a short list of big items – often it is about getting a whole list of basic things right. I call it the sins of neglect – accumulation of small things. Interview 47 GM.*

The general manager of a large international construction project management organisation also said:

> *When asked if I liked my job I would say yes it is a wonderful job except at 8.30am when all the day to day problems of running a business arise and then at 6pm in the evening I get to do the work I really like doing that should have started at 9am. Loved it before 8.30am and after 6pm. But later you realise that the small problems that arise each day are the most important ones – my desk and I have a lot of joint memories. Interview 46 GM.*

However, it was obvious that both of these general managers and other senior leaders spent an equal amount of time scanning situations from the ...

> ... *highest possible level – getting the best possible view – like being on*
> *a Mount Everest – as high as you can get. Interview 46 GM.*

It is only by taking the highest possible view of the situation, 'standing back' that leadership teams can start to discern patterns at the level of the wider system. Responding at a local level is sometimes important to restore and maintain trust. Immediately after responding at a local level leadership teams should step back to get as wide a view as possible. As discussed in Chapter 6, 'gut feel' is recognised as an important part of signal detection. It is an emotional response that somehow draws upon accumulated previous experience. Although anecdotal reports from leaders worldwide recognise the importance of 'gut feel', it has only recently been the subject of research (Lakomsky and Evers, 2009).

Sensemaking

> *It is the mark of an educated mind to be able to entertain a thought*
> *without accepting it.*
>
>   *Attruted to Aristotle, (384-322 BCE).*

Making sense of what is happening is the critical next stage following detection of weak signals that suggest something is not quite right. Sensemaking (Weick, 1988, 1995) (or sense-making; Dervin, 1992, 1996) was a termed coined to describe this important step. Making sense of what is going on is not straightforward. People's interpretation of events is bound up in who they think they are, their roles and their perceptions of themselves as the drama unfolds (Currie and Brown, 2003; Weick, Sutcliffe, and Obstfeld, 2005; Thurlow and Mills, 2009; Watson, 1995, 1998). Sensemaking is also to do with what people notice. How focused people are and what interruptions can affect the richness and accuracy of what people recall (Dunford and Jones, 2000; Gephart, 1993).

People take in the issues they face through stories and dialogue which help them understand what they think, organise their experiences and control and predict events (Isabella, 1990; Weick, 1995; Abolafia, 2010). Sensemaking can be both a social activity and an activity that involves individual reflection (Isabella, 1990; Maitlis, 2005) Sensemaking is also continuous (Thurlow and Mills, 2009), narratives change and evolve over time and people's understandings of the situation are continuously reshaped.

In reshaping their understanding of the situation people extract cues from the context to help them decide on what information is relevant and what explanations are acceptable. These cues are not necessarily the best ones. They have usually been determined by the particular context and focus (Salancick and Pfeffer, 1978; Brown, Stacey and Nandhakumar, 2007). One of the most interesting aspects is that, when making sense of a situation, people tend to favour *plausibility* over *accuracy* (Brown, 2005; Abolafia, 2010). This is important when communicating information during a crisis. If the leader can frame explanations in terms that people can relate to their experience, then people are more likely to believe the explanations.

CLARIFY WHAT CAN BE CLARIFIED

Nevertheless, not everything will be uncertain. The tension is somewhat relieved when at least some things can be clarified. Working out what can be clarified makes the whole mess seem less uncertain and people feel more able to cope. It always surprised me that after a half day's planning, with the right people present, we could estimate budgets and schedules to a very fine degree of accuracy, even with big projects, which appeared, at first, to be full of uncertainty. Most people do not realise how much they know and how quickly and accurately they can estimate outcomes from the knowledge they have. This is about breaking down the problem and asking the right questions.

A famous example was given by physicist and the Nobel laureate, Enrico Fermi, who asked his students to quickly estimate the number of piano tuners in Boston (many years before the worldwide web). Fermi started by asking the students other things about piano tuners that, while still uncertain, might be easier to estimate, such as: what is the population of Boston, the average number of people per household, the percentage of houses that might own a piano, how many pianos a tuner could tune in a day, how many days a year a piano tuner might work, and so on. Using this method, students found that they could quickly to come up with a figure that was surprisingly close to the actual figure (Hubbard, 2010, p. 12).

Innovating

> *Giving up was never a possibility for us so we had to think 'what can we do' – the absolute focus on the end delivery set the tone for everything else. I have to be the ultimate owner of that – you need a team around you but if I give way on any of the key goals we probably won't get there ... Interview 48 PD.*

Chapter 4 discusses the importance of encouraging innovation. Innovation often springs from adversity and never is innovative thinking more important than during a crisis. As the interviewee above recognises, it is the leader's job to link innovation with the project vision. Encouraging people to use their imagination also has much to do with keeping the teams motivated and focused on the end goals.

> *We kept it simple, focused on the larger issues, focused on the principles and fundamentals we were trying to achieve at every stage. Inteview 41 GM.*

And, so many leaders stressed, when under pressure, focusing on fundamental principles, the larger issues, usually meant that innovative solutions could be found. Going back to first principles can help to cut through much of the irrelevant material that obscures the goals.

Decision-making

Decision-making may be viewed as the process of reducing the gap between the existing situation and the desired situation through solving problems and making use of opportunities. It is goal-oriented. A decision is the conclusion reached after consideration. It occurs when one option is selected, to the exclusion of others through judgment. However, as discussed in Chapter 6, rarely is this pathway simple. The decision-making process is one that is shaped and formed by a variety of concerns and interests many of which are not based solely on formal evidence or 'facts' (Styhre et al., 2010). It is important for leadership teams to remember that under conditions of uncertainty people, including the leaders themselves, are operating under high levels of stress. Even under normal conditions decision-making, particularly decision-making involving groups, is highly influenced by emotions, values and available, as opposed to best, information. To recap, emotional impacts on decision-making can be simultaneously helpful and counter-productive.

Co-ordinating

This involves aligning all the key players in a co-ordinated effort to address the crisis. Even though a leadership team might have determined a suitable course of action, complex projects usually involve many layers of leadership and many key parties who need to be convinced of the proposed course of action. Each key person will bring to the table personal characteristics, cultural norms and organisational imperatives that will influence the way she or he sees the crisis and how the crisis and the proposed actions will affect their particular interests.

This is where effective leaders exert political influencing skills (see Chapter 8). Individuals and groups need to be lobbied and convinced and, due to the rapid emergence of risk patterns that characterise crises, all this must occur within a very short space of time. One of the major risks during a crisis is prevarication.

Meaning-making

In this respect meaning-making refers to how everyone involved internalises and comes to an understanding of the information presented to them. It is a key component in how successfully leadership co-ordinates key players in the decision-making process.

Ability to make and share meaning is determined by many factors: words and language used; emotions conveyed; people's ability to grasp and also their willingness to participate and try to understand. For example, the choice of words is critical. Words can be interpreted in multiple ways. In addition, many words and phrases have become platitudes because they are so overused that they begin to inspire derision and lose their impact. Facilitating conversations, in bigger and richer contexts, helps to create shifts in meaning. Meanings can shift when we get the chance to think about issues, worry about their consequences and then clarify what impact might be. Our values are at the root of meaning and for true change to occur we may need to review these terms that are deep, hidden inside our subconsciousness.

Using a number of methods; verbal reasoning, visual representation, narrative and metaphor, increases the probability that meanings are communicated. However, it is important to note again that in a crisis all this must occur very rapidly. Leaders do not have time to spend on building understanding. Ideally this occurs, at least with key people in the leadership teams, before a crisis occurs. A useful skill for leaders is the ability to state situations in plain language, avoiding jargon, and with language carefully targeted to people's concerns. The following example is a response to a question from the media by the Premier of Queensland, during the flood crisis in 2011. She said:

> *I'm not happy with the speed with which this is happening ... I've asked my director general to work with Centrelink [the government agency offering flood relief aid] to see if there's something we can do, maybe give some more resources to Centrelink, to process this more quickly ... Premier Anna Bligh: Source: NEWS.com.au 27/2/11; http://www. daylife.com/quote/0flr8Ly8t43lm?q=Anna+Bligh*

It is a good example of successful crisis communication from a senior leader. The leader first acknowledges fears and concerns and then states clearly what she is going to do about it. Her communication is also free from platitudes and unnecessary jargon.

Preparing

Doing the ground work so that all teams (executive through to project teams) are prepared for action cannot happen effectively during a crisis. It occurs well before, at the beginning of the project. If leadership teams are to effectively share meaning and create understanding and commitment during a crisis they have to rely on the ground work that they have put in before a crisis occurs.

Preparation for managing crises involves two main components; intellectual assessment of risk patterns and a foundation of trust in the leadership.

> *You cannot solve an intangible, if it happens it happens, you must have the optimum way of managing – something can come out of left field – don't know what or when – try to pick where are the likely areas where something odd could happen – scenario planning – straw man building – we had them in our back pocket therefore were able to respond quickly*

and calmly – best position to apply, the best management and stay calm
rather than panic. Interview 46 GM.

Useful techniques like scenario planning and cognitive mapping help prepare teams at all levels to manage risks. Nevertheless, many other risk management tools emphasise linear logic and often focus people's attention on the major risks while ignoring the myriads of small events that could escalate and emerge to create a crisis. Exploring what could go wrong with a project prepares people with a set of responses so that they can move quickly. Preparatory exercises that involve rich narrative and imagination also help to share meaning and understanding and to prepare people in advance for thinking differently.

Being able to help change the mindset of key stakeholders was mentioned earlier in this chapter as a key leadership capability in crisis situations. Individuals vary in the time they need to assimilate new ideas and new ways of doing things in different ways– some are quick adopters, others need a longer time to mull over ideas. If performed early, a range of exercises like scenario building, cognitive mapping and exercises in creative solution finding, help people prepare for doing things differently if and when a crisis occurs. Hence, meaning-making, which can be a slow process, can happen more quickly and the process of obtaining agreement to proceed during a crisis is accelerated. Although these exercises can never cover all emergent situations, they can often closely approximate future event patterns.

Implementing

Advice from leaders about implementing actions fell into four categories:

- Being seen to be taking action.

- Allocating the risk appropriately.

- Sustaining and enhancing communication.

- Maintaining focus on key goals.

During a crisis the teams and key stakeholders need strong leadership direction. Good leadership is not the same at all times. In crises tough leaders are often needed to get the job done and deal ruthlessly the situation. In the project environment, like in today's military environments, an ability to exercise tough leadership when the situation demands is less dependent on position power and more on:

- Trusting relationships and respect established with key players.

- Simple, sound, clear, shared and fully understood processes.

- Excellent preparation for crisis risk patterns so that people can move rapidly.

TAKING ACTION

Taking action and being seen and heard to take action, when people are anxious and uncertainty abides, is challenging but important because people can see that things are being done and that, in itself, restores confidence.

> *If you fix the broken windows it tends to restore the streetscape and people behave better. Interview 47 GM.*

ALLOCATING RISK WHERE IT CAN BE MANAGED

When something is too big, breaking it down is good advice. Key to this is making sure that the people handling the parts are capable of owning that part of the risk and dealing with it. Ownership of each part of the risk is essential to controlling it.

> *Identify areas of risk and do everything you can to gain ownership of that area of risk – if you don't own it you can't control it – don't give away your risk profile to someone who doesn't have the skills, abilities and authority to manage it. Risk often gets transferred from government to contractor to a subcontractor who is the least able to manage the risk and probably doesn't even know he has the risk. Interview 46 GM.*

However, this can only be done while keeping a hold on the big picture and there are times when radical holistic intervention is required.

SUSTAINING COMMUNICATION

While managing emergent risks, it is very easy to lose focus on what can be seen as non-core activities, such as communication. While implementing the actions communication is vital particularly if the outcomes are politically sensitive as it was in the following multi-national taxation project:

> *Proactive communications to all stakeholders. Having communications that is timely, tailored, and encompasses all stakeholders (e.g. have a 'to' list as well as a cc list so any stakeholder can understand whether the communication is aimed at them. Engage the media to show your side of the story. Interview 50 PM.*

MAINTAIN FOCUS ON KEY GOALS

> *Making sure that you do have the right strategy – very easy to dive straight in – time spent thinking about what you want and working back – asking what is the end state and rigorously working back is important. Focus on the end goal. Interview 48 PD.*

At critical times it is easy to be side-tracked by small issues and for people to become fixated on particular areas of focus or expertise. After all, we tend to retreat to our comfort zones when under pressure. Even when time is of the essence planning is important.

Monitoring

Working with crises is experimental. Leaps of faith are necessary. Therefore, testing the water with small interventions might be less risky than giant steps.

> *Sometimes it's like a search path when you are flying a plane. You test and correct ... test and correct. Interview 42 PD.*

Immediate feedback is essential so that the leader or the leadership teams are able to respond rapidly. Setting up clear reporting and honest feedback channels is a priority for complex projects when they are edging close to chaos.

Learning

Learning from crises is much harder than it looks. The aftermath of a crisis can become dominated by desire to allocate blame and there a real trade-off between blaming and learning can occur. The degree to which learning takes place is affected by how well accountability is understood and shared. A challenge for leadership, after the crisis, is to make the post-crisis period *safe* for learning. People will look for others to blame. It is part of dealing with crises. Attributing blame helps people make sense of what has happened and, of course, there are those with vested interests in attributing blame to secure compensation.

I have conducted several successful post-project reviews after project stakeholders' relationships have descended into a 'blame game'. The first thing I do is make it safe for people to exchange information. This requires several different approaches depending on my assessment of: the willingness of individuals and groups to work together; the level of commitment of senior executive leaders to learning; sensitivity of information (whether litigation proceedings are likely or in progress) and the cultures of the organisations involved.

If leadership can promote constructive learning from crises the learning process can also have a healing effect on teams and stakeholders. In my experience with facilitating post-project reviews, collecting and sharing valuable information helps people to move forward. Even in the most conflicted situations the learning process relieves tension and helps to rebuild relationships. Learning from crisis events places people back in control.

In Summary

Managing emergent risks can be akin to managing local crises. Through nonlinearity and emergence, groups of small risks and initial conditions can quickly escalate into vicious cycles with chaotic results. Leadership in a crisis might need to take a more direct form than leadership in everyday situations.

During periods of crisis leaders need to ensure that a rich mix of activities happen, including:

- Detecting signals – being alert to the 'weak signals' that indicate that a crisis is imminent and paying attention to the small events that might cause a landslide later on.

- Being on guard for tipping points signaling an approaching crisis.

- Sense-making – diagnosing the problem from as many perspectives as possible.

- Clarifying what can be clarified to reduce the perception of uncertainty.

- Decision-making – choosing a direction based on the evidence.

- Paying attention to the influence of emotions and personal values.

- Innovating – finding new ways to address problemsco-ordinating – aligning all the key players in a co-ordinated effortmeaning-making –persuading key players about the course of actionusing a number of methods: verbal reasoning, visual representation, narrative and metaphor to increase the likelihood that meanings are communicated.

- Preparing – setting the ground so that teams are prepared for action by buildingtrusting relationships and respect with key players before the crisis.

- Have simple, sound, clear, shared and fully understood processes in place.

- Make solid preparation for crisis risk patterns so that people can move rapidly if a cricis occurs.

- Implementing – planning and delivering the action needed to address the situation.

- Being seen to be taking action.

- Allocating the risk appropriately.

- Sustaining and enhancing communication.

- Maintaining focus on key high level goals.

- Monitoring – checking to see if it is working and making adjustments as needed.

- Encouraging immediate, honest feedback.

- Learning – sharing and understanding.

- Making the post-crisis period safe for learning.

References and Further Reading

Abolafia, M. (2010) Narrative Construction as Sensemaking. *Organization Studies*, 31(3), pp. 349–367.

Axelrod, R. and Cohen, M.D. (2000) *Harnessing Complexity. Organizational Implications of a Scientific Frontier*. New York, NY: Basic Books.

Boyd, B.K. and Fulk, J. (1996) Executive Scanning and Perceived Uncertainty: A Multidimensional Model. *Journal of Management*, 22(1), pp. 1–21.

Brown, A.D. (2005) Making Sense of the Collapse of Barings Bank. *Human Relations*, 58(12), pp. 1579–1605.

Brown, A.D., Stacey, P. and Nandhakumar, J. (2007) Making Sense of Sensemaking Narratives. *Human Relations*, 61(8), pp. 1035–1062.

Currie, G. and Brown, A. (2003) A Narratological Approach to Understanding Processes of Organizing in a UK Hospital. *Human Relations*, 56(5), pp. 563–586.

Dervin, B. (1992) From the Mind's Eye of the User: The Sense-making Qualitative-quantitative Methodology. In: Glazier, J. and Dervin, B. (1996) Given a Context by any Other Name: Methodological Tools for Taming the Unruly Beast. Keynote paper, ISIC 96: Information Seeking in Context, pp. 1–23.

Drayton, Bruce. W. (2004) Managing Crises in the Twenty-first Century. *International Studies Review*, 6(1), pp. 165–194.

Dunford, R. and Jones, D. (2000) Narrative in Strategic Change. *Human Relations*, 53, pp. 1207–1226.

Fink, S. (1986) *Crisis Management. Planning for the Inevitable*. New York, NY: American Management Association.

Gephart, R.P. (1993) The Textual Approach: Risk and Blame in Disaster Sensemaking. *Academy of Management Journal*, 36, pp. 1465–1514.

Gladwell, M. (2000) The Tipping Point: How Little Things Can Make a Big Difference. Boston, USA: Little Brown and Company.

Gleick, J. (1987) *Chaos: Making a New Science*. New York, NY: Viking.

Hambrick, D.C. (1981) Specialization of Environmental Scanning Activities Among Upper Level Executives. *Journal of Management Studies*, 18, pp. 299–320.

Herek, G.M. and Janis, I.L. (1987) Decision-making During International Crises. *Journal of Conflict Resolution*, 31(2), pp. 203–226.

Hubbard, D.W. (2010) *How to Measure Anything. Finding the Value of 'Intangibles' in Business*, 2nd. Ed. Hoboken, New Jersey: John Wiley and Sons.

Isabella, L.A. (1990) Evolving Interpretations as Change Unfolds: How Managers Construe Key Organisational Events. *Academy of Management Journal*, 33(1).

James, E. (Spring 2007). Leadership as (Un)usual: How to Display Competence In Times of Crisis. Leadership Preview, http://www.leadershipreview. org/2007spring/Article4.pdf. Retrieved 22/06/10.

James, E.H. (Vol. 10, No. 3, 2008). Linking Crisis Management and Leadership Competencies: The Role of Human Resource Development. Advances in Developing Human Resources, 10: 352. doi:10.1177/1523422308316450. http://adh.sagepub.com/cgi/content/short/10/3/352. Retrieved 22/06/2010.

Janis, I.L. (1989) *Crucial Decisions: Leadership in Policymaking and Crisis Management*. New York, NY: Free Press.

Kefalas, A. and Schoderbek, P. (1973) Scanning the Business Environment: Some empirical results. *Decision Sciences*, 4, pp. 63–74.

Lakomski, G. and Evers, C. W. (2009) Passionate Rationalism: The Role of Emotion in Decision-making. *Journal of Educational Administration*, 48(4), pp. 438–450.

Maitlis, S. (2005) The Social Processes of Organizational Sense Making. *Academy of Management Journal*, 48(1), pp. 21–49.

Park, C.L. and Folkman, S. (1997) Meaning in the Context of Stress and Coping. *Review of General Psychology*, 1(2), pp. 115–144.

Pearson, C.M. and Clair, J.A. (1996) Reframing Crisis Management. *Academy of Management Review*, 23(1), pp. 59–70.

Remington, K. and Pollack, J. (2007) *Tools for Complex Projects*. Aldershot, UK: Gower Publishing.

Rosenthal, U., Charles, M.T. and t'Hart, P.T. (1989) *Coping with Crises: The Management of Disasters, Riots and Terrorism*. Stanford University, SLAC Research Library.

Rosenthal, U., Boin, A. and Comfort, L.K. (2001) *Managing Crises: Threats, Dilemmas, Opportunities*. Springfield, Il: Charles C. Thomas.

Salancick, G. and Pfeffer, J. (1978) A Social Information Processing Approach to Job Attitudes and Task Design. *Administrative Science Quarterly*, 23, pp. 224–253.

Snowden, D. (2002) Complex Acts of Knowing: Paradox and Descriptive Self-awareness. *Journal of Knowledge Management*, 6(2), pp. 100–111.

Snowden, D. (2000) Cynefin: A Sense of Time and Space, the Social Ecology of Knowledge Management. In: *Knowledge Horizons: The Present and the Promise of Knowledge Management*. Despres, C. and Chauvel, D. (eds) Butterworth Heinemann.

Snowden, D.J. and Boone, M. (2007) A Leader's Framework for Decision-making. *Harvard Business Review*, November 2007, pp. 69–76.

Stern, D.K. (2000) *Crisis Decisionmaking: A Cognitive Institutional Approach*. Stockholm, Sweden, Swedish National Defence College.

Stern, E. and Sundelius, B. (2003) Crisis Management Europe: An Integrated Regional Research and Training Program. *International Studies Association: International Studies Perspectives*, 3(1), pp. 77–88.

Styhre, A., Wikmalm, L. Olilla, S. and Roth, J. (2010) Garbage-can Decision Making and the Accommodation of Uncertainty in: *New Drug Development Work. Creativity and Innovation Management*, 19(2), pp. 134–146.

Thurlow, A. and Mills, J. (2009) Change, Talk and Sensemaking. *Journal of Organizational Change Management*, 22(5), pp. 459–579.

Watson, T.J. (1998) Managerial Sensemaking and Occupational Identities in Britain and Italy: The role of Management Magazines in the Process of Discursive Construction. *Journal of Management Studies*, 35(3), pp. 285–301.

Watson, T.J. (1995) Rhetoric, Discourse and Argument in Organizational Sensemaking: A Reflexive Tale. *Organization Studies*, 16(5), pp. 805–821.

Weick, K. (1995) *Sensemaking in Organisations*. London: Sage.

Weick, K. (1988) Enacted Sensemaking in Crisis Situations. *Journal of Management Studies*, 25, pp. 305–317.

Weick, K., Sutcliffe, K.M. and Obstfeld, D. (2005) Organizing and the Process of Sensemaking. *Organization Science*, 16(4), pp. 409–421.

Williams, T. (2004) Why Monte Carlo Simulations of Project Networks can Mislead. *Project Management Journal*, 25(3), pp. 53–61.

SECTION TWO:

What Good Leadership Needs When Projects Are Complex

Once again the chapters in this section were derived from key themes emerging from the interviews with senior project leaders who had successfully led complex projects. The focus of this section is what leaders need in terms of organisational support. Chapter 10 explores the issue of governance, but from the perspective of complex, multi-owner, multi-national projects. Chapter 11 expresses a frequently repeated theme; the essential requirement for project leaders to have control over the structuring, including selection and removal, of key project roles. Chapter 12 derives its name from a comment made by one senior leader 'you must have partners for peace.' The chapter summarises the concept of partnering and relationship as a guiding principle on which complex projects can be delivered successfully.

Chapter 10: Governance That Matches the Complexity

Chapter 11: Authority Over Key Roles

Chapter 12: Partners for Peace

10

Governance That Matches
the Complexity

Sail forth! steer for the deep waters only!
Reckless, O soul, exploring, I with thee, and thou with me;
For we are bound where mariner has not yet dared to go,
And we will risk the ship, ourselves and all.
> From Passage to India, Leaves of Grass (1900)
> by Walt Whitman, (1819–1892).

Leaders cannot effectively mobilise the project (or steer the ship) without appropriate governance structures. Good governance can effectively move the project from a complex space to a complicated but manageable space.

> There was a high level BLT, business leadership team; if a decision was needed that couldn't be made on site or at coordinator level, it would go back to the BLT to make the decision about whether to take that step. The BLT at higher level made the decision on whether to proceed or not. That took a lot of uncertainty out. Interview 66 SE.

Any effective governance model aims to establish a process that steers the project to realise the benefits of the project for key stakeholders. Strategically, it is critical to establish the foundation for governance early so that governance team can make decisions and steer project (Fickenscher and Bakerman, 2011). Leaders interviewed stressed the relationship between good governance and clear accountability. In the following example of a police project the executive sponsor chose the project manager, kept a close interest and set some flexible boundaries, leaving the rest to the project manager in the understanding that a project like this is so full of unknowns that governance has to reflect the complexity:

> *It's how close you are to the accountability; it has to be very clear what you're asking people to do and that you're going to pay attention to what they're doing and not setting a direction and not checking that they're heading that way. The stolen motor vehicles project is an example. I nominated the key person, the project leader, and he was given accountability. We negotiated what the outcomes were, which was a reduction in stolen motor vehicles across the state. I also gave him a time frame for the reduction. It was also done without any financial support unless he could find it within his own budget. I was pretty confident that it wasn't about money, but focus, and how he would get the organisation to focus their energies and tactics. So he got set up with this target. He set a very small target for reduction, I went for a very large one. He went for 5 per cent, I said 20 per cent, in a twelve to eighteen month target. Up to that point 48,000 cars were stolen every year. He was also given responsibility to engage other stakeholders, vehicle manufacturers, car park owners, etc. As we got started he was given a couple of months to get people thinking about it, and he then nominated the ten top locations where vehicles were stolen and so we tracked over time to see if we could start to see a reduction in those ten locations. We designed the measures from the start. The fact that he had to broadly consult was also a requirement. That meant he had to go out and talk to people. They also talked to crooks. They interviewed fifteen kids charged with stealing motor vehicles. We reduced motor vehicle theft by 67 per cent. What it did was to get a lot of people saying look at this. It gave an impetus to the organisation, so they delivered and far better, but it was also part of a cultural change, getting people to see that they can make a difference. Interview 70 CEO.*

The complexity of achieving effective governance reveals itself when more than one organisation is involved; partnerships (such as public-private partnerships) and joint ventures. When, in addition, these multi-organisation projects are trans-national, local cultural differences are thrown into the mixing pot with organisational differences and the agendas, overt or covert, of individual stakeholders. It should be expected that a huge variance in motives and values will exist between the key players. Referring to a large mining project conducted in Asia, involving a foreign project team, a local client and local project teams, the following extract illustrates some of the challenges:

> *A bad decision to start off with was made on the Project splitting the responsibility of the project across Joint Venture Partners – half the*

project was given to one venture partner (civil works) with technology to the other. Seemed like a nice compromise at the time – a political decision but had exposed the project to a great deal of risk as quality and safety management has been atrocious – had to stop work for several months to get safety and quality people involved from our side –they were focused on as 'cheap as possible' and we were focused on getting the best value. The other JV partner focussed on cheap as possible – we were focused on best value. They were a part state owned enterprise so that has its own political machinations. Their strong focus on cost almost exclusively frustrated the technology side of the Project - trying to finish as quickly as possible to get a ROI they didn't appear to understand the time connection issues. In spite of being assigned overall project managers of the Project we effectively had little control. Cultural differences - cost, time, quality, safety – the client was very focussed on cost first, time second, and safety seemed to be their last consideration - our company is driven by safety as a primary objective – we look at safety, quality and then cost and time. It is absolutely fundamental that projects are structured well from the start – strong governance must be defined at the project front end and followed strongly -if you don't do it you will be exposed to a lot of complexity – people forget and change. Inteview 56 PD.

A Quick Overview of Project Governance

Project governance has been widely discussed in the professional literature. Most writers agree that project governance is separate from corporate governance and is concerned with steering the project or programme (OGC, 2009; Müller, 2009).

Classical project governance thinking aims to ensure the organisation level benefits are realised and is achieved through a number of activities:

- Evaluation and selection of proposals in relation to organisational strategic objectives.

- Defining critical success factors for the project.

- Gathering business support for the project.

- Defining key roles and responsibilities for the project.

- Enabling resources for the project.

- Ensuring that key stakeholders are managed.

- Monitoring progress – scope, quality, budget and schedule.

- Measuring outputs against the plan.

- Developing and enhancing delivery capability.

SIMPLE GOVERNANCE STRUCTURES

Governance for projects within organisations, such as the delivery of an IT capability within an organisation, or projects delivered for a clearly identified single client, such as a commercial property development project, generally require simple, straightforward approaches to governance. These projects and programmes can be complex but much of the complexity can be addressed if clear accountability can be defined. For these kinds of projects and programmes it is recommended that:

- A single point of accountability for the success of the project is determined. Ideally one person of high authority should be accountable for and drive the project. This person is usually the project sponsor.

- Responsibility for ownership of the project lies with whoever owns the outcomes. Several methodologies (for example Prince2 methodology) argue that the only sure method of ensuring that the project outputs meet needs of the end use is for ownership of the project to reflect this.

- Project governance is separated from corporate governance. Project governance structures should be established separately from the organisation's governance structure because organisation structures do not provide the necessary framework for project delivery. Projects require flexibility and speed of decision-making. The hierarchical decision-making mechanisms in most organisations generally do not support this. Project governance structures can overcome this by drawing the relevant decision-makers out of the organisation structure and placing them in a separate forum, the governance board or steering committee. Problems can occur when the decisions of the project governance board also need to be ratified by people in the organisation outside of that project decision-making forum (Garland, 2009; Müller, 2009; OGC, 2009).

- Project decision-making is separated from project stakeholder groups. This reflects the observation that advice from stakeholders can be sometimes be confused with decision-making bodies. As project decision-making forums grow in size, they have the capacity to be integrated with stakeholder management groups instead of being preserved as a forum for decision-making. When the project depends upon the committee to make timely decisions clarity of roles is essential (Garland, 2009, OGC, 2009).

These recommendations seek to minimise multi-layered or diffuse decision-making and minimise associated time delays and inefficiencies so that the project governance body is empowered to make decisions about the project in a timely manner.

Governance in Complex Environments

Whilst the principles cited above are very sound and should be easy to implement for a project conducted within a single organisation, or for a single client, sound governance is much more difficult to achieve when the project involves many more layers of authority.

Examples of multi-layered accountability might include:

- A project involving several countries in a cleanup after a nuclear disaster, like Chernobyl.

- A project to construct an oil and gas pipeline spanning several countries, like the Trans-ASEAN Natural Gas Pipeline Network in Southeast Asia.

- A project to provide international aid, involving three sponsoring countries, three on-the-ground aid organisations, many conflicted stakeholder groups and twenty local authorities.

- The construction of a multi-tiered educational facility in the Middle East, involving multiple foreign partners and local authorities for a government client that functions as an autocracy and operates within a legal system that does not acknowledge international arbitration procedures.

- A defence project involving multiple public service agencies, commercial partners and international suppliers.

- An international project to eliminate, or at least minimise, taxation fraud, involving multiple public agencies in many countries.

These projects are joint ventures or international partnerships of some kind. Ping Ho et al., (2009) argue that the choice of governance structure for a joint venture is largely influenced by four major variables, namely:

- Corporate cultural difference.

- Trust.

- Needs for procurement autonomy.

- Motivation for learning.

Many problems experienced by firms in joint ventures can be traced back to cultural differences (Meschi 1997; Horii et al., 2004). Project participants may find it hard to vary or adapt work practices and ways of thinking to which they are accustomed (Mahalingam and Levit, 2007). Increases in corporate cultural distance often mean greater differences in organisational and administrative practices, employee expectations, and interpretation of and response to strategic issues (Park and Ungson, 1997). In their study of how governance structures function in the different corporate cultures experienced in international joint ventures, Horii et al., (2004) emphasise the importance of variations in*practices* and *values.* regarding Corporate cultural difference plays an important part in the choice of governance structure because it often impacts the transaction costs, including information transmission cost, contracting cost, and monitoring and co-ordination costs. Complexity resulting from international and corporate cultural differences can become even more challenging because of project schedule constraints. Anomolies need to be identified and resolved very quickly.

When it comes to multi-owner projects, such as joint ventures, traditional governance models have a number of weaknesses. Implicit in traditional project governance models are the assumptions that:

- A single point of accountability for the project can actually be defined.

- It is possible for the people governing the project to have a clear idea of what is truly happening at project level at any one point in time.

- Decision-making is thorough and systemic rather than reactionary.

- People governing the project are able to define realistic success criteria.

- People at all levels of the project will report the truth.

- An atmosphere of co-operative problem-solving and learning will be inculcated at all levels of the project.

- The people governing the project are able to put aside their own vested interests in favour of the success of the project.

- Key executive stakeholders are managed successfully throughout the project.

- Key executive stakeholders understand that the project is complex and what contributes to the complexity.

- Decision-making by the governance team is mediated by external, impartial, multi-disciplinary advice.

- Transparency and accountability prevails.

- Governing executives respect and consider cultural differences.

- Disputes can be resolved on the basis of internationally acceptable dispute resolution frameworks.

When developing governance frameworks in complex project environments, such as international joint ventures, many of these assumptions can and should be challenged.

ACCOUNTABILITY

Projects have many stakeholders and complex projects may have a number of key stakeholders, often of equal importance. There might be one nominal owner of the project, but the key to satisfying the nominal owner of the project often lies in accommodating all of the key stakeholders. As the number of key interests in a project increase, finding points of accountability within each key stakeholder group can become more and more difficult, particularly if national or organisational cultures do not support single point accountability. For example, whilst the Australian Taxation Office (ATO) provides the official project management for Project Wickenby, a 'whole of government approach to financial crime', the ATO describes its relationship with the six other Australian agencies as 'first among equals'. Part of the success of this long term, multi-agency, international project is due to the ability of multiple agencies to govern co-operatively.

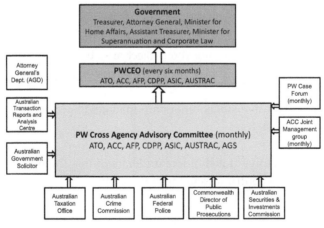

(http://www.ato.gov.au/corporate/content.asp?doc=/content/0022007; accessed 20/3/11; reprinted with permission)

Figure 10.1 **Project Wickenby governance arrangements (http://www.ato. gov.au/corporate/content.asp?doc=/content/0022007; accessed 20/3/11)**

ABILITY TO DEFINE SUCCESS CRITERIA

One of the major challenges for some truly complex projects is that it is difficult to define the outcome or the means of achieving the outcome. Additionally, the true nature of the outcome may only emerge with time, as interested parties reach accommodated positions, or as technical problems are addressed.

Particularly in volatile and unpredictable environments, if project goals do change it might also be difficult to anticipate how they will change and when. This kind of situation is frequently encountered in politically sensitive, public sector projects.

With any of these sources of complexity, whatever structure is put in place must be flexible enough adapt and respond appropriately. It is essential that a foundation of trust that supports flexible problem-solving is established early. The climate of trust necessary for the survival and productivity of all the teams associated with the project is modelled by the way the governance team behaves (Ngowi, 2007). Project vision statements and success criteria need to be drafted with the aim of making success a possibility!

ABILITY TO ASSESS THE STATUS AND MAKE DECISIONS WITH CONFIDENCE

Theoretically, a governance team determines whether a project is meeting certain key criteria. However, governors may not be in a position to be able to accurately assess a project against a pre-determined set of criteria in normal circumstances. As discussed in Chapter 6, ability to scan the environment diminishes during uncertainty and decisions are often made on the basis of reduced information. Value driven thinking, group thinking and emotional bias affects the quality of decisions. As the following leader argues, unless members of the governance team exercise high levels of self-awareness and reflection, rigorous decision-making can be difficult to achieve:

> *They're [the governance team] not in a position to know. That becomes a real problem. For that reason, personally, I think that governance works most effectively if there's a high degree of self-assessment and confidence and trust in the self-assessment process by the people who are being governed. Interview 54 PD.*

Also much data can be hidden from governance teams, either inadvertently or deliberately.

> *A recent project was experiencing difficulties. Over time it became apparent that the project team were reporting key status and traffic light information. The project team were trying to manage the governance process by providing information that they thought would allow the project team, themselves, to govern the project. For example, when a traffic light should've gone red, it didn't go red until the project team knew they could solve the issue. They didn't want to not have an answer to the problem. Interview 54 PD.*

Those governing the project can only have a limited perspective of the situation at any given time. Therefore, exercising effective project governance is dependent on breaking down barriers to communication, through building relationships with the project teams and through encouraging free and open dialogue between project teams and governors. Equally, the project teams only have a limited perspective of the project, particularly of its wider impacts. If the project teams are not made aware that what they are doing to address a project locally has wider implications the entire governance process may be undermined.

ENCOURAGING DIALOGUE

The previous examples also illustrate how inherited cultural norms can affect truthful reporting. Unfortunately, as our earlier research revealed, it is not uncommon to encounter environments where project teams are not encouraged to enter into dialogue with the governing bodies (Helm and Remington, 2004). A prevailing ethos of '... don't come to me with problems only solutions' has become a mode of operation at executive level in many organisations. Project teams may believe that accurate reporting of bad news will affect their jobs or prospects within the organisation, promulgating a climate that encourages people to say what they think people at the top want to hear.

> *I think quite often, particularly in some organisations, the very top leadership are shielded from some difficult decisions. They would be able to make a quick and educated decision if they'd been briefed in the right way. Often the guys below them think they're doing their job by protecting them from it. I've had those conversations, 'You're too important for this, you're too busy'. And I say, 'What do you think we*

do all day? This is why we're here, to make the right decision for the company or the country or whoever that puts us in this position'. So that's always an interesting one, persuading the middle tier to involve the top tier in the right decisions. Interview 61 GM.

Any of these behaviours closes the door on constructive dialogue and the possibility for truly creative problem-solving. Leadership that encourages open dialogue and problem-solving has to come from the top. If people are discouraged from reporting accurately, and instead report what they think people at the top want to hear, dialogue won't occur. Where strongly embedded cultural norms prevent honest reporting upwards, the governance team needs to take exceptional action to 'walk the talk'.

DECISION-MAKING IS THOROUGH AND SYSTEMIC RATHER THAN REACTIONARY

The governance team needs to know when issues arise. However, they must also have the discipline to know that project teams require adequate time to respond. Too often one hears project teams complaining that unreasonable demands are being made for immediate answers to problems that can only be described as 'wicked' – problems that require much more than an immediate 'patch-up' response. Because a local solution is unlikely to be a systemic response, a 'patch-up' solution will probably generate more risks as it produces unforeseen impacts on other parts of the system (Williams, 2004).

In turbulent and environments, if a governance team models a learning approach it becomes possible for people to say 'we've encountered this issue and don't have an answer yet'. During uncertainty, when there is no obvious solution, governance teams can take the lead by encouraging dialogue about options and approachs. This is much preferable to applying pressure to project teams to act, possibly inappropriately, when no one knows the answer.

As issues are put on the table the response people have a tendency to go directly to solution without fully structuring or understanding the problem (see Chapter 5). Because each person associated with the project, including those in the governance team, will only have a partial view of the situation, a systemically appropriate solution – one that has a good chance of addressing the issues in a sustainable manner – requires full participation of as many people as possible.

The governance team also needs to maintain a high level view of the issues and resist micromanagement in order to appreciate the implications of local risks for the system as a whole. A tendency for micromanagement by executive leaders is a way of coping with uncertainty by returning to previous modes of knowledge. Tunnelling down in this way localises the response range and interferes with systemic solution finding. As the following interviewee pointed out, for sustainable governance the focus must be on enabling self-governance at the team level:

> *If they're experienced they [the governance team] will have knowledge but they have to pass that knowledge on so the project team will assimilate that knowledge into their understanding of the problem. A critical review is required. You need to determine what the issues are and how well the processes are in place for self governance and whether those processes prove effective over time. Interview 54 PD.*

PERSONAL AGENDAS ARE PUT ASIDE

Leaders at the executive level should be skilled political players. Unfortunately not all political players use their skills for the good of the project or programme (see Chapter 8). There are several types of behaviour that can be particularly destructive.

> *I've seen this in every organisation I work in, people in the governance process who are motivated to make themselves look good, to show how clever they are, that they're smarter than the project team. That's very destructive behaviour ... Behaviour that doesn't encourage honest self-appraisal and dialogue is undermining the governance process. Interview 54 PD.*

Encouraging self-assessment, self-awareness and deep dialogue at project board level is important because it helps to reveal agendas. Once people get to understand what motivates and drives other key stakeholders, or executive board members, it is easier to reach accommodated positions and understanding, or at least be more alert to potentially disruptive behaviour. Often this is best achieved through skilled facilitation.

STAKEHOLDER ENGAGEMENT

It is the responsibility of the governance team to make sure that key stakeholders and changes in key stakeholders are identified and stakeholders' expectations are managed throughout the project. Unfortunately the following practice is not uncommon. Stakeholders are identified and contacted, asked for their input and then forgotten about (Grimsey and Lewis, 2004). A spectacular failure to understand and manage the real stakeholders can be found in Sydney's cross city road tunnel.

The cross city tunnel in Sydney has been a fairly spectacular failure as a Public Private Partnership – the operating company has gone into receivership less than two years after the tunnel opening in August 2005. The tunnel, built at a cost of about $800 million, failed to attract the traffic required to meet interest payments. Even when use of the tunnel was free, the traffic did not approach the forecast traffic levels of 90,000 vehicles per day. (Phibbs, 2007, p. 444)

In addition to optimism bias in traffic forecasting, which vastly overestimated the traffic flow and therefore the return on investment, the project owners did not expect the citizens of Sydney to react to the very high toll by refusing en masse to use. This was a self-organised boycott. Thousands of individuals, well informed by the media debates, made the decision not to use the tunnel. Further fuelled by the media the response spread like wildfire. The traffic authority then attempted to force motorists to use the tunnel by closing off roads. This further infuriated motorists who became even more determined not to use the tunnel. The Australian culture is characterised by a very healthy disrespect for authority and a disdain for officiousness and bullying. Motorists would take extraordinarily long detours to get around the road blocks and avoid the tunnel. To this day the tunnel has not come close to meeting the predicted traffic flow. People have long memories and many will still avoid the tunnel if at all possible. In an attempt to convince motorists of the benefits of using the tunnel a toll-free period was introduced. Even during this period tunnel use fell far below initial projections (Phibbs, 2007).

The Auditor General's Report (2006, p. 54) concluded:

> We found that the main objective of the road changes was to reduce through traffic in and around Central Sydney and to improve the public domain.

The report criticised the Government on two related issues:

> *Maining toll-free alternative routes was a key principle in the original design. But road restrictions added progressively meant that, in the end, there were no direct, convenient toll-free alternatives left' (and), 'There was extensive consultation with stakeholders about the road changes. But it did not capture the significant resentment among prospective toll payers.*

SHARED UNDERSTANDING ABOUT PROJECT COMPLEXITY OR A WILLINGNESS TO LEARN

Complex projects need governance protocols and procedures that respond flexibly and innovatively to emergent aspects of the project or programme. The governance team should understand enough about complexity to be able to resist imposing controls where they will only serve to exacerbate emergent situations.

> *It is up to the governance team to respond to deviation rather than expecting things to comply with some predetermined way forward – not failing to respond to the reality of the situation unfolding before you – people who don't understand that try to fight it by imposing more controls whereas actually if you are leading some complex project you should be doing the opposite... The failure to grasp this whole area is a major reason why these major projects do not succeed ... Interview 39 C.*

Even though divergence will occur at local levels in any complex adaptive system, such as a complex project, the system is not without structure. At any one time parts of the project or programme might be highly structured while other parts might be verging towards chaos. The one uniting factor is often a strong vision that is developed, sustained and clearly communicated by those governing the project.

> *In a public sector IT project we held the vision against a great deal of battering from different places – but the owner was very supportive all the way through because they understood what we were facing – the relationship I had with that client was always an open one and we kept an open mind – but you have to maintain a vision of what you want to achieve and although it will diverge. Interview 39 C.*

EXTERNAL, IMPARTIAL, MULTI-DISCIPLINARY ADVICE

Governing reflectively means being able to self-assess and take advice from a broad range of experts. A major contributing factor to the failure of the Sydney cross city tunnel project was optimism bias with traffic flow estimates. Unfortunately, startup optimism bias is not uncommon (Flyvberg et al., 2006). In the absence of impartial expert opinion it is easy to be swept along by the wave of optimism and excitement as the idea for a project germinates. With hindsight, knowledge of the national culture in which they were operating, might have set off alarm bells that restrictive road closures would have further inflamed public opinion about the project.

Without external, impartial and wide ranging advice, it is very easy for a governing body to succumb to 'group think' or to be mislead by inaccurate reporting. For example, the following interviewee was an outsider, invited from overseas to work with a British department, precisely because he had no existing network ties that would prevent him from reporting the truth upwards:

> I was brought in to review a crime reduction programme, which was a very bold attempt to try and implement an evidence policybased approach to criminal justice. They had a very substantial body of evidence of research over twenty or thirty years telling them what was good and bad about criminal justice currently and they believed they could reform it on the basis of research and evidence. So they set about five areas of reform and so things new and novel were tried, things ongoing were assessed, and at the end there was a three year programme which was extended to four. It was a fine example of scientists not understanding the business of policy implementation. They thought you do this because we say so; but people have to interpret it and place it in their personal experience and very often their skill base is better informed than that of the researchers. Within about twelve months they discovered that they had all this money lined up and ready to come down the chute, and the projects weren't getting implemented. So they wanted someone to look at implementation analysis, and that's what I did. Interview segment: 57 PM.

TRANSPARENCY AND CLEAR ACCOUNTABILITY PREVAILS

While transparency and clear accountabilities, with appropriate mechanisms for independent review, are absolute requirements for most large scale projects, the level of transparency and accountability is not always as high as it might be.

Joint ventures and partnerships are relationships. Relationships are sustained by trust, trust is sustained by honesty and transparency (see Chapter 12).

INTERNATIONALLY ACCEPTABLE DISPUTE RESOLUTION FRAMEWORKS ARE ACCEPTABLE

As illustrated by the following excerpt from one of our interviews, mutually acceptable processes for assessing claims and arbitrating disputes are not always achieved:

> *We would prefer, if we had a choice, to contract on our standard terms of engagement or an internationally recognised standard form, such as a FIDIC agreement or one of the many UK or other standard agreements developed by the relevant professional bodies (ICE, NEC, etc.) relevant to working in a country. For this project the applicable law is the State of ... There is no recognised arbitration body in ..., so all disputes are resolved in the local courts. Unlike the UK, there are no specialist courts or judges here for dealing with construction/engineering cases, so the judges often appoint experts to the court to assist them. These experts are locals and their experience and quality for dealing with the technical nature of disputes is often found wanting. Hence the outcome of your dispute is to be decided by a partially qualified engineer, but whose report is unlikely to be overturned by the court. Interview 63 PD.*

When managing projects in remote locations, differences should be expected; most project managers treat recourse to formal dispute resolution as the last resort, resulting from breakdown in communication, and ultimately, trust (Mohr and Spekman, 1994). However, in the event that relationships do break down, if one party is perceived by other parties to have behaved unprofessionally, mutually acceptable and enforceable legal frameworks must be available to help effect a resolution.

A recent study of multi-billion dollar international energy projects, by Sovacool (2010), reveals a complex network of agents above and below the state that, in conjunction with governments, influence the trajectory of the project. The projects exist in the 'murky waters of marginalised groups, contradictory interests, ambition, power, war, money, greed, guns, arrogance, monopolies, rebels and cartels ...' (p. 509).

In multi-owner projects, the fact that there are some stakeholder groups with benevolent intentions, some groups powerless to intervene and other groups acting only out of self-interest, is part of daily life for many project leaders. These are difficult landscapes to navigate. Multiple conversations up front, asking the right questions and listening carefully, will help to provide essential intelligence to executive project leaders; intelligence that might change an initially attractive proposition to a decidedly risky one.

CROSS-CULTURAL GOVERNANCE ISSUES

Many very complex projects are complex because they involve not only a number of different organisations, each with its own way of doing business, but also a number of different national cultures. Ideas of 'good project governance' as published in the professional literature (for example, APM, PMI) are infused with liberal democratic principles (Verspaandonk, 2001). The reality is that underpinning cultural values vary substantially from place to place (see Chapter 7). Whilst excellent governance is often difficult to achieve the problems become almost insurmountable in multi-national projects, such asinternational aid projects. One of the biggest challenges is developing a shared understanding of the motives and values of the various players and designing a governance structure that reflects and accommodates contradictory motives and values. Understanding local political processes that will drive reforms in accountability is critical (Nelson, 2009).

Implementing Governance

EARLY, DEEP DIALOGUE ABOUT VALUES

Governance policies and procedures are only as good as they can be effectively implemented. A project governance team must be able to achieve an accommodated position between all key parties at the beginning or the project will almost certainly experience serious difficulties downstream. This is challenging when the key parties operate from different value frameworks, as illustrated by a project engineering team working on an international joint-venture project, in a country where safety is not a priority:

> *Cultural differences – cost, time, quality, safety – the client was very focussed on cost first, time second, and safety is the last consideration – our company is driven by safety number one – we have a record of no injuries to anyone ever – we look at safety, quality and then cost and time.*

> *You need professionally facilitated workshops up front to share values (quality, safety, etc.) if you can't get that agreement and understanding before you are out of the blocks – once you are out of the blocks trying to impose rules is very difficult – part of the risk with a lot of projects is there is so much pressure from the customer 'what's holding you up – get on with it' – it is small bickies to bring international teams together for a short period at the beginning of the project compared with the overall budget – do your work up front and the back end will work smoothly. Interview 56 PD.*

It is essential that governance teams invest in time up front in order to explore differences and set boundaries of practice about deeply held values and standards some of which might be contradictory, including:

- Standards of interpersonal behaviour (honesty, trust, transparency).

- Problem-solving under conditions of certainty and uncertainty.

- Decision-making frameworks.

- Dealing with emergence (risk and learning opportunities).

- Roles, responsibilities and accountabilities.

- Procurement methods.

- Reporting protocols (owners, sponsors, project teams, stakeholders, including the media – internal and external reporting pathways).

- Security provisions (level of access to documents).

- Organisational values (safety, quality, budget, schedule).

Approaches need to take into account the organisational and local cultural practices that will enable satisfactory governance for the project or programme.

AGREEMENT TO BE FLEXIBLE

Also, from complexity theory we know that as projects become more complex boundaries must become more flexible. Rigid boundaries may send a complex system into chaos. The governance team must be able to respond flexibly by removing or adjusting boundaries if they don't work or if they seem to be too constrictive. Because of the nature of complex adaptive systems rules cannot be set in place too rigidly in advance. This doesn't mean that sound processes should be ignored. It means that governance teams must be vigilant about maintaining a watch on whether they are continuing to work.

When things are starting to look like being out of control the most common tendency is to tighten boundaries and move in the direction of micromanagement. We know from complexity theorists that adding more controls to complex adaptive systems can actually be counterproductive (Axelrod and Cohen, 2000; Snowden, 2002; Plowman and Duchon, 2008). It is more important to inject more variety into the system rather than restricting variety by tightening constraints.

Sovacool's (2010) study of some truly complex international projects, the Trans-ASEAN Natural Gas Pipeline Network in Southeast Asia and Baku-Tibilisi-Ceyhan Pipeline in the Caspian Sea concludes that completion is contingent on the right alignment of social, political and economic conditions and governance that is 'interpretively flexible in the sense that actors and institutions have different visions and views associated with each project' (p. 509).

The academic literature on governance has largely ignored the effects of power struggles on the governance process (Stoker, 1998). Achieving foresight and using participatory methods to achieve effective steering and decision-shaping by governance teams should be distinct from the use of politics as decision-making (Johnston, 2002) and ideally there should be genuinely inclusive participation at all levels (Loveridge and Street, 2005) however, we know this not to be the case. Vigilance, supported by the ability to listen, observe and the ability to respond flexibly are most important skill sets for governing in complex project environments.

USE OF LOCAL NETWORKS

One of the most important implementation tasks for multi-owner, multi-national governance teams, involves understanding the roles and emergence patterns of the local networks that might be involved or affected by the project. The strength of local networks is based on their proximity and capacity to integrate agents locally (Aranguren, et al., 2010). This is where flexibility of governance is essential. Local networks will have their own ingrained ways of operating. These should be respected. Like the Catholic Church, an organisation over 2000 years old, central governance works best when it concerns itself with mission, vision and values, leaving operational matters to the geographically dispersed parishes to interpret appropriately for their communities. Respectful and responsive governance with strong local autonomy of this kind has proved to be very successful in multi-national telecommunications roll outs (Lilliesköld, et al., 2005; Taxén, 2003).

BEGINNING A CONSTRUCTIVE CONVERSATION ABOUT GOVERNANCE FOR THE PROJECT

Many leaders interviewed observed that successful projects had governance teams with well constructed charters or protocols for how they would work together as a governance team. Again and again the leaders we interviewed stressed the importance of the governance team being able to work together to constructively steer the project. A governance team is made up of individuals, each with many concerns and interests. The following questions are intended as a stimulus for conversations that governance teams might need to conduct in order to explore potential differences and look for constructive ways to work together. Taking time to explore these questions will not solve all problems, but will certainly provide a platform for a more robust governance charter. I have found from experience that if project teams ask enough questions and listen long enough, hitherto, hidden agendas will nearly always reveal themselves.

Responses to questions like the following in Table 10.1, also help to surface potential partnership risks and after all, forewarned is forearmed.

In Summary

Some of the assumptions implicit in traditional project governance models that need to be challenged when dealing with complex projects and programmes include whether:

- A single point of accountability for the project can actually be defined.

- It is possible for the people governing the project to have a clear idea of what is truly happening at project level at any one point in time.

Table 10.1   Exploratory questions to stimulate the conversations that
              governance teams need to conduct to explore potential
              differences and find constructive ways to work together

	Questions to consider by members of governance teams Based on the responses to any of these questions the questions to follow might be: What are the differences or barriers for the organisations involved? What enablers could help us overcome potential issues? How can we achieve a satisfactory outcome?
1.	Do all key parties fully recognise the levels and types of complexity that are likely to impact the project or programme?
2.	Do all key parties understand how complexity (emergent patterns) and related effects can affect the project?
3.	Are values shared between participating organisations/entities? What is most important for each participating organisation? For example, does each organisation place the same value on cost, time, quality and safety?
4.	Do members of the governance team share a clear understanding of the critical success factors?
5.	How does the expected complexity impact our ability to accurately define success criteria for the project?
6.	What actions can members of the governance team commit to ensure: timely decision making? effective resolution of differences?
7.	What do we need to do to make the governance process consensus driven?
8.	What is the nature of participation needed from key partners to govern this project?
9.	Are all key parties able and willing to participate as equal shareholders in the governance process?
10.	How do we prevent a short-sighted or narrow views predominating? Do we have access to a wide range of expertise to advise us which go well beyond the key technical disciplines associated with the project?
11.	Are all key parties able and willing to be informed/seek multi-disciplinary expertise?
12.	How do we achieve and maintain honest reporting from project teams?
13.	How do we as a governance team engage and continue to engage key stakeholders throughout the project?
14.	How do we work to establish a climate of trust and sharing amongst the governance team? with external stakeholders? within project teams? between project leaders and the governance team?
15.	How do we put in place a framework that encourages us to challenge our assumptions?
16.	What do we need to know about differences (inter-organisational; interdepartmental; international) in local: cultures? work practices? knowledge? procurement standards? auditing standards? dispute resolution protocols?
17.	Are the available dispute resolution frameworks acceptable to all partners? Do they comply with international standards? Are decisions enforceable?

- People governing the project are able to define realistic success criteria.

- People at all levels of the project will report the truth.

- An atmosphere of co-operative problem-solving and learning can be inculcated at all levels of the project.

- The people governing the project are able to put aside their own vested interests in favour of the success of the project.

- Key executive stakeholders are able to be managed successfully throughout the project.

- Key executive stakeholders understand that the project is complex and what factors contribute to the complexity.

- Decision-making by the governance team is mediated by external, impartial, multi-disciplinary advice.

- Transparency and accountability prevails.

- Governing executives respect and consider culture differences.

An effective governance charter needs to be informed by deep enough dialogue between all members of the governance team(s) to reveal and explore differences in:

- Values, motivations, constraints of key stakeholders.

- Knowledge and experience with complex projects.

- Local project delivery capability.

- Ability to seek and take advice – willingness to learn.

- Propensity for flexibility in response to emergence.

References and Further Reading

Aranguren, M.J., Larrea, M. and Wilson, J. (2010) Learning from the Local: Governance of Netwoks for Innovation in the Basque Country. *European Planning Studies*, 18(1), pp. 47–65.

Axelrod, R. and Cohen, M.D. (2000) *Harnessing Complexity. Organizational Implications of a Scientific Frontier.* New York, NY: Basic Books.

Fickenscher, K. and Bakerman, M. (2011) Leadership and Governance for IT Projects. *PE Journal*, February, pp. 72–76.

Flyvbjerg, B., Skamris Holm, M. and Buhl, S.L. (2006) Inaccuracy in Traffic Forecasts. *Transport Reviews*, 26(1), pp. 1–24.

Garland, R. (2009) Project Governance – a Practical Guide to Effective Project Decision-making. London, Philadelphia: Kogan Page.

Grimsey, D. and Lewis, M.K. (2004) *Public Private Partnerships: The Worldwide Revolutions in Infrastructure Provision and Private Finance.* Cheltenham, UK: Edward Elgar.

Horii, T., Jin, Y. and Levitt, R.E. (2004) Modeling and Analyzing Cultural Influences on Project Team Performance. *Comput. Math. Org. Theory*, 10(4), pp. 305–321.

Johnston, R. (2001) Foresight – Refining the Process. *International Journal of Technology Management*, 21, no. 7/8, pp. 711–725.

Johnston, D.J. (2002) Better Values for Better Governance, *OECD Observer*, Issue 234, pp. 234–237.

Lilliesköld, J., Taxén, L. and Klasson, M. (2005) Managing Complex Development Projects – Using the System Anatomy. Proceedings of the Portland International Conference on Management of Technology and Engineering, PICMET'05, July-Aug.

Loveridge, D. and Street, P. (2005) Inclusive foresight. *Foresight*, 7, 3, pp. 31–47.

Mahalingam, A. and Levitt, R.E. (2007) Institutional Theory as a Framework for Analyzing Conflicts on Global Projects. *Journal of Construction Engineering Management*, 133(7), pp. 517–527.

Meschi, P. X. (1997) Longevity and Cultural Differences of International Joint Ventures: Toward Time-based Cultural Management. *Human Relations*, 50(2), pp. 211–228.

Mohr, J. and Spekman, R. (1994) Characteristics of Partnership Success, Partnership Attributes, Communication Behavior, and Conflict Resolution Techniques. *Strategic Management Journal*, 15(2), pp. 135–152.

Müller, R. (2009) *Project Governance.* Aldershot, UK: Gower Publishing.

NSW Auditor-General (2006) *Performance Report – Cross City Tunnel.* Sydney, NSW.

Nelson, F. Conservation and Aid: Designing More Effective Investments in: Natural Resource Governance Reform. *Conservation Biology.* 23(5), pp. 1102–1108.

Ngowi, A.B. (2007) The Role of Trustworthiness in the Formation and Governance of Construction Alliances. *Build. Environ.*, 42(4), pp. 1828–1835.

OGC, (2009) Managing Successful Projects with PRINCE2, London: TSO 2009.

Park, S.H. and Ungson, G.R. (1997) The Effect of National Culture, Organizational Complementarity, and Economic Motivation on Joint Venture Dissolution. *Academy of Management Journal*, 40(2), pp. 279–307.

Phibbs, (2007) Driving Alone- Sydney's Cross City Tunnel.SOAC, http://www.fbe.unsw.edu.au/cityfutures/SOAC/drivingalone.pdf; retrieved 14–3-11, pp. 444–454.

Ping Ho, S., Lin, Y-H, Chu, W. and Wu, H-L. (2009) Model for Organizational Governance Structure Choices in Construction Joint Ventures. *Journal of Construction Engineering and Management*, June, pp. 518–530.

Plowman, D.A. and Duchon, D. (2008) Dispelling the Myths About Leadership: From Cybernetics to Emergence. In: M. Uhl-Bien and R. Marion (eds), *Complexity leadership. Part I: Conceptual Foundations.* Charlotte, North Carolina: Information Age Publishing Inc., pp. 129–153.

Snowden, D. (2002) Complex Acts of Knowing: Paradox and Descriptive Self-awareness. *Journal of Knowledge Management*, 6(2).

Sovacool, B.J. (2010) Exploring the Conditions for Cooperative Energy Governance: A Comparative Study of the Two Asian Pipelines. *Asian Studies Review*, 34, pp. 489–511.

Stoker, G. 1998. Governance as Theory: Five Propositions. *International Social Science Journal*, 50(155), pp. 17–28.

Taxén, L. (2003) A Framework for the Coordination of Complex Systems Development, Dissertation No. 800. Linköping University, Dept. of Computer and Information Science, Available at http://www.eliu.se/diss/science/08/00/index/html, accessed Oct. 2006.

Verspaandonk, R. (2001) Good Governance in Australia.Research Note11 2001–02, Commonwealth Government of Australia, Politics and Public Administration Group, 25 September 2001, http://www.aph.gov.au/library/pubs/rn/2001–02/02rn11.htm; accessed 27/1/11.

Williams, T. (2004) Why Monte Carlo Simulations of Project Networks can Mislead. *Project Management Journal*, 25(3), pp. 53–61.

11

Authority Over Key Roles

If you have to be in a soap opera try not to get the worst role.
Attributed to the American actress.

Judy Garland, (1922–1969).

Not all complex projects can be likened to soap operas but unfortunately some evolve into something remarkably similar. In order to get the best out of people, leaders must have the authority to place the right people in the right roles.

Key Points in This Chapter:

- Leadership roles and layers.

- Linking roles to level and type of complexity.

- Assigning key roles.

- Authority to select and replace key personnel.

- Accountability and assessment.

Part 1: Leadership Roles and Layers

RIGHT PEOPLE, RIGHT TEAM SIZE, RIGHT TIME

If leadership is to be effective it is critical that the right people are assigned to the right roles and for the right period of time. Leadership roles in large complex projects are often diffuse. This is particularly so in public sector projects. Leadership might be thought of in terms of leadership layers rather than individual roles. The success of a complex project is primarily dependent upon the leadership layers working in synergy. Leadership layers or groups need to be very carefully established with the right range of expertise. The size of each leadership group contributes to effectiveness.

> *The projects which tend to have characteristics of lack of clarity generally have poor governance and unclear roles and responsibilities, ambiguities ... So with the leadership structures I've set up, I make things thin until someone says you need more people. Because on long term projects more people tend to turn up anyway. The challenge is to keep it thin ... In one project the government stuffed it full of the great and good from British and international engineering creating titles for people without clear roles, so some left because they didn't feel they were adding any value and the project also underwent significant reorganisation. The government did the right thing in employing good competent people, but they employed too many with poorly defined roles. Interview 60 C.*

LEADERSHIP ROLES IN COMMERCIAL PROJECTS AND PUBLIC SECTOR PROJECTS

In the commercial world having a single sponsor is someone in the organisation with high leverage who can take responsibility for project success is viable. In other industry sectors, particularly in the public sector, the sponsorship level can be a fairly weak construct. Leadership roles are to some extent undertaken in aggregate and how roles are manifested depends very much on the context.

> *There are two leadership roles that are absolutely critical. They're not individual roles but part of the leadership construct. First, the topmost leadership tier within the project team; they are the directors, senior project managers. Second, there is a leadership tier outside the project team; not considered a formal part of the project team, but the leadership*

layer that the senior project tier interact with. They are critical, and the relationship between them is binary in terms of its criticality. If that relationship is poor, the project has a high chance of failure. If it's effective, there's a high chance the project will be successful. If that binary part of the leadership construct is effective, they have a high degree of influence on the rest of the leadership as a whole. They influence or manage the rest of the leadership environment, whether sponsor, owners, end users, or just interested stakeholders. Interview 54 PD.

Defence projects, like the one referred to above, are delivered in a multi-faceted sponsorship environment. There will be an executive leadership layer from the services who will be responsible for capability, it might be one person or several; there will be executive leadership from the organisation that will acquire the facility, the army, navy or airforce, for example; executive leadership also comes from other organisations, such as government departments, that have responsibility for certain related policies and the things that flow from those; as well as executive leadership from the organisations who are the major contractors. Large defence projects offer valuable contracts for the major contractors and there will be high level representation from head contractors on the executive project board. As a result the leadership layers can become quite diffuse. Other public sector projects, such as the international tax fraud example discussed in Chapter 10, have similar, multi-layered executive leadership stuctures.

CLEARLY DEFINED ROLES AND ACCOUNTABILITY

All standard project management text books mention the importance of clearly defined roles, responsibility and accountability. However, there is a noticeable lack of discussion on some of the really important issues around performance – how do project owners and sponsors make sure that: people with suitable leadership behaviour capabilities are in leadership roles, leaders take an appropriate level of responsibility and are fully accountable for their actions? The key requirements following might seem to be obvious but, based on our research, they are not always achieved:

- Role capabilities defined based on the assessed level and type of complexity.

- People and teams are assigned who can really do the job.

- Redundancy for key roles is built-in.

- The hero syndrome is avoided.

- Project leaders are given the authority to make changes to roles where needed based on the complexity.

- Assessment criteria is developed to ensure accountability as well as outcomes.

Part 2: Linking Roles to Level and Type of Complexity

As discussed in Chapter 3, roles should be defined according to the leadership teams' assessment of the complexity of the project. Complex projects require higher order leadership and management skills at every level of leadership. Research indicates that, additional to specific expertise in the field, the following role capabilities, as in Table 11.1, have been identified as essential for complex projects. The following tables can be used to assist in identifying which capabilities are needed for the project, beyond discipline-specific knowledge.

Table 11.1   Executive leadership – essential role capabilities (Helm and Remington, 2005a, 2005b)

Attribute	Yes	No	Notes from the research on executive leadership of complex projects
Understands or is willing to explore how complexity can manifest in projects of this kind.	☐	☐	*Recognising that the project is more than just difficult is the first essential step in creating a learning climate that fosters enquiry and collaborative problem-solving. Our research indicates that while project leaders often had some understanding of what contributed to making the project complex, many executive leaders did not, and many were also unwilling to engage in discussions about the complexity.*
Exhibits a high capability for self-reflection and willingness to engage other experts in problem-solving.	☐	☐	*Many examples of poor problem-solving can be traced to group decision-making practices such as over optimism and group-think, inadequate environmental scanning and desire to reduce complexity by over-simplification.*

Develops and fosters high level connections within the organisation. Communicates relevant organisation-wide issues to the project teams.	☐	☐	*These are essential skills on which project relationships depend. Partnering, as opposed to adversarial relations, should be established and maintained at executive level. Being essentially involved with the day to day issues of project delivery it is important that the project teams are kept abreast of external events that might impact the project. Executive knowledge and support is essential if risks are to be managed systemically.*
Holds a sufficiently senior position within the organisation.	☐	☐	*This attribute relates to the degree of formal power the executive leader or sponsor holds within the organisation, which might be important for escalation and rapid decisions about issues, especially where the project is time dependent. Formal authority due to position is also essential in establishing important, high level, external relationships.*
Demonstrates high level and diverse communication skills.	☐	☐	*This attribute is linked with most others and refers to communication skills with a wide range of stakeholders, ranging, for example, from team member or contractor on the job to senior politician).*
Exhibits courage to support the project team to deliver the project objectives. Courage to make timely decisions when necessary.	☐	☐	*This refers to the willingness to go into battle with other key stakeholders to smooth the way for the project team to overcome any obstacles that might be beyond the power of the project leader to negotiate. It also refers to the ability to make timely decisions, avoiding prevarication when things are critical.*
Can provide motivational support for the project team to deliver the vision when the going gets tough.	☐	☐	*If risks are triggered team members often spend very long hours working on the project and morale levels drop. Twelve hour days are not uncommon for these kinds of projects. Executive leaders can provide valuable support to the project teams by being visible and available for consultation, and by offering encouragement during stressful times.*
Compatible with a broad range of people.	☐	☐	*Compatibility with the project leaders and project teams is important in establishing the mutual respect necessary especially if the project is particularly difficult and long term.*
Willingness to partner the project manager and team to deliver the project objectives.	☐	☐	*Senior project directors and managers found that executive leaders and sponsors who were willing to take a partnering approach to problem-solving achieved better results than those who exerted authority in a formal way. Our research indicated that executive leaders were sometimes excluded from the decision-making processes by project managers and teams who tended to 'work around' those executive leaders who put up barriers or discouraged collaborative problem-solving. Barriers put up by senior executives were often associated by project leaders with the executive leader being 'out of his depth'.*

Table 11.1   *Concluded*

Attribute	Yes	No	Notes from the research on executive leadership of complex projects
Provides ad hoc support to the project team rather than micromanages.	☐	☐	*Support should be available when needed. The level of support offered should vary according to the experience of the project leader. Micromanagement is de-motivating for senior project leaders and the often excessive level of reporting required can prevent project leaders from focusing on important management activities. Micromanagement was associated by followers with fear on the part of executive leaders, who lacked experience in executive leadership and who relieved their fear by focussing on detail ...*
Takes a holistic view and seeks broad advice as appropriate.	☐	☐	*Few, if any, leaders will have a complete perspective of the complexity at any one time. Project executives must be able to view the project from multiple perspectives remaining at a high level and be willing to seek diverse opinions.*
Provide objectivity to the project team and challenge assumptions.	☐	☐	*Senior project managers interviewed generally appreciated being challenged by the executive leaders or the sponsor. Objectivity did not require the sponsor to have a detailed knowledge of the project or sometimes even the field.*
Detailed technical knowledge of the project is not always necessary.	☐	☐	*Very few project mangers reported that a detailed knowledge of the technical aspects of the project was required by executive leaders. In some cases detailed technical knowledge led to micromanagement with insufficient attention to the other, wider concerns.*
Understands and can comment constructively on schedule at a high level.	☐	☐	*Ability to analyse, at a high level, the relationships between interdependent activities is particularly relevant to projects exhibiting structural complexity (see Remington and Pollack, 2007). In structurally complex projects there should at least be familiarity with the use of advanced scheduling software.*
Understands and can comment constructively at a high level on cost management.	☐	☐	*Projects exhibiting structural complexity would require high level cost analysis and management skills, such as Earned Value Management, which tracks cost in relation to schedule and cost and can be used to predict final project costs.*

Table 11.2   Project leadership – essential role capabilities (Helm and Remington, 2005a, 2005b; Remington and Pollack, 2007)

Attribute	Yes	No	Notes from the research
Uses high level communication skills in ways appropriate to individual stakeholders and groups.	☐	☐	*Senior project managers valued the ability to communicate informally as well as formally with a broad range of people, from senior executives to specialist team members and with different stakeholders within and outside their organisations.*
Builds strong relationships based on transparent communication and trust with all stakeholders.	☐	☐	*This emerged as a key capability from current research. Project leaders who spend the time building trusting relationships are more likely to be able to manage difficult risk patterns as they emerge. Also contractual issues were managed more easily if strong relationships had been developed earlier in the project.*
Manages the interfaces within the organisation to achieve project outcomes.	☐	☐	*Awareness and ability to work with the internal politics of the organisation to achieve project goals is highly valued by senior project managers working on complex projects.*
Accepts and works with ambiguity.	☐	☐	*A project leader working on a project which is likely to exhibit characteristics of technical, directional or temporal complexity needs to be comfortable with uncertainty because the project may seem to be 'out of control' at times. This kind of project is unsuited to project managers who prefer strict adherence to rules in order to maintain a sense of control.*
Translates ambiguity in ways appropriate to the needs of various stakeholders so that they can participate effectively.	☐	☐	*It is part of the project leader's task to communicate those aspects of the complexity that are relevant to the needs of particular senior managers, team members, specialist consultants, clients, customers and interested parties, so that they can contribute their part of the project in a productive way. The project leader needs to be able to communicate an impression of confidence and 'can do' to others who might be experiencing stress due to uncertainty and ambiguity.*
Views the project from a holistic perspective.	☐	☐	*The project manager must be able to view the project from multiple perspectives so that s/he can move around the project and intervene as required and at the appropriate level of detail.*
Uses flexible, multi-paradigm approaches, suiting the style of management to purpose and the group.	☐	☐	*Particularly where the project involves technical, directional and temporal complexity successful project managers reported that they used a multitude of methods and approaches, ranging from traditional (control-based) project management methods to approaches which derive from 'soft systems thinking'.*

Table 11.2   *Concluded*

Attribute	Yes	No	Notes from the research
Uses divergent thinking to solve problems and negotiate obstacles.	☐	☐	*Ability to think 'outside the square' to find imaginative ways around obstacles was one of the most highly valued attributes by senior project managers.*
Able to motivate the teams to deliver the project milestones whilst allowing them space to work effectively.	☐	☐	*Motivation involves achieving a balance between maintaining focus on milestones, using a range of interpersonal skills to keep up pace and spirits. This is especially important in projects that exhibit technical complexity. Design or research teams must have the space to do their creative work and generally resist micromanagement.*
Employs high level holistic, analytical and organising skills.	☐	☐	*This ability is particularly relevant to projects exhibiting structural complexity. The project manager must be able to 'see' the complex picture of interrelationships in order to manipulate the interdependencies to achieve optimum time and cost outcomes and be able to recognise and respond to emergent risk patterns.*
Uses high level scheduling skills.	☐	☐	*Scheduling large numbers of activities and being able to analyse the relationships between interdependent activities is an essential skill set for projects exhibiting structural complexity. The project leader should be familiar with advanced scheduling software.*
Uses advanced cost management and analysis skills.	☐	☐	*Projects exhibiting structural complexity would require high level cost analysis and management skills, such as Earned Value Management, which tracks scope, schedule and cost and can be used to predict final project costs.*

ASSIGN PEOPLE AND TEAMS WHO CAN DO THE JOB

Chapter 3 begins this discussion. A quick appraisal of the capabilities listed above might suggest that one person is unable to fulfil all capabilities. However, the right teams can.

> *Pick your people, there are people that deliver on time and people who deliver shortcuts. It is important that you get the right people in your team and the right personalities. The Spanish were going to benefit from the change whereas the Italians and French were going to lose product, so availability and obtaining information was difficult, due to resentment. And we had technical challenges. We had to put in a liquid nitrogen cooling system to pack the product – 270°C is a bit cold! Interview 67 GM.*

For example, a project leader with advanced technical capabilities and scheduling and cost management skills might be needed for a project which is highly structurally or technically complex. However, if the same project is affected by other sources of complexity, such as lack of shared direction, political, cultural or market pressures, a project leader with the necessary facilitation and political skills might be needed. The costs involved in setting up project teams are usually minimal in comparison with possible losses if risks are poorly handled. Many risks, like those associated with inadequate communication and relationship management, are not identified as project risks. If risks are triggered because the project leader was focusing on meeting the schedule rather than managing the relationships, both the reputation of the project leader and the project outcomes suffer. It is possible to provide all capabilities but rarely do they exist in one person. Project leadership teams should be resourced on the basis of benefits realisation and return on investment.

Part 3: Assigning Key Roles

BUILD IN REDUNDANCY FOR KEY ROLES

Complexity theorists in all kinds of different fields stress the need for redundancy in complex systems in order to ensure robustness of the system (see for example, Beard, 1971; Kim and Yum,1993; Randles et al., 2010).

> *If the project manager is taken out there must be someone else of similar capability to take over – you need a co-pilot- you would not fly a plane without a co-pilot – it is dangerous – but it is not uncommon in the oil and gas industry for a 32 million dollar project not to have appropriate backup. One person can control a small project 1–5 mill but a mega project (over 250 mill) you need a project organisation. In the oil and gas industry it seems to be projects in the gap between these sizes of project 5 and 250 mill, which can be equally complex, that don't have adequate resourcing, organisation and redundancy. Interview 45 PM.*

Redundancy Engineering is a branch of engineering that attempts to eliminate the need for human intervention by designing redundancy into the system components (Marcus and Stern, 2003). The two kinds of redundancy incorporated are *passive redundancy* and *active redundancy*. Passive redundancy aims to achieve high availability by including enough excess capacity in the design to accommodate a performance decline. The simplest example is a plane with at least two separate engines. The plane can continue to fly if one engine is disenabled. Similarly, electrical power plants have built in redundancy enabling continuity of power to the region as a whole even when one section has been disabled, for example due to storm activity. Active redundancy is used in complex systems to achieve high availability with NO performance decline. Multiple items of the same kind are incorporated into a design that includes a method to detect failure and automatically reconfigure the system to bypass failed items using a voting scheme. This approach is used with complex computing systems that are linked. The Internet is the most obvious example.

While we are now reasonably adept at achieving 'zero down time' in mechanical and information systems, project executives seem to be consistently poor at providing the necessary redundancy when it comes to human components in complex systems. Too often insufficient skilled resources are allocated to complex projects. This is a major source of risk for the project.

Lack of redundancy in key roles, means that projects are vulerable. Compared with the cost of failure, the cost of providing adequate redundancy in key roles is usually minimal. However, effective project resourcing requires an understanding of the potential complexity and some hard-nosed planning. Complex projects are renowned as extremely stressful and it has been demonstrated that decision-making can be adversely affected when people are under stress. Making sure there is redundancy in key roles safeguards against the risk of losing a key leader due to an accident, as in an earlier example, or from the risk of the leader being poached by other parts of the organisation or from outside the organisation. From a human resources management perspective redundancy is the one of the most effective forms of future proofing as less experienced personnel can work with and be mentored by experts.

MANAGE HEROES CAREFULLY

Project leaders who successfully deliver complex projects rapidly become heroes; not only legends in their own minds but legends in their organisations. Although thereappears to be little academic research about this phenomenon, anecdotal evidence suggests several dangers inherent in the 'hero syndrome'. The hero can become over confident leading to mistakes. Alternatively, others in the organisation might treat him or her as the number one problem-solver, the 'get X, she or he will fix it' syndrome. This can contribute to lazy management practices, knowing that the hero can be relied upon to save the day. In the long term executive leaders are let off the hook with regard to establishing appropriate project support processes. It would also be interesting to map the job trajectories of heroes. It is likely that the reputation they develop beyond the organisation means that they can be easily lured away by better offers.

As a result of extraordinary performance the hero and his or her team can become distanced from the rest of the organisation. Extraordinary performance sets a new benchmark for the organisation. This should be beneficial, but like any change it must be carefully managed by executive leaders or resistance might be encountered from those who are not performing at such a high level. During some of our conversations with people within one large organisation it was interesting to note frequent criticism about the project leader of a team that was performing exceptionally well. Other senior leaders seemed to be going to sometrouble to find fault with the project leader in question, even though he had been generally well-regarded prior to taking over leadership ofthe project. It appears that his exceptional success with such a seemingly impossible assignment might have been putting other senior leaders to shame and the project leader now found he was being marginalised as a result of his superb efforts. As the laid-back organisational culture will probably be allowed to predominate it is likely, in the near future, that the organisation will lose an excellent project leader.

Part 4: Authority to Select and Replace Key Personnel

If a leader is to have carriage of the project, s/he must also have the authority to select and replace key personnel. It is essential that a forum exists for input into project-specific decisions about the personnel at every level of the project. These recommendations seem to be obvious for the project level but it is equally important that executive leaders can be replaced if they are not contributing. However changing members of the executive leadership team usually requires a critical level of support from key stakeholders.

> I've seen several examples where the executive leadership didn't work in practice and a change in leadership was needed. We've just been through a process like that ourselves and it was quite interesting because we detected early that the project was having challenges at executive leadership level and with the customer. My experience told me that those problems were probably not rectifiable without changes in the leadership team. I sit in the executive leadership structure outside the

> *project team, and other people within that structure felt it shouldn't be*
> *changed immediately, and we debated that and agreed on an approach*
> *that allowed us to give a broader range of stakeholders an opportunity*
> *to understand that there was a need for a change in leadership. We built*
> *a consensus for change. People don't necessarily agree first off, they*
> *have to agree there are issues in the first place, they have to understand*
> *what's driving them, and they have to agree there's a rationale for*
> *change to fix the problem. Initially there isn't that consensus. You have*
> *to bite the bullet and make changes anyway and manage the process as*
> *effectively as possible through good communication. If you can allow*
> *a consensus for change to accelerate, then when you come to make the*
> *change, a broader range of people will understand the reason for it and*
> *concur with this necessity. Interview 54 PD.*

At any level of leadership teams can become too large, too unwieldy. Oversized teams arise can from trying to get as much expertise involved as possible. Alternatively they can come from the desire to make sure everyone who thinks they need to be involved is involved, a way of managing the politics. Team composition and size are both critical to project success. Not all team members need to be permanently assigned to ensure expert input to the project.

> *There are a lot of people who think they need to be involved but don't.*
> *One of the skills of managing public sector projects, as opposed to*
> *private sector, is telling people they're not involved when they think*
> *they are. If you involve too many people everything slows down, you*
> *can't make an effective decision, people get confused, it undermines the*
> *speed and effectiveness of the delivery of the project. I think we got the*
> *team selection right; no one ever thought for one minute of giving up.*
> *That determination has had a number of practical impacts. There have*
> *been numbers of stages when we realised things were going off track,*
> *and we altered course and did things differently. Interview 60 C.*

At the project level it is essential that project leaders have the authority to select staff so that the team has the range of experience needed for the project and works together as required. Without that level of authority progress can be completely stifled.

> *The key to a complex project is having the right people in the right*
> *positions with the necessary skills, budget and power to deliver on the*
> *project. Interview 50 PM.*

It is also vital that the project leaders have the authority to replace team members if they are not working out.

> The team of people you have a round is most important – making sure you have people with the right mix of experience so you have the flexibility to change the project team project through different phases. Quality of the team you select and flexibility. Interview 48 PD.

However, if any one of the sponsoring organisations has a low level of project maturity the project team may be forced to rely on others in the organisation for team member selection. Resulting allocations may be unsympathetic to the project needs. Turner and Müller (2003) argue that large projects be resourced as if they are temporary organisations with the project leaders as the quasi CEO of the temporary organisation.

> The team of people you have is important. So that's making sure that you have people with right mix of skills and experience, and that you have flexibility on the project to change the composition of the teams through different phases ... you first start off with the planning phase, then through into the construction phase and handover. It's the quality of the team that you select, and you select that team to reflect the status of the project. Interview 48 PD.

Also leadership needs to assess when an experienced external consultant can cut through some of the organisational cultural issues in a way that an internal appointee cannot do.

> In my position working in but not employed by the public sector ... I didn't have the restrictions that they did. So I didn't have to worry about how much I was getting paid or whether I was getting promoted or made redundant. I was simply there to get the project done. So in a roundabout way that element of the leadership is not having someone do it internally but having someone do it externally because they're more like to get the job done than if they're internal. In my role, I didn't have any preconceptions about being nice to people because it was on a short term basis, it's all about getting people to work together effectively, without the constraints their normal processes and hierarchies and redundancy and payment and promotion cycles. Interview 60 C.

A complex project will always be subject to emergence. As the project needs change it is likely that the project personnel needed in one phase will not be appropriate in later phases, and that also applies to the executive leaders.

Part 5: Accountability and Assessment

Accountability is the litmus test for project human resource management. As a concept in ethics and governance *accountability* has several meanings. It is often used synonymously with words like responsibility, answerability, blameworthiness, liability and other terms associated with the expectation of account-giving (Dykstra, 1939). In leadership roles, accountability is the acknowledgment and assumption of responsibility for actions, products, decisions, and policies. It includes the governance, admnistration and implementation within the scope of the role position. It encompasses the obligation to report, explain and be answerable for resulting consequences (Williams, 2001). Traditionally, accountability did not apply to the top layers of leadership and while a few dysfunctional corporate leaders may still hold this belief (Blumen-Lippman, 2004), the tide is turning (Price, 2005).

AVOIDING ACCOUNTABILITY

People in organisations can avoid accountability in many different ways: people can point out other people's inadequacies; tell others what they want to hear rather than what is true; leave out important details (lying by omission); be vague (speaking or writing in general terms rather than in specifics); divert attention (introducing irrelevant material or focusing on details, obfuscation, minimising the importance of the situation, paying selective attention, making a big fuss about a minor point); avoid getting round to a decision; put others on the defensive by degrading them, or quibbling over words, or embarrassing others, and unfortunately common in projects, agreeing verbally but refusing to sign off.

> *If the upmost layers of leadership are not accountable, how can you expect anyone else to be. There is a real lack of courage at the top in some sectors; a reluctance to put anything in writing; a real unwillingness to make hard decisions. It is childish really - making sure they can duck for cover rather than applying intelligence to the problem and we get the blame. Interview 22 PM.*

CLARITY AND FULL AWARENESS OF ACCOUNTABILITY

If people are either unaware of what they are supposed to do, or there is no clear method for assessing what they have done, they cannot be held accountable for their performance.

Assessment and role definition must be developed together. In Chapter 10, it is suggested that the accountability of the executive leadership team be linked to delivery of sustainable business benefits. Nevertheless, any attempt to do this must encourage systemic thinking rather than obfuscation which seeks to hide anything that might be personally disadvantageous to the executive or project leaders in question. Admittedly this is very difficult to achieve when some people act primarily from self-interest.

ACHIEVING ACCOUNTABILITY IN A COMPLEX ENVIRONMENT

Linking accountability to outcomes and ultimately benefits in a complex project that is characterised by nonlinearity might, at first assessment, appear to be problematic, if not impossible. Such the link normally requires a direct causal relationship to be established. The confusion of cause and effect observed in complex relationships due to nonlinearity means that clear linkages are often not apparent. When clear causal relationships are not evident it is best to go to the next highest level of the hierarchy to define accountability. If it is impossible to link accountability with cause and effect, the trick is to move up a notch, stand back and take a more holistic view of the situation, look at the end benefits rather than focus on pathways and processes. For example, a project executive sponsor might be accountable for a mutually agreed KPI, such as 'no litigation proceeding from negative stakeholder action', and that KPI might be linked to a share of profit or loss. Multiple interrelated management actions will be needed at the project level to achieve that KPI but the clearly defined accountability at sponsor level should ensure that the project team gets the support it needs from the sponsor to achieve the particular KPI.

Even if the project is full of uncertainties achieving accountability is assisted by:

- Clear definition of roles and responsibilities according to the level and type of complexity. If the project is full of uncertainty it is preferable to describe role statements in terms of general capabilities (see Tables 11.1 and 11.2) rather than terms of specific tasks.

- Visibility of tasks assigned and responsibilities – if someone is causing a delay the fact that colleagues are watching and waiting is a strong motivator. Transparency is the basis of achieving effective partnerships and alliances.

- Honest reporting – plain language is preferable to words designed to obscure.

- Accountability linked to project benefits, particularly at the executive level (however, caution needs to be applied in case rewards start to drive process).

- Induction material for new leaders and team members defining accountability as well as responsibility.

- Attention to accountability arrangements across organisational and cultural boundaries (see Chapter 7).

- Clear communication and documentation available to the whole team, especially clarifying responsibilities (such as, missed deadlines and who is responsible) – this also provides an audit trail if needed later.

- Modelling a culture of 'no blame, but no excuses'. Experience has shown that the 'no blame culture' needs to be coupled with the requirement to demonstrate that everything has been done to avoid the issue.

- Suitable forums for transmitting 'bad news' – these can be informal or formal or anonymous, depending upon the organisational culture.

In fact, clear accountability and clear role responsibility is fundamental to leadership of complex projects even if detailed precise role definition is hard to achieve because of changing states. In a highly complex environment the role responsibility and accountability may become the only secure elements in the system.

In Summary

Leadership roles in some complex projects may be diffuse. Particularly in multi-organisational or multi-national projects leadership may take the form of leadership layers rather than single points of leadership.

However, clearly defined responsibilities and accountabilities for groups and individuals are the foundation on which a complex project is managed. The following guidelines are explored to assist project leaders in this important aspect and illustrate examples of issues to avoid:

- Role capabilities are defined based on the assessed level and type of complexity rather than in detailed terms.

- People and teams who can do the job are assigned.

- Redundancy for key roles is built-in at the planning stage.

- Heroes are managed.

- Project leaders are given the authority to make changes to roles where needed based on the complexity.

- Accountability is clear and assessed.

References and Further Reading

Australian Crime Commission, (2009) What is the Difference Between Project Wickenby and Operation Wickenby? http://www.crimecommission.gov.au/media/faq/wickenby.htm; accessed 10/2/11.

Beard, R.V. (1971) *Failure Accommodation in Linear Systems Through Self-Reorganization*. Dept. MVT-71–1, Man Vehicle Laboratory, Cambridge, MA.

Blumen-Lippman, J. (2004) *The Allure of Toxic Leaders: Why We Follow Destructive Bosses and Corrupt Politicians – and How We Can Survive Them*. NY: Oxford University Press.

Dykstra, C.A. (February 1939) The Quest for Responsibility. American Political Science Review. *The American Political Science Review*, 33(1), pp. 1–25.

Helm, J. and Remington, K. (2005a) Adaptive Habitus – Project Managers' Perceptions of the Role of the Project Sponsor. Proceedings of EURAM Conference, May, Munich: TUT University.

Helm, J. and Remington, K. (2005b) Effective Sponsorship, Project Managers'
Perceptions of the Role of the Project Sponsor. *Project Management Journal*,
36(3), 51–62.

Kim, J-H and Yum, B-J. (1993) A Heuristic Method for Solving Redundancy
Optimization Problems in Complex Systems. *IEEE Transactions on Reliability*,
44(4), pp. 572–578.

Marcus, E. and Stern, H. (2003) *Blueprints for High Availability*, 2nd ed.
Indianapolis, IN, USA: John Wiley and Sons, Inc.

Price, T.L. (2005) *Understanding Ethical Failures in Leadership* (Cambridge Studies
in Philosophy and Public Policy), Cambridge University Press.

Randles, M., Lamb, D., Odat, E. and Talebb-Bendiab, A. (2010) Distributed
Redundancy and Robustness in Complex Systems. *Journal of Computer and
System Science*, 77(2), pp. 293–304.

Remington, K. and Pollack, J. (2007) *Tools for Complex Projects*. Aldershot, UK:
Gower Publishing.

Turner, J.R. and Müller, R. (2003) On the Nature of the Project as a Temporary
Organization. *International Journal of Project Management*, 21(1), pp. 1–7

Williams, C. (2001) *Leaders of Integrity: Ethics and a Code for Global Leadership*.
Amman: UN University Leadership Academy.

12

Partners for Peace

 *Other than the fact that it is a board game it is as different from Chess as cats are from dogs. In Chess, you have to kill to win. In Go, you have to build to win ...The aim of the game is not to eat your opponent but to build the biggest territory. Excerpt from Muriel Barbery (2006) The Elegance of the Hedgehog, p. 108. [Go, an ancient board game that originated in China more than 2,000 years ago, is played by two players who alternately place black and white stones. Part of the strategic difficulty of the game stems from finding a balance between conflicting interests of expansion and sustainability.]*

As one of the main characters in the novel tries to point out that adversarial relationships demand there is a loser as well as a winner. There are more subtle and effective ways to develop and through support, influence and balance.

Key Points in This Chapter:

- The case for partnering.

- Mindsets that get in the way of partnering.

- Procurement strategies for partnering.

- Developing a partnering relationship.

Part 1: The Case for Partnering

As a project becomes more complex the need for strategic partnering increases. A partnership can go under many different titles; alliances, joint ventures, strategic partnering arrangements. In essence, they all amount to the same thing – an agreement to work together to get the best outcomes for all key stakeholders. It is the intention that counts.

> *You need partners for peace – in a highly disputed environment you need a partner for peace on the other side – if you get two leaders who understand that it is the project that is in trouble not the people you can actually turn that to a force for good with the other party – and people feel that they will get justice. Interview 47 GM.*

The project leader who made this statement is a general manager and project sponsor in the defence industry whose projects involve international suppliers, more than one partner country and often several government departments, in addition to the end-user, within the client country. These are large budget projects which may extend over many years. They have to survive changes of government, changes in regulatory environments, changes in technology and changes in requirements. They have many different sources of complexity.

As a number of authors have demonstrated (Williams, 2002; Ackerman et al., 1997), when nonlinear risk patterns develop in complex projects things can spiral out of hand very quickly, escalating into disputes. Resulting viscious cycles can produce what complexity theorists refer to as a phase change, or a tipping point, like falling over a cliff with no way to get back up again. In this kind of situation combative, or tribal, relationships between parties promote aggressive, adversarial or confrontational behaviours. Conflict that descends into litigation can rapidly bring the project to a halt. As some of our research has demonstrated (Remington and Pollack, 2007) nonlinear processes can force contractors and suppliers into cash flow crises, and even bankruptcy, due to delays and disputes. Rarely can a project sustain these kinds of effects. Almost everyone loses.

Part 2: Mindsets That Get in the Way of Partnering

Walker and Hampson (2003, p. 8) argue that a number of mindsets get in the way of establishing effective partnerships. Subsets of each other, these mindsets tend to stress short term compared with long term or sustainable outcomes. They include:

- Conformance to requirements and focus on cost minimisation that can overshadow innovation and opportunities to add value are lost.

- Focus on the 'cheapest' initial price instead of a focus on value and sustainability.

- Win-lose mentality which can result in a litigious atmosphere, locking out many creative solutions and win-win possibilities. They recommend using an agreed problem-solving and resolution mechanism that recognises the validity of diversity of opinion and approaches.

- Short term profit gain or capital cost-reduction focus – stakeholder-value generating possibilities are seldom revealed through this approach which constrains solutions to a win-lose outcome. A focus on the needs of the stakeholders with development and maintenance of long term relationships fosters release of creative synergies that in the long term reduce wasted energy and builds shared knowledge for all parties involved.

- Focus on short term profit maximisation or initial cost reduction often has a detrimental quality-of-life impact on project team members and other supporting groups who can pay high indirect costs for short term profit gains.

- Cheapest initial cost and bottom line profits that are relentlessly pursued can result in environmental degradation as a whole. The consequences of waste generation are often borne by the community rather than those who were responsible.

Additionally the following attitudes should be questioned:

- A focus on local quick fix rather than holistic approaches to problem-solving usually means that solutions are non-systemic and have repercussions on other parts of the project or organisations involved.

- Local problem-solving focus that does not involve all key stakeholders is less likely to produce sustainable long term solutions.

Individual organisations should recognise that in the long term they are subject to judgement of their actions by a wide community of interests. Project initiators need to appreciate a broader range of community values, and address them, to truly achieve long term success through sustainability. The judgement of corporate or project success is increasingly seen as a function of financial, environmental and social performance (Elkington, 1997).

Part 3: Procurement Strategies for Partnering

Partnering can take place within the most traditional of procurement systems. The attributes associated with establishing good partnering relationships are similar to those discussed for relationship management in Chapter 3. Tony Lendrum (2003), who has spent much of his professional life helping organisations to build and maintain strategic partnerships, describes strategic partnering as a core competency. Based on our research with senior leaders, partnering, with key stakeholders, clients, customers, suppliers, contractors and other affected parties, appears to be an essential ingredient for success when a project is complex, whatever the procurement system chosen.

Partnering has the potential to change an entire industry, as the following comment illustrates. A project leader in a large public infrastructure organisation, which has been responsible for several very successful alliances in recent years, reported:

> We had a review yesterday, with a number of alliance partners from different alliances plus a number of our own people to discuss some of the challenges for our alliances. It was good to realise that some people, who are competitors in the industry, were quite open and transparent. There was a lot of commonality in some of the issues and challenges in our approach to developing alliances and how we establish them. A lot of it does come down to leadership in the form of being able to provide clarity, particularly across the spider web of this kind of organisation. You can probably imagine the multiple departments all with different areas of corporate responsibility. It makes the role of the project leader

in our organisation even more critical to ensuring the effectiveness of
project delivery strategies. Interview PM 65.

Most experienced project managers, whether working with traditional or
non-traditional contracts, value relationship management as one of their
prime skillsets (Kokotovich and Remington, 2009). They know that having to
resort to the contract in order to leverage power is a sign of failed relationship
management. When it comes to complex projects however, the choice of
procurement system can severely hamper the propensity for developing
constructive partnerships, simply because some systems encourage adversarial
behaviour or are very inflexible. Some procurement systems are more
appropriate to conditions of uncertainty.

To apply fixed sum procurement systems that depend on specifying
elements with certainty to parts of a project that are still unclear is a
recipe for disaster. Interview 35 C.

The following is by no means a comprehensive summary of procurement
systems. It is included simply to explore how some of the main procurement
systems in use apply to complex projects.

Traditional Procurement Strategies

FIXED PRICE CONTRACTING

One of the major criticisms is that fixed price procurement systems invite
an inherently confrontational approach over disputes (NBCC, 1989). A huge
industry has evolved, dedicated to advising contractors how to claim for extra
work and clients how to counter these claims. Walker and Hampson (2003)
also note that this traditional approach 'casts roles in stone' making it difficult
to solve problems that cross boundaries. Although fixed price, or lump sum,
contracts have well researched and documented disadvantages they remain
popular. One reason is lack of experience with other systems and although
'none of these parties particularly like "the game" as played ... each at least
knows the rules' (Latham, 1994, p. 2).

The illusion of certainty that lump sum contracting brings is probably its
most attractive feature. However, the illusion of certainty is the crux of the
problem. This kind of procurement approach encourages a culture in which

contractors tender a low price on the assumption that there will be changes in the specifications, or later changes to scope, that will permit variations to the initial tender sum. The contractor makes up the initial 'loss in profit' from highly priced variations. A complex project will always have aspects of uncertainty. A fixed sum contract is really only appropriate when it is possible to exactly specify outcomes. Because of the chaordic nature of complex projects, fixed price contracts might be suitable for some parts of a project or programme but probably not for all parts. Therefore, with a programme management approach which differentiates those parts that are straightforward from those that are not, simple procurement methods can be applied to those elements that can be specified exactly, leaving others to be managed with more sophisticated procurement methods.

END-TO-END PACKAGES – FOR EXAMPLE BOO (BUILD-OPERATE-OWN), BOT (BUILD-OPERATE-TRANSFER), BOOT (BUILD-OPERATE-OWN-TRANSFER – USUALLY BACK TO CLIENT)

These procurement approaches can deliver outcomes at a fixed initial cost. They also entail an alliance or joint venture group that identifies, assigns and manages risks (Walker and Smith, 1995). This arrangement is frequently adopted for major infrastructure projects, like motorways, tunnels, bridges, hospitals and prisons, which are able to incur future revenues for the financiers through tolls or charges. Other applications include facilities that are used for a fixed period of time such as Olympics facilities, which are renovated and leased back or otherwise returned to the sponsoring body such as the local council or government authority. This kind of system encourages a life cycle approach to quality but there have been numerous failures, particularly associated with estimation of revenues. As discussed in Chapter 10, the sponsoring organisation for the Sydney cross city tunnel failed to take into account that motorists in Sydney would be capable of boycotting the tunnel. Other failures have been due to poor communication and loss of trust between key parties (Ogulana, 1997; Smith, 1999).

DESIGN AND IMPLEMENT (ALSO REFERRED TO AS DESIGN AND CONSTRUCT, NOVATION, OR CONTRACTOR-FINANCED PROJECTS)

The contractor is engaged to manage the design development as well as the implementation of the project. As Walker and Hampson (2003) explain, there are several possible advantages including cost-effectiveness and the possibility that innovative solution scan be tested by the market prior to final fabrication. Through a single point of contact for the client and project team, integration can be enhanced by combining the expertise of design, technical and implementation professionals (Dulaini and Dalziel, 1994).

However, Gunning and McDermott (1997) found a number of disadvantages. As this type of procurement still involves traditional competitive tendering the tender may be based on less than fully resolved designs with inflated estimates to cover variations to scope. There is little incentive to focus on life cycle and sustainable design and the quality of the design is heavily dependent upon the adequacy of the client brief. Additionally, the professionalism of the project teams can be challenged by economic pressures or inadequate or one-way communication. Also there is often little opportunity to work with and educate clients about the importance of the brief development phase, which is often prepared separately and prior to engagement of key parties.

Novation, which involves transfer of the responsibility for design development, after an initial conceptual design stage, allows for a more thorough conceptual design to be carried out after the contract has been awarded. This reduces much of the uncertainty about precise client requirements. However, there are several disadvantages with this system also. By accepting a novated design, errors and omissions are also accepted and the novated design might eventually prove unworkable. In addition, the original designers are no longer able to supervise quality and once novation occurs communication with the original designers, which might be important for continuity, is also lost (Chan, 1996).

Contractor financed projects (often referred to as Turnkey projects) are similar to BOT projects with the exception that the contractor does not operate the facility. This kind of procurement system allows clients to make payment only upon delivery of an acceptable product; however, there is substantial risk for the contractor.

Non-traditional Procurement Choices

PROJECT MANAGED CONTRACTS

Walker and Hampson (2003) place this approach in the non-traditional category of procurement, somewhere on the risk spectrum (for both client and contractor) between fixed tender price and variable price. In the construction industry these are referred to as construction management procurement systems. The two main forms are agency and direct. Agency project management is performed by a consultant who co-ordinates the implementation. Direct project management is where a firm undertakes management and execution of the contract, usually for a guaranteed minimum fee or contract price.

From a complexity perspective project managed contracts allow an overlap of design and implementation which is necessary when design is evolving and technical solutions might not yet have been determined. They also encourage a stronger learning environment with the possibility for earlier involvement of those who are executing the project. On large projects which can be parcelled into smaller elements, increased competition for sub-contracted elements or amongst suppliers is also a possibility (Sidwell and Ireland, 1989). One of the most important advantages is that there is no contractual severing of formal client input after the tender has been let, as can occur in other, more traditional procurement methods. Key stakeholders, including client or sponsoring organisation(s) and end users, can be brought on board to inform the project early and remain close to the project in an advisory capacity throughout the project. There exists the possibility for key stakeholders to partner with the project team as the project evolves.

This is a very flexible option but, at first glance, it appears to carry high risks for the client or sponsoring organisation. The success hinges on the project management capability. However, it must be considered as a viable option when there are extreme technical challenges, where goals or goal-paths are undetermined or unshared and in volatile environments involving rapid change of technology, for example. Most experienced project leaders who advocate this type of procurement approach also stress the need for high levels of trust and accountability. Trust comes from a demonstrable honesty and this requires excellent communication, absolute transparency, stringent monitoring and independent auditing.

GAIN-PAIN SHARE (COST PLUS ADJUSTMENTS FOR AGREED GAINS AND LOSSES)

A number of approaches come under this heading. The principle is that partners share both the wins and the losses. When these procurement systems of this type are conducted effectively the participating parties, including sub-contractors and suppliers, co-operate to support each other to achieve the best because everyone loses if one section fails.

The North Sydney Storage Tunnel was procured as an alliance mostly because it was technically complex; how to achieve the desired outcomes was not fully understood at the commencement of the project. Sydney Water procured the contract under an alliance with the Head Contractor, selected after in-depth, round-table meetings. Sydney Water and the Head Contractor agreed on key success indicators. Profit to the Head Contractor was set at a maximum with deductions if any of the key success indicators were not met. (NSW LC Report, 2001; Sydney Water Northside Storage Tunnel, accessed 21/3/11).

Another variant, a Collaborative Working Agreement, has been used on complex construction and defence projects involving a huge number of sub-contractors. The main purpose of Collaborative Working Arrangements (CWA) is to engage the client, design consultants, contractors, sub-contractors, and vendors into one team, with incentives to establish a structure to ensure that everyone works together to achieve agreed shared targets. The aim is to build a unified team with the purpose of creating an environment whereby players are motivated through incentives expressed as a Gain Share / Pain Share arrangement. If the project is successful there will be Gain Share, if it is not then there may well be Pain Share. There cannot be a win-lose result because of the way Gain Share and Pain Share is structured. The most important aspect is that there are no contracts based on adversarial principles. It relies on careful and collaborative estimation and control of costs, defined in terms of Targeted Outturn Cost (TOC) hours, which are negotiated with each sub-contractor in the partnership (Dua, 2006). Sophisticated systems like Earned Value Management are essential to monitor and control costs in order to accurately calculate and monitor the actual value of the work performed in relation to schedule and budgeted cost (Budd and Budd, 2005; AS 4817–2006).

The management of the CWA is usually undertaken by two groups; the first is the Principals Group which is made up of the most senior manager (for example, the CEO) of the various major partners in the Arrangement. They oversee and are responsible for the strategic guidance of the project. The second group manages the day to day aspects of the project and is usually known as the Project Executive Group and takes direction from the Principals Group.

Particularly with these more innovative forms of procurement, there is the opportunity for many additional features, such as 'guaranteed maximum price' which gives some degree of certainty to the client, and sharing pain and gain, which offers an incentive to partners involved in the project to work towards key success factors. The main point is that as the project becomes more complex, more flexibility is required and the choice of procurement system is critical.

Flexibility of Procurement Style: Complexity and Trust

Whatever procurement system is chosen, or imposed, complex projects must have 'partners for peace' if they are to succeed. As mentioned earlier in this book, uncertainty can breed reduction in trust and loss of faith, which in turn contributes to cultures of blame, as opposed to cultures of co-operation needed for collaborative problem-solving.

As these simple graphical relationships illustrate, the higher the uncertainty that is being experienced, the higher the level of flexibility in procurement is needed.

Only some procurement options allow for very high levels of flexibility. A similar exponential relationship is found between flexibility needed and the level of trust between partners needed to sustain the flexibility in procurement options.

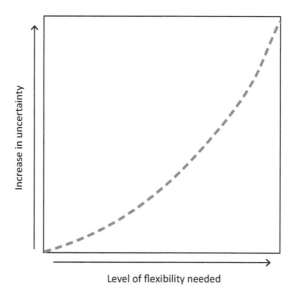

Figure 12.1   Uncertainty graphed against flexibility needed

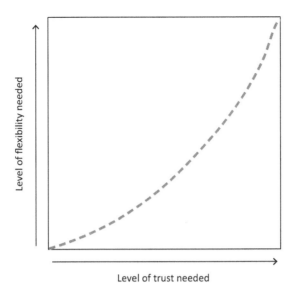

Level of trust needed

Figure 12.2   Level of flexibility required against trust needed

Part 4: Developing a Partnering Relationship

Practitioners across industries agree that trust is the basis on which successful partnerships are built (Lendrum, 2003; 2004; Contractor and Lorange, 2002; Robbins and Krakow, 2000; Glaser, 1994). The following steps are offered as a very brief summary of the process:

Step 1: Is trust important to the relationship? Lendrum (2004, p. 37) offers a simple set of questions illustrated as follows:

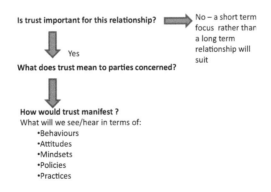

Figure 12.3   Questions and steps for partnering

Step 2: Moral versus legal agreement Lendrum (2004, p.38) argues that partnerships put the 'handshake back into business'. The agreement is as much a moral agreement as a legal agreement. He suggests that good questions to ask are: 'what comes first, the moral or the legal agreement and which should be acted on first?'.

Step 3: Assess the cultures of the partnering organisations. The cultures of the partnering organisations matter enormously in assessing whether a truly open, trusting relationship is possible (see Chapter 7). All participating organisations might not be able or willing to enter an honest trusting relationship. Some organisations are hampered by embedded cultural practices, such as procurement departments that favour adversarial relationships, inherent distrust because of differences in values, and so on. In one very successful alliance the auditors (at both government and organisation level) became the major initial stumbling block to entering a partnership in which all partners wanted to develop a transparent relationship. They had not done business in that way before.

Step 4: Create a partnering charter based on what level of trust is needed or possible; the behaviours, attitudes, mindsets, policies and practices that would demonstrate trust (Step 2), it is useful to spend the time documenting how the partnership will perform in the form of a charter. This is best done in a facilitated workshop. A well-facilitated workshop provides further opportunities to explore differences that might remain undisclosed in formal meetings.

Step 5: Identify champions 'partners for peace' from all parties who will continue to give high level support to the partnership, making sure that it is maintained, being alert to potential fractures and be prepared to act at a high level for the success of the project.

Repairing Broken Relationships

In my consulting and teaching I have been often asked how to save a project when relationships have broken down and litigation seems to be the only option. Usually relationships 'break down' because they have never been established as strong trusting relationships in the first place. Establishing a trusting relationship is not a fuzzy concept. Nevertheless it does require the parties concerned to take time up front – usually a relatively small amount of time in relation to the total project duration. In ancient and sophisticated cultures, such as Asian, Middle Eastern and some European societies, people understand the importance of taking time to establish relationships and listen to each other, before getting down to business, as one English project director related about a highly sensitive project involving a multi-national consortium:

> *The French Consortium leaders were very adept at dealing with the politics, they took time to build relationships, but other members had a lot to learn. Interview 49 PD.*

In fact, in some cultures, it is considered insulting if you don't invest time in building the relationship before business. Where you decide to build a relationship is also important. Some cultures separate the act of relationship building in both a spatial and temporal sense – a meeting is a business meeting and relationship building occurs before or after the meeting in a less formal setting. As one German project manager, working on an international project in the USA, put it:

> *When we set up meetings, in Germany, we tend to plan and organise them very carefully and thoroughly. But for people from other areas, that is not the case, they just arrive and chat, when we are supposed to be concentrating on the business. We do a lot of preparation upfront that we take to the meeting. But the approach over here, in the USA, is first chat, then do the work. That causes problems when the practice is not addressed upfront. When a complex project involves various countries, they have to think about the cultural communication differences. In Germany we tend to be quite upfront and direct, but that is not always the case in the US. And meetings are not facilitated in a way that takes these differences in expectation into account. Interview 53 PM.*

Nevertheless, the reality is many relationships fail. The recourse is usually to alternative dispute mechanisms, such as mediation, or ultimately litigation. If the project is being conducted in a country that operates under a very different legal system, or has an autocratic form of government, and/or a culture characterised by high power-distance (see Chapter 7), formal litigation procedures may not result in satisfactory outcomes. Outcomes may seem to be unfair and biased in favour of the party who holds the power, usually the host country client or senior sponsor.

In almost all cases, it is preferable to stop and invest time in trying to regain trust. Obviously this is very difficult to achieve because, by this time, trust is at its lowest. However, it is not impossible and, with a skilled facilitator, trust can be re-established.

First it is important to establish rapport. Rapport can be achieved very quickly if the following happens:

- At least one side opens the dialogue by admitting that trust has broken down and expresses a willingness to regain a trusting working relationship. This must be seen as a sincere attempt. In most cases, all parties generally want the project to succeed and want a win-win outcome, so stating the reality will help to open up the dialogue.

- Then the opening party should refrain from dominating the conversation. Exploratory questions are asked to allow others to talk about how they see the situation, and what they are facing. It is important to really listen to what the others are saying.

- Then listen for values and beliefs in the dialogue (Coster, 2011). This is essential. Rapid rapport building depends on being able to relate to people's values and beliefs RATHER THAN focusing on the surface issues at hand. Most people make the mistake of going directly to the surface issues without exploring the underlying value differences first.

- Paraphrase what the other parties are saying about what is important to them rather than the actions or details. A focus on the values and beliefs that they have expressed takes the dialogue to a higher level. When one party indicates that they have heard the values and beliefs that underpin the other side's concerns, rapport is established very rapidly (Coster, 2011).

- Continue to listen deeply.

- Establish the benefits of resolving the conflict without recourse to litigation.

- Once some level of rapport has been established it is worth testing to see if trust can be re-established by exploring how the issues that seem to be the most important can be resolved using a collaborative, problem-solving approach.

- Go slowly. Don't try to tackle all issues in one sitting. Chip away slowly – one issue at a time until trust between all parties is stronger.

Try to avoid putting your issues on the table until you have listened deeply to the other party's position:

- Once broken down a relationship takes time to mend. However, the alternative to attempting to repair a relationship is often not worth contemplating. When we are not operating on our home territory, by familiar rules, the odds are generally against us if we decide to choose adversarial approaches.

- Ultimately an agreement or charter to work together needs to be drafted up but this only comes after some trust had been established.

In Summary

Partnering is an attitude of mind rather than a procurement system:

- Complex adaptive systems are chaordic. There will be elements that are highly structured, which might be able to be procured through traditional frameworks. There are elements that are highly unstructured which should be procured through one of the many procurement approaches. Key points to remember are:

  - When uncertainty prevails higher levels of flexibility in procurement are needed.
  - In order to obtain high levels of flexibility there must be equally high levels of trust.
  - In reality partnering involves building relationships and no matter which procurement system is chosen or enforced sound, trusting relationships will almost always work to the advantage of the key stakeholders.
  - Even broken relationships can be repaired and previously adversarial relationships can be made to work if at least one party takes the first step towards reparation.

References and Further Reading

Ackerman, F., Eden, C. and Williams, T. (1997) Modelling for Litigation: Mixing Qualitative and Quantitative Approaches. *Interfaces*, 2, pp. 48–65.

AS 4817-2006, Project Performance Measurement Using Earned Value. Sydney: Standards Australia.

Budd, C.I. and Budd, C.S. (2005) *A Practical Guide to Earned Value Project Management*. Vienna, Va: Management Concepts.

Chan, A.C. (1996) Novation Contract – Client's Roles Across the Project Life Cycle. Procurement Systems North meets South – Developing ideas, CIB W92, Durban, RSA.

Contractor, F.J. and Lorange, P. (eds) (2002) Cooperative Strategies in: International Business. Joint Ventures and Technology. Partnerships between Firms. *International Business & Management*, Ghauri P.N. (Series Editor) Kidlington, Oxford: Pergamon.

Coster, K (2010) Conversations with a enior coach. Dialogue in preparation for this book.

Dua, R. (2006) Making Performance Happen Using Collaborative Working Arrangements in the Construction Industry. Proceedings of the IRNOP VII Conference, Xi'an, China: Northwestern Technical University, pp. 119–132.

Dulaini, M.F. and Dalziel, R.C. (1994) The Effects of the Procurement Method on the Level of Management Synergy in Construction Projects. East meets West – CIB W92 Symposium, Hong Kong, University of Hong Kong.

Elkington, J. (1997) Cannibals with Forks: The Triple Bottom Line of 21st Century Business. *Journal of Business Ethics*, 23(2), pp. 229–231.

Glaser, M. (1994) Economic and Environmental Repair in the Shadow of Superfund: Local Government Leadership in Building Strategic Partnerships. *Economic Development Quarterly*, 8(4), pp. 345–352.

Gunning, J.G. and McDermott, M.A. (1997) Developments in Design and Build Contract Practice in Northern Ireland. Procurement – A Key to Innovation, CIB W92 Procurement Systems Symposium, The University of Montreal, CIB.

Kokotovich, V. and Remington, K. (2007) Enhancing Innovative Capabilities: Developing Creative Thinking Approaches with Tomorrow's Project Managers. IRNOP VIII, Brighton, UK, Conference Proceedings.

Latham, M. (1994) Constructing the Team. Final Report of the Government/ Industry Review of Procurement and Contractual Arrangements in the UK Construction Industry. London, HMSO.

Legislative Council of New South Wales (LC NSW) (2000) Report on Inquiry into the Northside Storage Tunnel-Scotts Creek Vent. Parliamentary Paper No. 453. General Purpose Standing Committee No. 5.

Lendrum, T. (2004) *The Strategic Partnering Pocket Book*. Sydney, Australia: McGraw-Hill

Lendrum, T. (2003) *The Strategic Partnering Handbook,* 4th Ed. Sydney, Australia: McGraw-Hill.

Limerick, D., Cunninton, B. and Crowther, F. (1998) *Managing the New Organisation: Collaboration and Sustainability in the Postcorporate World*. Warriewood, NSW: Business and Professional Publishing.

NBCC (1989) Strategies for the Reduction of Claims and Disputes in the Construction Industry – No Dispute. Canberra, Australia: National Building and Construction Council.

Ogunlana, S.O. (1997) Build Operate Transfer Procurement Traps: Examples from Transportation Projects in Thailand. Procurement – A Key to Innovation, CIB W92 Procurement Systems Symposium, The University of Montreal, CIB.

Robbins, H. and Krakow, M. (2000) Evolution of a Comprehensive Tobacco Control Programme: Building System Capacity and Strategic Partnerships – Lessons from Massachusetts. *Tobacco Control*, 9, pp. 423–430.

Sidwell, A.C. and Ireland, V. (1989) An International Comparison of Construction Management. *The Australian Institute of Building Papers*, 2(1), pp. 3–12.

Smith, A.J. (1999) *Privatized Infrastructure – The Role of Government*. London, UK: Thomas Telford.

Sydney Water. Northside Storage Tunnel. http://www.sydneywater.com.au/Oursystemsandoperations/WastewaterSystems/NorthsideStorageTunnel/; retrieved 21/3/11.

Walker, D. and Hampson, K. (2003) (eds) *Procurement Strategies. A Relationship Approach*. Oxford, UK: Blackwell Publishing.

Walker, D. and Smith, A.J. (1995) *Privatised Infrastructure – The BOT Approach*. London, UK: Thomas Telford.

Williams, T. (2002) *Modelling Complex Projects*. (Sussex, UK: John Wiley and Sons).

SECTION THREE:

How Good Leadership Behaves When Projects Are Complex

Based on observations of the 70 leaders interviewed by the research team between 2004 and 2011, this section attempts to describe the key characteristics observed in the leaders interviewed. The observations come from in-depth interviews and from observations made by both researchers independently. Although, as would be expected, many different personalities were represented in the sample of leaders interviewed, the observations that form the basis of this section come from overwhelming impressions gained by both observer/ interviewers. Chapter 13 introduces the concept of humility, not in a demeaning sense but in accordance with dictionary definitions which emphasise 'knowing oneself'. After much discussion the title 'humble iconoclasts' emerged as a title that seemed to encapsulate the idea of a leader not being without ego, but also being perpetually open to learning, and, at the same time willing to break down barriers in search of what he or she believes to be the right way. Chapter 14 really summarises the impression the leaders made. They are people-oriented (some are even charismatic, in its positive connotation) but above all they exhibit enormous courage, resilience and determination, even when times are very, very tough. These were the qualities that helped them lead teams through the most complex challenges.

Chapter 13: As Humble Iconoclasts

Chapter 14: With Charisma, Resilience, Determination and Courage

13

As Humble Iconoclasts

Rough work, iconoclasm, but the only way to get at truth. Oliver Wendell Holmes.
American physician, poet, writer and Professor at Harvard, 1809–1894.

Finding a title to this chapter was a struggle because the word humble has taken on many meanings in recent years, some of them associated with low self-worth and that is certainly not what we found in the leaders we met.

Key Points in This Chapter:

- A right estimate of oneself.

- Iconoclasm – the capacity to break down barriers.

- Discussed in terms of psychology.

- Traits not associated with effective leadership.

A Right Estimate of Oneself

There are many quotations on the subject of humility but this one by the nineteenth century English preacher, Charles Spurgeon (1834-1892), seems to best sum up the quality we observed:

Humility is to make a right estimate of one's self.

A person with a right estimate of self neither underestimates his or her ability nor inflates it. During the course of the interviews we became conscious of this as pervasive quality. At first we described the quality as 'lack of ego' however, it would be wrong to say that the leaders we met lacked ego. They were proud of their successful projects and pleased to talk about them. Eventually it became apparent that what we were really observing was *humility*. Almost without exception these leaders possessed very high degrees of humility, and it seems that this was an important part of what made them effective leaders for the very complex projects with which they had been involved. Humility seems to be one of the essential qualities that enable them to guide and sustain a diverse group of stakeholders through the uncertainty associated with often not knowing all the answers. It gives them the ability to lead flexibly, to listen to and take advice from a vast number of people associated with the project, to lead alongside the teams, stepping back to allow others to lead but with the presence of mind to take on a more overt leadership role if the situation demands.

LEADERSHIP DIVERGED FROM CLASSICAL LEADERSHIP MODELS.

Our evidence seems to be at odds with the prototypical image of a military or political leader (Exline and Geyer, 2004) but it is very much in line with what complexity leadership theorists are saying (see for example, Plowman et al., 2007; Marion and Uhl-Bien, 2001; Schwandt and Marquardt, 2000). Nevertheless, the leaders we interviewed came across as assured individuals with a very clear sense of self and strong levels of self-confidence. It was also apparent to both researchers that interviewees tended to pursue what they considered to be the right thing in the circumstances in spite of opposition. They were iconoclasts, not in the traditional sense, of course. As far as we know they are not in the practice of destroying religious images, but in the sense of being willing to challenge cherished beliefs or traditional institutions if they consider them to be founded on error or if they find they are inappropriate to meet the needs of the project. To be iconoclastic and to get away with it requires a leader to be able to make a very clear assessment of a situation and then have confidence in his or her own ability to carry through radical ways of addressing a problem.

Without subjecting our interviewees to a barrage of IQ tests it was quite obvious that they were highly intelligent individuals, with a strong capacity for integrating complex information (see Chapter 6). However, at no time did the interviewees betray any of the language or traits that could be associated with an inflated sense of one's own importance. In fact, quite the opposite was the case. Some of the interviews were close to 1.5 hours in length. During such a protracted length of time it is difficult for interviewees to 'mask' their values so we came to the conclusion that we were getting pretty honest responses to our questions.

WHAT HUMILITY BRINGS TO LEADERSHIP

Humility is a relatively old-fashioned word these days when we are constantly taught that developing self-confidence is the key to achievement. Nevertheless, it is an interesting quality because it opens up the possibility for so many behaviours that are often associated with good leadership.

Humility promotes the capacity to listen. The literature on the importance of listening abounds but many people find it very hard to listen well. Listening to hear another's point of view depends to some extent on being humble enough to hear an opinion which might be different from one's own.

Humility enhances the capacity to observe. Like listening, the ability to stand back and observe is vital to any leader but even more so when what you are dealing with is 'messy' or unstructured.

The very state of humility presupposes that the leader knows that she or he does not have all the answers. It opens up the capacity to be wrong and to entertain the possibility that other approaches might have value.

The quality of humility seems to be related to the ability to reflect, which includes the ability to take in information, compare what has been heard or observed to other experience and theory and reframe it in such a way that it is either stored for the future or responded to in the present. Reflection is, of course, an essential part of a learning cycle.

One essential aspect that has been well-researched and documented is the capacity for a leader to learn (Schwandt and Marquardt, 2000). Successful leaders seem to have enormous capacities to learn. In order to learn we need to be able to listen, observe, we need to allow ourselves to be wrong and we need to be able to reflect on the situation. It also opens up the possibility for others to learn.

Humility, as Charles Spurgeon put it, is to be able to assess your own capabilities accurately. Presumably it follows that if we have a clear picture of our own abilities we will also have a clear understanding of the gaps, understand what others can offer and make sure the gaps are filled by others (see Chapter 3).

At a time when we are becoming increasingly aware of executive leaders who exhibit extreme psychotic and narcissistic tendencies, talking with the leaders who took part in this research was refreshing, and at times, inspirational.

Humility Discussed in Terms of Psychology

Although there are many references to 'humility' in management and leadership, articles tend to be either anecdotal or polemical. The most revealing research literature comes from psychological studies of leadership behaviour. Recently, a number of examinations of humility as a personal attribute have appeared in the psychological literature that has associated humility with virtue or personal strength. Emmons (1999), for example, argues that humility involves:

- Accuracy.

- Self-acceptance.

- Understanding one's imperfections.

- Keeping one's talents and accomplishments in perspective.

- Freedom from both arrogance and low self-esteem.

In a list of key features of humility, Tangney (2000, 2002) includes:

- An accurate sense of one's abilities and achievements.

- The ability to acknowledge one's mistakes, imperfections, gaps in knowledge, and limitations.

- Openness to new ideas, contradictory information, and advice.

- An ability to keep one's abilities and accomplishments in perspective.

According to Landrum (2002), humility involves:

- An open-minded attitude.

- A willingness to admit mistakes and seek advice.

- A desire to learn.

Exline et al., (2004) add to these that humility involves:

- A non-defensive willingness to see the self accurately, including strengths and limitations.

They propose that humility is likely to stem from a sense of security in which feelings of personal worth are based on stable, reliable sources (for example, feeling unconditionally loved; belief in the value of all life) rather than on transient, external sources such as achievement, appearance, or social approval. Such a sense of security might stem from personal values, religious views, or life experiences (Crocker and Wolfe, 2001).

THE EFFECT OF HUMILITY ON OTHERS

According to a study by Exline and Geyer (2004), the word 'humility' now has predominantly positive connotations and is associated with the ability to honestly accept one's humanity and the knowledge of one's own imperfections (Kurtz and Ketcham, 1992). Exline and Geyer (2004) found participants with high self-esteem were more likely to link humility with good adjustment and less likely to associate it with shame, embarrassment or humiliation.

In its positive sense the word humility might be associated with a sense of security, an accurate view of self, and a non-defensive, open attitude. Humility would also lead to modest self-presentation as opposed to grandiosity or self-promotion. Finally, it seems reasonable to predict that humble people would be seen as likeable as research shows that traits like grandiosity and self-promotion are more likely to be disapproved of by others (Colvin, Block, and Funder, 1995; Godfrey, Jones, and Lord, 1986; Leary, Bednarski, Hammon, and Duncan, 1997).

WHEN HUMILITY HAS NEGATIVE CONNOTATIONS

A dominant concept in modern Western culture is that people should see themselves in a positive light. A myriad of self-help books exist on how to increase self-esteem (for example, Branden, 1994). Low self-esteem has been blamed for many serious social problems (Baumeister, et al., 1996). When faced with personal weaknesses or failings, people may need to distort the truth in order to feel good about themselves. Favourable self-views generate confidence and positive emotion, which can have other positive effects on social adjustment. Some evidence suggests that favourable distortions, used in moderation, are associated with good mental health—and possibly physical health as well (for example, Taylor and Brown, 1988; Taylor, et al., 2000).

On the other hand, some people associate the quality of humility with humiliation and low self-esteem. In competitive situations or when dealing with highly aggressive, dominant people, those who fail to self-promote or demonstrate their superiority run the risk of being short changed. Exline and Geyer (2004) found that narcissists, in particular, did not associate humility with self-confidence, either in themselves or in others. By definition, the trait of narcissism seems antagonistic to humility. Individuals who are narcissistic are preoccupied with seeing and presenting themselves in a positive light. They often react defensively to self-esteem threats (Baumeister et al., 1996; Bushman and Baumeister, 1998; Rhodewalt and Morf, 1998) and are motivated by desires for dominance in interpersonal relationships (Emmons, 1984; Raskin, Novacek, and Hogan, 1991; Raskin and Terry, 1988).

Traits NOT Associated with Effective Leadership

It may also be helpful to look at those traits that are NOT associated with effective leadership. In an investigation of ineffective police leaders, Schafer (2010) found that respondents identified the following traits and habits as common among the ineffective police leaders. In particular, 'focus on self over others', 'ego/arrogance', 'closed mindedness', 'micromanagement', and 'capriciousness', 'poor work ethic', 'failure to act', 'ineffective communication', 'lack of interpersonal skills', and 'lack of integrity' emerged as recurrent themes in the survey responses.

EGO AND ARROGANCE

Ego and arrogance represent a fine line for leaders to tread. On the one hand, it is desirable for a leader to have a measure of confidence in themselves and their abilities (Lipman-Blumen, 2005; Maccoby, 2000). In order to secure followers, a leader needs to convey to others that their objectives and methods are appropriate and followers need confidence that their leader is working to achieve a proper goal using a sound plan. However, taken too far, a leader's behaviour might be deemed 'selfish, stubborn, self-righteous, [and] egotistical'. One-third of the respondents in Schafer's (2010) study identified ego and arrogance as characteristics displayed by ineffective leaders. These characteristics had presumably gone beyond the normal realms of confidence and self-assurance that might be considered healthy and productive.

In Summary

Successful senior project leaders in the study were distinguished by their ability to have an accurate (apparently neither inflated nor deflated) knowledge of their capabilities:

- At the same time they were not afraid to break with traditions if that meant they could achieve the outcomes more effectively.

- Humility has been shown to be a quality that assists in development of positive relationships with most people, though people who either have low self-esteem themselves, are combative by nature or have inflated self-esteem (narcissism) may not see humility as a positive trait.

- Humility is a personal characteristic that increases the capacity to listen, observe, be wrong, reflect and learn – all essential qualities for leading complex projects.

- Displays of ego and arrogance have been associated with ineffective leadership in recent studies.

References and Further Reading

Baumeister, R.F., Smart, L. and Boden, J. M. (1996) Relation of Threatened Egotism to Violence and Aggression: The Dark Side of High Self-esteem. *Psychological Review*, 103, pp. 5–33.

Branden, N. (1994) *The Six Pillars of Self-esteem*. New York: Bantam Books.

Bushman, B.J and Baumeister, R.F. (1998) Threatened Egotism, Narcissism, Self-esteem, and Direct and Displaced Aggression: Does Self-love or Self-hate Lead to Violence? *Journal of Personality and Social Psychology*, 75, pp. 219–229.

Colvin, C.R., Block, J. and Funder, D.C. (1995) Overly Positive Self-evaluations and Personality: Negative Implications for Mental Health. *Journal of Personality and Social Psychology*, 68, pp. 1152–1162.

Crocker, J. and Wolfe, C.T. (2001) Contingencies of Self-worth. *Psychological Review*, 108, pp. 593–623.

Emmons, R.A. (1999) *The Psychology of Ultimate Concerns*. New York: Guilford.

Emmons, R.A. (1987) Narcissism: Theory and Measurement. *Journal of Personality and Social Psychology*, 52, pp. 11–17.

Emmons, R.A. (1984) Factor Analysis and Construct Validity of the Narcissistic Personality Inventory. *Journal of Personality Assessment*, 48, pp. 291–300.

Exline, J.J., Campbell, W.K., Baumeister, R.F., Joiner, T. and Krueger, J. (2004) Humility and Modesty. In: Peterson, C. and Seligman, M. (eds), *The Values In Action (VIA) Classification of Strengths*. Cincinnati, OH: Values in Action Institute.

Exline, J.J. and Geyer. A (2004) Perceptions of Humility: A Preliminary Study, Self and Identity, 3, pp. 95–114.

Godfrey, D.K., Jones, E.E. and Lord, C.G. (1986) Self-promotion is not Ingratiating. *Journal of Personality and Social Psychology*, 50, pp. 106–113.

Kurtz, E. and Ketcham, K. (1992) *The Spirituality of Imperfection: Modern Wisdom from Classic Stories*. New York, NY: Bantam Books.

Landrum, R.E. (2002, May) Humility: Its Measurement and Impact on Person-perception. Poster presented at the annual meeting of the Midwestern Psychological Association, Chicago, IL.

Leary, M.R., Bednarski, R., Hammon, D. and Duncan, T. (1997) Blowhards, Snobs, and Narcissists: Interpersonal Reactions to Excessive Egotism. In: R.M. Kowalski (ed.), *Aversive Interpersonal Behaviors*, pp. 111–131. New York: Plenum.

Lipman-Blumen, J. (2005) Toxic Leadership: When Grand Illusions Masquerade as Noble Visions. *Leader to Leader*, 36, pp. 29–35.

Maccoby, M (2000) Narcissistic Leaders: The Incredible Pros, the Inevitable Cons. *Harvard Business Review*, January-February.

Marion, R. and Uhl-Bien, M. (2001) Leadership in Complex Organisations. *The Leadership Quarterly*, 12, pp. 389–418.

Plowman, D.A., Baker, L.T., Beck, T.E., Kulkarni, M., Solansky, S.T. and Travis, D. (2007) The Role of Leadership in Emergent Self-organization. *The Leadership Quarterly*, 18(4), pp. 341–356.

Raskin, R.N., Novacek, J. and Hogan, R. (1991) Narcissistic Self-esteem Management. *Journal of Personality and Social Psychology*, 60, pp. 911–918.

Raskin, R.N. and Terry, H. (1988) A Principal-components Analysis of the Narcissistic Personality Inventory and Further Evidence of its Construct Validity. *Journal of Personality and Social Psychology*, 54, pp. 890–902.

Rhodewalt, F. and Morf, C.C. (1998) Self-aggrandizement and Anger: A Temporal Analysis of Narcissism and Affective Reactions to Success and Failure. *Journal of Personality and Social Psychology*, 74, pp. 672–685.

Schafer, J.A. (2010) The Ineffective Police Leader: Acts of Commission and Omission. *Journal of Criminal Justice*, 38, pp. 737–746.

Schwandt, D.R. and Marquardt, M.J. (2000) *Organizational Learning: From world-class Theories to World's Best Practice*. New York, NY: St Lucie Press.

Tangney, J.P. (2002) Humility. In: Snyder, C.R. and Lopez, S.J. (eds), *Handbook of Positive Psychology*, pp. 411–419. Oxford: Oxford University Press.

Tangney, J.P (2000) Humility: Theoretical Perspectives, Empirical Findings and Directions for Future Research. *Journal of Social and Clinical Psychology*, 19, pp. 70–82.

Taylor, S.E. and Brown, J.D. (1988) Illusion and Well-being: A Social Psychological Perspective on Mental Health. *Psychological Bulletin*, 103, pp. 193–210.

Taylor, S.E., Kemeny, M.E., Reed, G.M., Bower, J.E. and Gruenewald, T.L. (2000) Psychological Resources, Positive Illusions, and Health. *American Psychologist*, 55, pp. 99–109.

14

With Charisma, Resilience, Determination and Courage

When I left the dining room after sitting next to Mr. Gladstone, I thought he was the cleverest man in England. But after sitting next to Mr. Disraeli, I thought I was the cleverest woman in England.
A 19th century hostess after dining with both Prime Ministers.

From this observation we get the impression that charisma, for Prime Minister Disraeli, stemmed from a desire to bolster others whereas Prime Minister Gladstone's charisma was tinged with an inflated sense of his own importance. We observed that many of the project leaders interviewed tended towards the former more positive kind of charisma, to which they added resilience, determination and courage.

Key Points in This Chapter:

- What is charisma?

- How is charisma assigned?

- Charismatic communication.

- Resilience, determination and courage.

Charisma

Charisma has become a loaded term of late because it has also become associated with dysfunctional behaviours, such as narcissism. In its original meaning charisma is associated with transformational leadership; the ability to motivate, encourage and get the very best out of people. Max Weber (1947),the great German sociologist, famously divided sources of authority into three types: the traditional, the charismatic and the legal-bureaucratic. For Weber, as well as many contemporary social psychologists, charismatic leaders have special gifts, potentially learned and 'manufactured' (Glassman, 1975, p. 615), that allow them to invigorate and inspire followers to transcend conventional practices in pursuit of new visions of future possibilities (Bass, 1985b, 1988).

Charismatic (or transformational) leaders tend to exhibit:

- High self-confidence.

- Superior verbal ability.

- Ability to express themselves non-verbally.

- High need for influence or power.

- Exceptionally strong convictions that what they are doing is ethically justifiable.

- Determined and able to persist in the face of high risks and major obstacles.

- Satisfaction from the process of leading others.

- A high need for influence and to be influential.

- More need for flexibility and change.

One particularly interesting finding is that interpersonal characteristics by themselves, such as pleasantness and caring (see Chapter 3), do not necessarily increase perceptions of charisma (Yagil, 1998). It is possible to be pleasant and caring and also be weak or indecisive.

Many, but certainly not all, of the leaders we interviewed could be described as having some level of charisma. Most were personable and seemed to like interacting with people. All, without exception, were effective communicators. Some were outstanding in their ability to frame and reframe their messages to suit different audiences. They all expressed firm opinions, and confidently, but they could not be described as overbearing or dogmatic. As a result of this observation a digression to explore the concept of charisma and extraordinary leadership and how it might apply to leadership of complex projects follows.

Compared with non-charismatic leaders, charismatic leaders are reported to (House, 1977):

- Show more concern for the professional growth of their followers.

- Engage in more developmental efforts such as coaching, role modelling by personal example, and providing guidance and developmental experiences.

- Be more inclined to nurture people around them.

- Have high levels of pragmatism.

- Be more compassionate.

- Be more insightful.

- Show lower levels of dominance and aggression.

- Be less critical of others.

Also charismatic leaders characteristically derive satisfaction from the process of leading others and being influential. They need to have a high need to influence if they are to receive intrinsic satisfaction from leading (House, 1977).

CHARISMA IS ASSIGNED TO LEADERS BY THEIR FOLLOWERS

Charisma is often associated with transformational leadership behaviour that can motivate others to follow a leader to achieve extraordinary tasks; nevertheless, there has been a shift in thinking about how charisma is assigned (Bass, 1985a, 1985b). It is now generally agreed that:

- Followers attribute charisma to the leader.

- Once attributed to a leader, charisma does seem to enhance followers' satisfaction and performance.

- Without followers' attribution, the extraordinary influence of charisma does not occur.

Charismatic leaders (if they are socially functional – like Prime Minister Disraeli) have the following effect on their followers:

- Inspiring

- Motivating

- Empowering.

Of particular interest to project management, which is essentially a team-based enterprise, is the importance of the group or team. A group will be more likely to see the leader as charismatic if:

- There is evidence of the leader's self-sacrifice in pursuit of collective goals.

- The leader is recognised as having performed successfully in the group.

- The leader emphasises the group identity in language used (such as the use of 'we' instead of 'I').

- The leader is seen to be acting in the best interests of the group.

- The members want to be part of the group – for the group to support the leader in his/her endeavours there should be strong group cohesiveness and purpose.

The implication is that it is vital for the leader to do everything in his/her power to establish and maintain group cohesion and preserve a sense of wanting to belong to the team. Any charisma that is attributed to the leader by the group is dependent upon the group being cohesive.

In initial encounters with groups or teams, the following conditions help a group to perceive a leader as charismatic:

- Groups often recognise charisma in a leader after the leader has done something which is self-sacrificing on behalf of the group (Choi and Mai-Dalton, 1999; De Cremer, 2002; De Cremer and van Knippenberg, 2002).

- The leader expresses a vision that is important and relevant for the group (Yorges, Weiss, and Strickland, 1999).

- If the group performs successfully the leader is more likely to be seen as charismatic, even if the performance is coincidental to the leadership (Ensari and Murphy, 2003; Haslam et al., 2001; Howell and Avolio, 1993; Meindl, 1993; Shamir, 1992).

- It is helpful if the leader uses depersonalised rewards (not contingent on behaviour) instead of individuating rewards (contingent on behaviour) and contingent punishments (Atwater et al., 1997). This is particularly interesting and at first appears to be contrary to common sense.

- The leader is representative of the group. If the leader is not liked in the group, in terms of social background, professional experience and length of experience in the field, then leaders' specific behaviours (such the language and metaphors they use to communicate) become important, with an increased onus on leaders to act in a manner which identifies them with the group norms in terms of their behaviour (Platow and van Knippenberg, 2001).

- The leader promotes the group's best interests. As noted above, recent thinking suggests that being charismatic is to do with being representative of the group. It 'is not simply about being one of us, it is about being representative of us' (Platow, et.al., 2006, p. 315).

In the project environment charismatic leadership is important when there is a need to motivate teams to perform seemingly impossible tasks, usually in equally impossible time-frames. However, for leaders to continue to be supported in their endeavours, group members need to continue to want to be part of the group.

CHARISMATIC COMMUNICATION

Charismatic messages (see also Chapter 3) have been shown to have particular characteristics in common. When analysed they are found to:

- Contain strong images that people relate to.

- Emphasise collective purpose, values, beliefs and ethics.

- Be delivered with strength and conviction.

Both the content of a message and the communication of the message seem to be important in achieving a message that followers interpret as charismatic (Awamleh and Gardner, 1999; Holladay and Coombs, 1993, 1994; Kirkpatrick and Locke, 1996; Sidani, 1993). House (1977) identifies nonverbal expressiveness and the ability to be verbally articulate as necessary for communicating vision and mission in compelling ways to followers. When the communication of a message is strong it increases subjects' perceptions of a leader as charismatic (Awamleh and Gardner, 1997; Holladay and Coombs, 1993, 1994; Kirkpatrick and Locke, 1996). For example, the use of powerful language containing images that are understood by the majority, and to which most people in the audience can relate, (Emrich et al., 2001) really does enhance perceptions that a leader is charismatic.

Charismatic messages emphasise collective purpose, values, beliefs, and morality (House and Shamir, 1993). Even if the message is not particularly well formed or visionary, strong communication of the message can also result in the perception of a leader as charismatic (Awamleh and Gardner, 1997; Holladay and Coombs, 1994; Sidani, 1993). Holladay and Coombs (1993) also found that strong delivery increased subjects' perceptions of charisma to a greater extent if the message was visionary than if the communication just contained non-visionary messages. Thus, the highest perceptions of charisma were obtained with strong delivery of a visionary message and the lowest with weak delivery of a non-visionary message. As mentioned above, choice of language that emphasises the group in communication is important, such as use of 'we' instead of 'I' (Fiol, et al., 1999; Hunt, Boal, and Dodge, 1999; Shamir, Arthur, and House, 1994; Shamir, Zakay, et al., 2000, 1998).

THE DOWNSIDE OF CHARISMA

Dysfunctional charismatic leaders (often referred to as narcissists) exhibit leadership behaviours that:

- Are based on personal dominance and authoritarian behaviour.

- Serves the self-interest of the leader.

- Is self-aggrandising.

- Is exploitative of others.

- Shows disregard for others.

- Can be impetuous.

- Impulsively aggressive.

- Can be associated with narcissistic characteristics.

Narcissistic behaviour is often associated with high levels of charisma, particularly in the short term. Characteristics include:

- High extraversion.

- Dramatic levels of risk taking and associated high variance of performance.

- Need for self-aggrandisement and continuous nurturing of self-esteem.

- Lack of interest in forming and maintaining caring relationships.

- Relationships with followers deteriorating over time.

- Low levels of integrity.

- Willingness to endorse unethical practices for personal gain.

- Poor interpersonal management skills.

- Frequent need to move on to establish new relationships in order to nurture ego.

- Belief in self as a leader (a legend in their own mind).

- Negatively perceived as a leader by others.

- Aggression or other negative behaviours if threatened (this is an important sign for followers that the leader's behaviour is dysfunctionally charismatic behaviour).

Unfortunately the dysfunctional behaviours listed above are not uncommon in senior leaders. It is therefore helpful to be alert to the differences between functional and dysfunctional charismatic behaviour. Functional charisma seems to be beneficial both to leaders and to followers.

SELF-REFLECTION SEPARATES FUNCTIONAL FROM DYSFUNCTIONAL CHARISMA

Self-reflection appears to be the differentiating attribute between those leaders who are functionally charismatic and those who are dysfunctional. For leaders to exhibit functional forms of charisma they must be highly self-reflective and invite regular feedback and criticism from colleagues and teams. It is easy to slip into some of the negative behaviours to the eventual disadvantage of all concerned.

Resilience

> *I have always said that if all else fails I could drive a bus. Interview 70 CEO.*

Resilience is discussed in more depth in Chapter 3. Suffice to say here that toughness and resilience were characteristics that came through again and again in the interviews. We got the impression that none of these leaders would be knocked over easily and if they were they would be able to bounce back very rapidly. The following comment comes from a former Police Commissioner who was responsible for long overdue and extensive reforms but who, at one stage, was attacked mercilessly by a media being fed information by those who did not want the reforms to go ahead. It illustrates the kind of resilience that senior leaders need in order to carry out their responsibilities:

> *I think part of it is not being ego driven. It's not about me. I'm doing a task and if you took my early days in the police, it was all about achieving reform and being focused on the task helped. When people try to attack you personally ... I kind of look at it and think 'that may be your opinion but here is the reality'. Or I may not even value their opinion. There are people whose opinion I don't respect at all so why should I give them the capacity to get under my skin. What you're there for is to achieve the goals, or to focus on the task - you need to stay focused on that. And if you stuff it up then it is about saying, 'oh, you've stuffed that up, what can you learn from it,' and that creates a sense of optimism, that this too will pass, and we need to work out way through these issues. I had great advice years ago which was, 'let some things go through to the keeper'... It's important to understand that your whole self is not invested in this role or task, but you'll do your best. In that sense you know you have to protect yourself as well. Interview 70 CEO.*

Determination and Courage

Related to resilience, determination and the courage to take on, or work around any obstacles that were placed in their way, was also an overriding impression.

> *On a merger between two organisations in the telecommunications industry, involving over 4000 people, I had access to the right people in that steering committee to drive decisions and I didn't let up. I asked who I could and couldn't touch and they said you can touch anyone. That was my remit and off I went. Interview 63 CPM.*

I think the final statement should be left to another of the leaders interviewed:

> *Giving up was never a possibility for us. You have to think of what else you can do. So I think that absolute focus on end delivery which is how we started right at the beginning just set the tone for everything else. That means for me personally, I have to be the ultimate owner of that. You need a team around you who share that view, but if I give way on the key elements, I'm setting a dreadful example for the teams and I really have to watch that. Interview 48 PD/GM.*

In Summary

Charismatic (and transformational) leaders tend to have:

- High self-confidence.

- Superior verbal ability.

- Ability to express themselves non-verbally.

- High need for influence or power.

- Exceptionally strong convictions that what they are doing is ethically justifiable.

- Determined and able to persist in the face of high risks and major obstacles.

- Satisfaction from the process of leading others.

- A high need for influence and to be influential.

- More need for flexibility and change.

Compared with non-charismatic leaders, charismatic leaders are reported to:

- Show more concern for the professional growth of their followers.

- Engage in more developmental efforts such as coaching, role modelling by personal example, and providing guidance and developmental experiences.

- Be more inclined to nurture people around them.

- Have high levels of pragmatism.

- Be more compassionate.

- Be more insightful.

- Show lower levels of dominance and aggression.

- Be less critical of others.

Charismatic leadership is a group phenomenon, assigned by the group and dependent upon group cohesion.

Charisma can also be dysfunctional – associated with destructive tendencies based on personal self-interest that do not benefit the group in the long term.

The differentiator between functional and dysfunctional charisma seems to be the leader's propensity for self-reflection and willingness to invite honest feedback about themselves as leaders.

Resilience, determination and courage were also dominant traits that came through in the interviews – not least amongst the key essential attributes.

Final Note

Conducting the research for this book, especially having the opportunity to meet and interview so many exceptional project leaders was a real pleasure. I would like to thank them for giving so freely of their time and knowledge.

References and Further Reading

Atwater, L.E., Camobreco, J.F., Dionne, S.D., Aviolio, B.J. and Lau, A.N. (1997) Effects of Rewards and Punishments on Leader Charisma, Leader Effectiveness and Follower Reactions. *Leadership Quarterly*, 8, pp. 133–152.

Atwater, L.E. and Yammarino, F. (1989) Transformational Leadership Among Midshipmen Leaders at the U.S. Naval Academy. Technical Report No. ONR-TR-6. Office of Naval Research, Arlington, Virginia.

Awamleh, R. and Gardner, W.L. (1999) Perceptions of Leader Charisma and Effectiveness: The Effects of Vision Content, Delivery, and Organizational Performance. *Leadership Quarterly*, 10, pp. 345–373.

Bass, B.M. (1988) Evolving Perspectives on Charismatic Leadership. In: Conger, J.A. and Kanungo, R.N. (eds), *Charismatic Leadership: The Elusive Factor in Organizational Effectiveness*, pp. 40–77. San Francisco, CA: Jossey-Bass.

Bass, B.M. (1985a) *Leadership and Performance Beyond Expectations*. New York, NY: The Free Press.

Bass, B.M. (1985b) Leadership: Good, Better, Best. *Organizational Dynamics*, 13, pp. 26–40.

Binning, J., Zoba, A. and Whatham, J. (1986) Explaining the Biasing Effects of Performance in Terms of Categorization Theory. *Academy of Management Journal*, 29, pp. 521–535.

Calder, B.J. (1977) An Attributional Theory of Leadership. In: Staw, B.M. and Salancik, G.R. (eds), *New Directions in Organizational Behavior*, pp. 179–204. Chicago, IL: St. Clair Press.

Choi, Y. and Mai-Dalton, R.R. (1999) The Model of Followers' Responses to Self-sacrificial Leadership: An Empirical Test. *Leadership Quarterly*, 10, pp. 397–421.

Clover, W.H. (1988) Transformational Leaders: Team Performance, Leadership Ratings and First-hand Impressions. In: Clark. K.E. and Clark, M.B. (eds), *Measures of Leadership*. West Orange, NJ: Leadership Library of America.

Conger, J.A. and Kanungo, R.N. (1998) *Charismatic Leadership in Organizations*. Thousand Oaks, CA: Sage.

Conger, J.A., Kanungo, R.N. and Menon, S.T. (2000) Charismatic Leadership and Follower Effects. *Journal of Organizational Behavior*, 21, pp. 747–767.

De Cremer, D. (2002) Charismatic Leadership and Cooperation in Social Dilemmas: A Matter of Transforming Motives? *Journal of Applied Social Psychology*, 32, pp. 997–1016.

De Cremer, D. and van Knippenberg, D. (2002) How do Leaders Promote Cooperation? The Effects of Charisma and Procedural Fairness. *Journal of Applied Psychology*, 87, pp. 858–866.

Deluga, R.J. (1995) The Relationship Between Attributional Charismatic Leadership and Organizational Citizenship Behavior. *Journal of Applied Social Psychology*, 25, pp. 1652–1669.

Emrich, C.G., Brower, H.H., Feldman, J.M. and Garland, H. (2001) Images in Words: Presidential Rhetoric, Charisma, and Greatness. *Administrative Science Quarterly*, pp. 46, 527–557.

Ensari, N. and Murphy, S.E. (2003) Cross-cultural Variations in Leadership Perceptions and Attribution of Charisma to the Leader. *Organizational Behavior and Human Decision Processes*, 92, pp. 52–66.

Fiol, C.M., Harris, D. and House, R. (1999) Charismatic Leadership: Strategies for Effecting Social Change. *Leadership Quarterly*, 10, pp. 449–482.

Fuller, J.B., Patterson, C.E.P., Hester, K. and Stringer, D.Y. (1996) A Quantitative Review of Research on Charismatic Leadership. *Psychological Reports*, 78, pp. 271–287.

Glassman, R. (1975) Legitimacy and Manufactured Charisma. *Social Research*, 42, pp. 615–636.

Haslam, S.A., Platow, M.J., Turner, J.C., Reynolds, K.J., McGarty, C., Oakes, P.J., Johnson, S., Ryan, M.K. and Veenstra, K. (2001) Social Identity and the Romance of Leadership: The Importance of Being Seen to be Doing it for us. *Group Processes and Intergroup Relations*, 4, pp. 191–205.

Holladay, S. J. and Coombs, W.T. (1993) Communicating Visions: An Exploration of the Role of Delivery in the Creation of Leader Charisma. *Management Communication Quarterly*, 6, pp. 405–427.

Holladay, S.J. and Coombs, W.T. (1994) Speaking of Visions and Visions Being Spoken. *Management Commilrnication Quarterly*, 8, pp. 165–189.

House, R.J. (1977) A 1976 Theory of Leadership. In: Hunt, J.G. and Larson, L.L. (eds), *Leadership: The Cutting Edge*, pp. 189–207. Carbondale, IL: Southern Illinois University Press.

House, R.J. and Howell, J.M. (1992) Personality and Ship. *Leadership Quarterly*, 3, pp. 81–108.

House, R.J., Spangler, W.D. and Woycke, J. (1991) Personality and Charisma in the U.S. Presidency: A Psychological Theory of Leader Effectiveness. *Administrative Science Quarterly*, 36, pp. 364–396.

House, R.J. and Shamir, B. (1993) Toward the Integration of Transformational, Charismatic, and Visionary Theories. In: M.M. Chemers and R. Ayman (eds), *Leadership Theory and Research: Perspectives and Directions*, pp. 81–108. San Diego, CA: Academic Press.

Howell, J.M. and Avolio, B.J. (1993) Transformational Leadership, Transactional Leadership, Locus of Control, and Support for Innovation: Key Predictors of Consolidated-business-unit Performance. *Journal of Applied Psychology*, 78, pp. 891–902.

Hunt, J.G., Boal, K.B. and Dodge, G.E. (1999) The Effects of Visionary and Crisis-responsive Charisma on Followers: An Experimental Examination of Two Kinds of Charismatic Leadership. *Leadership Quarterly*, 10, pp. 423–448.

Kirkpatrick, S.A. and Locke, E.A. (1996) Direct and Indirect Effect of Three Core Charismatic Leadership Components on Performance and Attitudes. *Journal of Applied Psychology*, 81, pp. 36–51.

Lowe, K.B., Kroeck, K.G. and Sivasubramaniam, N. (1996) Effectiveness Correlates of Transformational and Transactional Leadership: A Meta-analytic Review of the MLQ Literature. *Leadership Quarterly*, 7, pp. 385–425.

Maslow, A.H. (1943) A Theory of Human Motivation. *Psychological Review*, 50(4), pp. 370–396.

Meindl, J.R. (1993) Reinventing Leadership: A Radical, Social Psychological Approach. In: Murnighan, J.K. (ed.), *Social psychology in organizations: Advances in theory and research*, pp. 89–118. Englewood Cliffs, NJ: Prentice Hall.

Oberg, W. (1972) Charisma, Commitment, and Contemporary Organization Theory. *MSU Business Topics*, 20, pp. 18–32.

Oommen, T.K. (1967) Charisma, Social Structure and Social Change. *Comparative Studies in Society and History*, 10, pp. 85–99.

Paul, J., Costley, D.L., Howell, J.P., Dorfman, P.W. and Trafimow, D. (2001) The Effects of Charismatic Leadership on Followers' Self-concept Accessibility. *Journal of Applied Social Psychology*, 31, pp. 1821–1844.

Pillai, R. and Meindl, J. (1991) The Effect of a Crisis on the Emergence of Charismatic Leadership: A Laboratory Study. *Academy of Management Proceedings*, pp. 235–239.

Platow, M.J., van Knippenberg, D., Haslam, S.A., van Knippenberg, B. and Spears, R. (2006) A Special Gift we Bestow on you for Being Representative of us: Considering Leader Charisma from a Self-categorization Perspective. *British Journal of Social Psychology*, 45, pp. 303–320.

Platow, M.J. and van Knippenberg, D. (2001) A Social Identity Analysis of Leadership Endorsement: The Effects of Leader in Group Prototypicality and Distributive Intergroup Fairness. *Personality and Social Psychology Bulletin*, 11, 1508–1519.

Podsakoff, P. and Todor, W. (1985) Relationships Between Leader Reward and Punishment Behavior and Group Processes and Productivity. *Journal of Management*, I l(l), pp. 55–73.

Rogers, C. (1961) *On Becoming a Person: A Therapist's View of Psychotherapy.* Boston: Houghton Mifflin.

Shamir, B. (1992) Attribution of Influence and Charisma to the Leader: The Romance of Leadership Revisited. *Journal of Applied Social Psychology*, 22, pp. 386–407.

Shamir, B., Arthur, M.B. and House, R.J. (1994) The Rhetoric of Charismatic Leadership: A Theoretical Extension, a Case Study, and Implications for Research. *Leadership Quarterly*, 5, pp. 25–42.

Shamir, B., House, R.J. and Arthur, M.B. (1993) The Motivational Effects of Charismatic Leadership: A Self-concept Based Theory. *Organization Science*, 4, pp. 577–594.

Shamir, B., Zakay, E., Brainin, E. and Popper, M. (2000) Leadership and Social Identification in Military Units: Direct and Indirect Relationships. *Journal of Applied Social Psychology*, 30, pp. 612–640.

Shamir, B., Zakay, E., Breinin, E. and Popper, M. (1998) Correlates of Charismatic Leader Behavior in Military Units: Subordinates' Attitudes, Unit Characteristics, and Superiors' Appraisals of Leader Performance. *Academy of Management Journal*, 41, pp. 387–409.

Shea, C.M. and Howell, J.M. (1999) Charismatic Leadership and Task Feedback: A Laboratory Study of their Effects on Self-efficacy and Task Performance. *Leadership Quarterly*, 10, pp. 375–396.

Sidani, Y.M. (1993) Perceptiom of Charisma: The Influence of Leader Attributes, Leader Speech, and Follower Self-esteem. Unpublished Doctoral Dissertation, University of Mississippi, Oxford, MS.

Waldman, D., Bass, B. and Yammarino, F. (1990) Adding to Contingent Reward Behavior: The Augmenting Effect of Charismatic Leadership. *Group and Organization Studies*, 15, pp. 382–395.

Weber, M. (1947) *The Theory of Social and Economic Organization* (Parsons, T., Ed.) (Henderson, A.M. and Parsons, T., Trans.). New York: Oxford University Press.

Yagil, D. (1998) Charismatic Leadership and Organizational Hierarchy: Attribution of Charisma to Close and Distant Leaders. *Leadership Quarterly*, 9, pp. 161–176.

Yammarino, F. and Bass, B. (1990) Long-term Forecasting of Transformational Leadership and its Effects Among Naval officers. In: Clark, KE. and Clark, M.B. (eds), *Measures of Leadership*, pp. 151–169. West Orange, NJ: Leadership Library of America.

Yorges, S.L., Weiss, H.M. and Strickland, O.J. (1999) The Effect of Leader Outcomes on Influence, Attributions, and Perceptions of Charisma. *Journal of Applied Psychology*, 84, pp. 428–436.

Index

Abolafia, M. 218, 219
abstract concepts 136
accountability 175, 178, 181, 203
   avoiding 270
   awareness of 271
   and governance 233, 234, 236, 237,
      239, 240, 247, 254
   and key roles 259–60, 270–72, 273
accuracy 32, 299
achievement 168, 172
Ackerman, F. et al. 276
actions 40, 92, 114, 153, 157,170
   and crises 212, 213, 214, 223ff.
   political 200
adaptability 4, 5, 6, 123, 127, 128, 129,
      131, 147, 157
adaptive systems 16, 17, 110, 117, 151,
      211, 212, 213, 246, 251, 289
adversarial relationships 261, 275,
      276, 279, 286, 289
adversity 36, 37, 38, 70, 171, 220
advice 247, 254, 299
   network 44, 45
affiliative attributes 168, 172
agency project management 282
aggression 204–5, 307, 311, 312, 315
aggressive-defensive cultures 168,
      169, 172
agreeableness 56, 200
agreements 196, 286, 289
   see also charters
Agrell, A. and Gustafson, R. 134

Albrecht, T.L. and Adelman, M.B. 59
alliances 177, 191, 200, 272, 276, 278,
      280, 283, 286
alternatives 54, 148, 149, 151, 153, 246
altruism 57
ambiguity 3, 20, 22, 24, 26, 59, 122,
      130, 263
   strategic use of 58
analysis skills 123, 137, 140, 264
Annabile, T.M. 138
Annabile, T.M. and Gryskiewicz, S.S.
      138
anti-social behaviour 83
anxiety 35, 36, 41, 55, 59, 138, 152
apologies 200
appropriateness 32, 81
approval 169, 172
Aranguren, MJ. et al. 251
argumentativeness 50, 53
Argyris, C. and Schön, D. 133
Aristotle 43
arrogance 182, 299, 301, 302
artefacts, cultural 170, 171, 173, 174,
      176, 177
arts 181
Ashby, W.R. 103, 104
Ashurst, C. et al. 107
Asia 234, 237, 287
assertiveness 199
assessment 19, 82, 191, 194, 198, 202,
      222, 260, 271, 296
associative thinking 123, 124

assumptions-busting 134
assuredness 50, 52, 55
attractors 157–8, 212
audacity 199
auditing 192, 282
Australia 87, 179–80, 214, 221, 240,
    245 *see also* Sydney
authority 25, 184, 224, 236, 237, 245,
    257, 260, 261, 267–70, 273, 306
avoidance 58, 169, 172, 194, 270
Avolio, B.J. et al. 56
Awamleh, K. and Gardner, W.I. 31,
    51, 52, 53, 310
Axelrod, R. and Cohen, M.D. 17, 211,
    251

Babrow, A.S. et al. 19
baby boomers 184
Baccarini, D. 5, 16
backstabbing 195, 204
Backström, T. 111
Bacon, Francis 1
'bad news' 242, 272
barriers *see* obstacles
Bass, B.M. 306, 307
Baumeister, R.F. et al. 300, 301
Bechara, A. 153
Bechara, A. et al. 153
behaviour 39, 83, 84, 86, 92, 121, 149,
    151, 243, 250, 297, 307, 309
  cultural 168
  dysfunctional 64, 204–5, 244, 270,
    306, 311–12, 315
  emergent 87
  ingratiating 196–7, 199
  pathological 205, 207
  political 190, 194, 202; *see also*
    political activity
  transformational 56
  and uncertainty 58

Belbin, R.M. 85, 86
beliefs 36, 37, 38, 56, 59, 154, 160, 310
benefits 107, 108, 235, 265, 271, 272
  business 105
  integrated approach 105
Bennis, W. 90
Berger, C.R. 36
Berger, C.R. and Bradac, J. 35
Berger, C.R. and Calabrese, R.J. 35
biases 60
'big picture' view 103, 105
Billikopf 166
blame 203, 207, 226, 270
Blomqvist, K. et al. 60
Blumen-Lippman, J. 270
Board 96–7, 98, 99, 108, 196, 259
Borgatti, S.P. and Cross, R. 57
BOT projects 280, 281
bottlenecks 34, 112
boundaries 171–8, 212, 233, 250, 251,
    272
bounded rationality 148
Boyd, B.K. and Fulk, J. 155, 156, 216
Bradley, G. 105
brain 148, 153
brainstorming 134
Branden, N. 300
Brashers, D.E. 35, 57, 59
Brashers, D.E. et al. 58
brevity 52, 53
Brown, A.D. 61, 219
budget 3, 5, 104, 105, 177, 250
bullying 204
Burke, R.J. 83
Bushman, B.J. and Baumeister, R.F.
    301
business management 108
business support 235

Caldeira, M. and Dhillon, G. 108

calmness 200
Canada 180
career advancement 196
career pathways 113
caring 306, 311
Carpenter, G.A. 150
catalytic probes 157
cause and effect 4, 18, 20, 271
causes 21, 22, 24, 124, 134, 148, 271
Cavaleri, S.A. and Fearon, D.S. 114
central figures 48
CEOs 196–7, 205, 234
    see also executive project leaders
certainty 17, 18, 34, 55, 58, 250, 283
    illusion of 279
challenge 6, 84, 128, 129, 133, 139,
        140, 296
Chan, A.C. 281
change 3, 7, 8, 15, 20, 22, 24, 25, 33, 35,
        87, 105, 110, 124, 133, 157, 241,
        306
    of leaders 203–4
    overcoming obstacles 129
    see also organisational change
chaos 17, 18, 111, 211, 212, 246, 250
    'edge of' 216
    see also crisis management
charisma 49ff., 200, 305–19
    assignment of 307–9
    and communication 310
    definition of 306–7
    functional 312, 314, 315
    and groups 308–9, 315
    negative aspects 311–12, 315
charters 201, 252, 254, 286, 289
Cherulnik, P.D. et al. 56
China 180, 181
choices 148, 149, 153
Christensen, C.R. et al. 121
Christiaans, H. 137

Cialdini, R.B. 197
clarification 219, 227
clarity 52, 53, 55, 93, 214, 258, 271
Cleland, D. 89
Clements, C. and Washbush, J.B. 83
clients 21, 278, 281, 282, 283, 284
Clift, T.B. and Vandenbosch, M.B. 23
'climate' 166, 170, 171; see also
        organisational cultures
cliques 195
Clore, G.L. and Huntsinger, J.R. 153
club atmosphere 171
coaching 206, 207, 307, 314
coalitions 200
co-dependent tasks 25
codes 45
cognition 123, 148–9, 151
cognitive complexity 148–9
cognitive mapping 223
Cohen, M.D. et al. 153
Cohen, W.M. and Levinthal, D.A. 157
collaboration 126, 288
Collaborative Working Agreement
        283
command-control notions 4, 5
commercial organisations 33, 107, 258
common patterns 45, 71
communication 4, 7, 25, 31–72, 184,
        242, 281
    and charisma 310
    and complexity 32–4
    in crisis 219, 222, 225
    and cultural differences 176, 182–3
    formal 60–61
    interpersonal 35
    in large projects 32–3
    and leadership 31, 32, 48–53
    networks 32, 41–8
        informal 42–4
        patterns 45–7

pathways 43
planning 61–70, 72
problems 46–8, 66–7
'rich' 42, 212, 214
risks 61, 62ff.
see also communication skills;
    communication styles
communication gap 108, 111
communication skills 126, 261, 263
communication styles 48–9, 59, 71–2
  and knowledge sharing 54–7
  and programmes 111
  in teams 56–7, 84
    personality differences 86
  verbal 49–51ff.
community 132, 278
compassion 307, 314
compatibility 84, 261
competence 92, 93, 167
competition 169, 170, 172, 181, 192, 282
complex problems 122, 123
complex projects 1–2, 11, 24–6
  accountability in 271–2
  communications planning 61–70
  and control 5
  definition of 3
  duration of 6, 8
  failed 3, 14, 108, 280
  indicators of 13, 19–21
  multi-partner 60
  and political influencing 197ff.
  recognition of 13, 14–16
  specific factors 13, 21–4
  and uncertainty 34–7ff.
complex systems 17
complexity 26, 87, 105, 135, 246
  assessment of 22, 239
  aversion to 15
  cognitive 148–9
  and communication 32–4
  directional sources of 106

early recognition of 13, 14–16
lack of understanding of 15
levels 110, 112, 257, 260ff., 271
and procurement 276, 282, 284
programme management 112–13
sources of 8, 62, 105, 106, 241, 265,
276 *see also* directional sources;
    temporal sources
strategies 110
temporal sources of 106, 155
types 110, 112
  and personnel 114
complexity theory 4, 7, 20, 22, 104–5,
    111, 157–8, 216, 217, 250, 251,
    265, 276, 296
complicated projects 13, 14, 16, 17, 18
  and problems 123
computers 109, 184, 266
confidence 19
conflict 4, 169, 190, 276, 279
  minimising 6
conflicts of interest 192–3
confusion 130
connections 6, 21
consequences 149
consistency 92, 93
constraints 34, 58, 93, 99, 104, 110,
    125, 130, 138, 175, 239, 251, 254
construction projects 87, 128, 133, 217
  project managed contracts 281–2
  and team selection 83
constructive cultures 168, 172
consultants, external 269
consultation 199
context 19, 22, 60, 92–3, 99, 134, 219
contingency 309
contracting process 60, 279ff.
contractors 259, 278ff.
  financing 281
control 4, 5, 16, 17, 18, 33, 93, 94, 104,
    251

conventions 169, 172
convergence 123, 124
'conversation models' 52
conviction 306, 310, 314
Cooke, R.A. 168, 169, 172, 175, 181
cooperation 56, 59, 91, 168, 283, 284
co-optation 200
co-ordination 215, 221, 239
coping 37, 38
corporate governance 235, 236
    see also project governance
cost-effectiveness 280
Coster, K. 288
costs 21, 23, 113, 151, 238–9, 262, 264,
        265, 283
    minimisation 277
    sharing 282–3
courage 206, 212, 214, 261, 293, 305,
        313, 315
Crawford, L. et al. 14
creativity 23, 35, 131, 157, 168, 223,
        277
    and learning 133
    and problem-solving 121, 123–5,
        126, 130
        technical and design 131–2
    stifling of 36, 70
    and time pressure 137, 138–9, 140
crime reduction programme 247
crisis management 211–30
    decision-making 214, 215, 219, 220
    implementation 215, 223–5, 227
    leadership qualities 213–18, 226–8
    preparation for 215, 222–3, 224,
        227
    research 214
critical thinking 123–4
criticism 171, 307, 312, 315
cronyism 193
Cross, N. 136
Cross, N. and Clayburn, A. 137

cross-agency projects 25
cross-cultural factors 25, 65, 66,
        165, 179, 249 see also cultural
        differences
cultural audit 172–3
cultural differences 36, 51, 106, 165,
        166, 182, 183, 185–6, 202, 203,
        234, 235, 239, 287
    and communication risks 66–7
    corporate 238
    and governance 238–9, 248, 249
    and joint ventures 238
    national, inventory of 179–81
    and negative political actions
        202–3, 207
    and time 174–5
    within organisations 176, 178
    see also cultural sensitivities;
        project cultures
cultural inventory 168–70
cultural misfits 172, 173
cultural norms 66, 168, 169, 178, 202,
        207, 242, 243
    see also cultural differences
cultural practices 175, 250, 286
cultural sensitivities 3, 26, 36, 51, 88,
        168ff., 269, 272
    see also cultural differences
cultures see cultural differences;
        national cultures;
        organisational cultures
Currie, G. and Brown, A. 218
cycles 21, 22, 56
    virtuous 23
    viscious 276
Czepiel, J.A. 47

Damasio, A.R. 153
Damasio, A.R. et al. 153
De Janasz, S.C. et al. 206
De Meyer, A. et al. 5, 24

De Vries, R.E. et al. 49, 50, 51, 52, 54, 56, 57
Dearborn, D.C. and Simon, H.A. 122
decision theory 148–9
decision-making 8, 20, 43, 61, 147, 236, 237, 239, 241–2, 250, 254
    in crises 214, 215, 219, 220
    and cultural practices 175, 177
    delay 20, 22
    and emotions 148, 151, 153
    and knowledge sharing 54
    rational 148–9
    and risk 157
    testing 154, 155
    and time 23
    and uncertainty 35, 150, 158
decomposition techniques 123
defence projects 22, 31, 32, 85, 130, 138, 206, 212, 217, 238, 259, 276, 283
deference 179
delays 20, 22, 34
Delhi Airport project 179
Den Hartog, D.N. and Verburg, R.M. 31
DePaolo, C.A. 92
departments 114, 176
dependence 36, 47, 53, 70, 169, 172
Dervin, B. 218
Deshpande, R. and Webster Jr., F.E. 166
design 22, 23, 124, 126, 136–7, 140, 281, 282
design problems 122
design solutions 131–2
despair 133
determination 128, 268, 293, 305, 306, 313, 315
development 109, 112, 135, 136, 277, 281, 307, 314
Dewan, T. and Myatt, D.P. 52, 55

dialogue 39, 47, 242–3, 249, 254, 288
differences 59–60, 63, 84, 85–6, 149, 182
    see also cultural differences
differentiation, cognitive 148
difficulty 18, 133
diffuseness 4, 25, 45, 48, 63, 124, 155, 175, 177, 203, 216, 237, 258, 259, 273
DiMaggio, P. and Powell, W.W. 157
direct project management 282
direction 52, 53, 110
directional complexity 106, 112, 113
directional sources 106
disciplines 2, 47, 51, 85, 111, 131, 239, 243, 253, 260
disorder 5
disparate concepts 138
dispute resolution 240, 248, 287
distraction 138
distress 38, 58
distrust 190, 286
divergence 123, 124, 246, 264
Dolan, R.J. 151
dominance 307, 311, 315
Dorner, D. 122
Dorst, K. 137
double loop learning 133
DuBrin, A. 192, 194, 195
Dulaini, M.F. and Dalziel, R.C. 281
Dwivedi, R.S. 90
Dykstra, C.A. 270

Earley, P.C. 90
Earned Value Management 86, 264, 283
Eco, Umberto 13, 19
ecology 104
economic models 155
education 111, 129, 132
effects 22, 26, 36, 106, 271

efficiency, internal 134
ego 296, 301, 312
Einstein, Albert 121
Eisenberg, E.M. 35, 58
Eisner, H. 17
elaboration 123
electronic communication 67
Elkington, J. 278
Ellis, S. and Shpielberg, N. 156, 157
Ely, R.J. et al. 206
emergence 4, 6, 22, 26, 33, 70, 87, 105, 107, 110, 133, 139, 147, 213, 250, 251, 270
    see also risk patterns
Emmons, R.A. 299, 301
emotions 38, 39, 50, 56, 71, 159, 160, 182, 194, 197, 207, 220, 221
    and decision-making 148, 151, 153
    and stress 151–2
empathy 131
employees 138, 178, 192
    and trust 91
empowerment 308
Emrich, C.G. et al. 310
encouragement 59, 61, 92, 93, 99, 137, 168, 172
end-to-end packages 280
energy 88, 95ff.
Engeström, Y. 133
engineering projects 89
engineers 136, 138
enthusiasm 56, 57
entrepreneurs 24
environmental degradation 277
environmental impacts 20, 21, 24, 25, 34, 87, 104, 107, 108
environmental scanning 155–6, 216
errors 17, 60, 156, 169, 281, 296
ethics 190, 306, 310
Europe 287
evaluation 59, 108, 124, 137, 235

events 12, 18, 20, 25, 26, 37, 105, 155, 213
evidence 152, 154, 155, 215, 220, 227, 247
examples 40
executive project leaders 83, 86, 173
    and cultural practices 175
    energising 95–7ff.
    negative qualities 298, 301–2
    and organisational change 109
    political behaviour 191, 197, 204
    replacement of 267–8
    role capabilities 260–62
    see also Board 96
executive sponsors 6, 14, 21, 26, 84, 88, 89, 93, 105, 191–2, 204, 213, 258
    and accountability 271
    and governance 233
executives 1, 2, 14, 15, 21, 41, 155, 239
    see also Board; executive project leaders executive sponsors
Exline, J.J. and Geyer, A. 296, 300, 301
Exline, J.J. et al. 300
expansive learning 133
experience 14, 15, 21, 35, 86, 153, 192
experiment 93, 158
expertise 21, 113, 157, 200, 260
experts 18, 114, 136, 157, 247, 248, 260, 266
    and knowledge sharing 57
explorative learning 133
expressiveness 49, 50, 51
extraversion 56, 311

face-saving 203, 205, 207
facilitation 47, 131, 212, 221, 265, 286, 288
fairness 90, 91
faith 20, 94, 225
    loss of 20, 22, 113, 190, 284
favourable distortions 300

favouritism 193, 204
favours 196, 197, 199
fear 69, 93, 94, 152, 155, 262
feedback 112, 184, 193, 225, 228, 312,
     315
Feldman, M.S. and March, J.G. 156
Fermi, Enrico 219
Ferris, G.R. et al. 199
Fiol, C.M. et al. 310
'firefighting' 139
first principles 136
fixed price contracting 279–80
flattery 196, 197, 199
flexibility 4, 6, 70, 87, 103, 104, 110,
     111, 123, 126, 236, 289
   and governance 250–51, 254
   need for 306, 314
   and procurement 284–5
Florian, V. et al 38
Flyvberg, B. et al. 247
focus 61, 108, 111, 124, 138, 139, 140,
     152, 159, 201, 225, 234
followers 307–9, 311, 314
Fonseca, J. 105
Ford, L.A. et al. 59
forecasting 86
formal channels 157
formal communication process 59–61,
     71
forums 237, 267, 272
France 179
Frankl, V. 167
Fredrickson, B.L. and Levenson, R.W.
     38
Fredrickson, J.W. 156
Fredrickson, J.W. and Mitchell, T.R,
     156
freedom 46, 93, 167, 184, 190, 299
Frese, M. et al. 31
Frey, D. et al. 57

friendliness 51, 53
fun 133
functional roles 112, 114
future 5, 6, 134, 149, 153

gain-pain share 282–4
Galford, R. and Seibold Drapeau, A.
     92
gaming industry 88
Gareis, R. 170
Garland, R. 237
gatekeeper 47
Gehring, D.R. 2
gender 153, 181, 197
generalists 115
Generation X 184
Generation Y 184
generational culture 183–5, 186
generative learning 133
genuineness 199
geography 68
Geraldi, J. 19, 20, 190
Geraldi, J. and Adlbrecht, G. 19, 20,
     190
Germany 179, 287
Gersick, C.J.G. 24
Giarni, O. and Stahel, W.R. 35
Girmscheid, G. and Brockman, C. 34
Gladwell, M. 216
Glassman, R. 306
Gleick, J. 211
Global Financial Crisis (GFC) 87
globalisation 185, 186
goal-path 8, 16, 25, 33, 106, 113
goals 5, 6, 7–8, 16, 49, 59, 113, 124,
     125, 126, 154, 220, 223, 225
   changing 241
   collective 308
   and communication 33
   inspirational 199

multiple 149–50
uncertainty about 24, 25, 130
Goldsmith, D.J. 36
governance *see* corporate governance;
    governance teams; project
    governance
governance teams 241, 242, 245, 250,
    251, 252
  and dialogue 243
  questions for 252–3
governments 96, 97, 111, 175, 245,
    259, 276
Green, G.C. 149
Grimsey, D. and Lewis, M.K. 245
groups 4, 7, 42, 43, 45, 136, 149, 180,
    203, 220, 237, 241, 248–9
  and charisma 308–9, 315
  communication 46
    risks 62
  and extraversion 56
  imploded 46
  and project management 283
  size of 258
  team selection 85
  see also teams
growth 6, 38
guidance 307, 314
Gunning, J.G. and McDermott, M.A.
    281
'gut feeling' 153, 218

Hambrick, D.C. 155, 216
happiness 85
hardiness 37–8
Hards, R. 138
harmony 85
Hatch, M.J. 108
Haunschild, P.R. and Sullivan, B.N.
    114, 115
Hauschildt, J. et al. 149

health 301
health sector 35, 107
Heath, L. 157
Helm, Jane 2
Helm, J. and Remington, K. 14, 15, 83,
    242, 260, 263
'heroes' 47, 260, 266–7, 273
hidden agendas 106
high level view 107, 218, 244
Hillson, D. 134, 135
history 170, 171, 185
Ho, C. 136
Hofstede, G. 179, 180, 181, 202
holistic view 262, 271
Holladay, S.J. and Coombs, W.T. 310
Holmquist, M. 133
honesty 92, 248, 250
Horii, T. et al. 238
House, R.J. 307, 310
House, R.J. and Shamir, B. 310
Hovarth, D. et al. 157
humiliation 300, 301
humility 295, 296–301
  effect on others 300
  negative aspects 300–301
  in psychological research 299–300
hunches 153
Hunt, J.G. et al. 310

Ibarra, H. and Hunter, M. 197
iconoclasm 296
ideas 5, 6, 123, 136, 137, 149, 157
imagery 123, 310
imagination 149, 199, 223
immaturity, emotional 200, 207
implementation stategies 110–14
  in crisis management 215, 223–5,
    227
  and governance 249–52
improvisation 149, 199

inclusivity 4, 251
independence 167
individualism 179, 180–81, 184, 203
individuals 4, 7, 46, 47, 57, 60, 114,
        115, 180, 223
    and political activity 194
induction material 272
influence, personal 45, 306, 314
influencing, political 6–7, 37, 43, 199
    upwards 97
    see also political skills
informal networks 40, 42–8
    central figures in 48
    imploded 46
    patterns in 45–6
    problems 43, 45, 46
information 7, 15, 19, 49, 57–61, 91,
        98, 195, 219, 242
    access to 59
    and communication 32, 43, 47
    in crises 213, 216, 226
    and decision-making 148
    discounting negative 58
    environmental 155–6
    exchange 46–7
    formal exchange of 59–61
    gathering 57, 59
    integration 149, 160
    misuse of 57–8
    networks 22, 32, 41–8
    overload, and stress 156
    and personality differences 84
    and problems 122
    reliability of 147, 155–9
    'rich' 36, 158
    roles of 57
    security 115
    selection of 58–9
    sources 58, 59, 155, 156, 198
    validating 59

information flows 6, 135
    formal 157
    informal 157
    and reducing uncertainty 36
information transfer 32, 34, 57ff., 72
infrastructure projects 43, 111, 158,
        170, 176, 278, 280
innovation 18, 23, 47, 114, 121–46,
        157, 158, 159, 199
    and crisis management 215, 220,
        227
    and problem-solving 123
    and project leaders 126–8
    and time pressure 138–9
    see also creativity
insecurity 193, 194, 197
insight 307, 314
Insko, C.A. et al. 56
inspiration 51, 308
instability 6, 23
insularity 171
integration 105, 107, 114
    cognitive 148
intelligence (information) 199, 200,
        203, 207, 249
intentional forgetting 58
interconnectedness 135, 216
interdependence 21, 22, 25, 33, 42,
        216, 264
internal development programmes
        109
international aid 3, 238, 249
international projects 179–83, 202–3,
        205
    governance 234–5, 237ff., 248, 249,
        251
Internet 54, 69, 184, 185, 212, 217,
        266
interviewees 2–3, 25, 49, 58, 65, 85, 89,
        96, 126, 247, 293, 297

interviews 1, 14, 26, 40, 43, 54, 61, 82,
        83ff., 111, 112, 125, 136, 147,
        158, 165, 176, 183, 189, 191, 196,
        202, 204, 205, 206, 213, 216, 217,
        220, 224, 225, 235, 242, 244, 246,
        248, 250, 258, 259, 268, 269, 276,
        313
    length of 297
intuition 153–4, 159
inventory 112
investment 3, 168
    appraisal 109
invincibility 171
Isabella, L.A. 218
IT projects 109, 112, 236, 246
Italy 180
iterative process 124
Ivory, C. and Alderman, N. 5, 16

Jaafari, A. 5, 16
James, E. 213, 214
Jamieson, A. and Morris, P.W. 107
Japan 180, 181
jargon 111, 174
Jensen, J.A. 111
job performance 196
job satisfaction 57, 91
Johnston, D.J. 251
joint ventures 238, 239, 240, 249, 276,
        280
Jones, R. and Deckro, R. 23
justification 200

Kaghan, W.N. and Lounsbury, M.D.
        60
Kefalas, A. and Schoderbek, P. 155,
        216
Kellerman, B. 83
Kelloway, B. 89
Keltner, D. and Bonanno, G.A. 38

Kerzner 114
key issues 59
key players 14, 42, 45, 192, 198, 213,
        215, 221, 224, 227, 234, 236, 240
key roles 257–74
    and accountability 259–60, 270–72
    assignment of 265–7
    authority for 257, 260, 261, 267–70,
        273
    and levels of complexity, 259,
        260ff.
    and redundancy 266
Kirkpatrick, S.A. and Locke, E.A. 31,
        310
Kitchen, P.J. and Daly, F. 35
knowledge 15, 19, 36, 54, 58, 86, 108,
        153, 213, 219, 262
    of consequences 149
knowledge management 114, 115, 117
knowledge sharing 54–7, 86, 115, 128,
        134
    barriers to 69
    human-oriented 54–5
    and trust 56
    willingness for 56
    see also new knowledge
Kobasa, S.C. et al. 37
Koestler, A. 138
Kokotovich, V. 137
Kokotovich, V. and Remington, K.
        126, 127, 279
Kolnai, A. 150
Kooyman, B. and Steel, J. 107, 108,
        111
Kotter, J.P. 5
KPI 271
Krackhardt, D. and Hanson, J.R. 41,
        44, 45, 47, 48
Kramer, M.W. 35, 58
Kreitner, R. 190

Krimmel, J.T. and Lindenmuth, P. 93
Kruglanski, A.W. 57
Kulunga, G.K. and Kuotcha, W.S. 115
Kurchner-Hawkins, R. and Miller, R. 190
Kurtz, E. and Ketcham, K. 300

Lakomsky, G. and Evers, C.W. 153, 218
Landrum, R.E. 299
Langer, E. 57
language 40, 66, 65, 86, 97, 111, 174, 182, 183, 200, 221, 222, 272, 308, 310
large projects 22, 25, 111, 122, 130, 217, 219
    communication in 32, 33
    culture of 170
    decision-making in 158
    team selection for 269
lateral thinking 124
Latham, M. 279
laughter 38, 133
leaders 1, 2, 4, 99, 266
    assignment of charisma to 307–9
    comprehending complexity 14–15
    and control 5
    and cultural misfits 173, 176, 178
    emotionally immature 200, 207
    ineffective 93, 94, 130, 301–2
    and informal networks 44–5
    interviews with 2
    knowledge sharing 54–5
    limited knowledge of 7
    negative behaviour of 193, 195, 196–7
    non-charismatic 307
    performance 54, 55, 267
    and problem-solving 134
    promoting resilience 37, 41

qualities of 81, 85–6, 90, 264–5, 297–8ff.
    tough 223–4
    see also charisma; project leaders
leadership 1–2, 9, 89, 270, 296, 306, 314
    bottom-up 212
    charismatic 49, 50, 51, 52, 53, 54, 55
    communication styles 48–53
    for complex projects 2, 4, 21, 22
    and complexity levels 259, 260ff.
    for crisis management 213–18, 222, 223–4, 226–8
    distrust of 36
    empowering 54, 55
    human-oriented 48, 49, 51, 54–5, 92
    layers 258, 259
    multi-faceted view 81
    myths about 4–7
    research 48
    role capabilities 260–64
    task-oriented 48–9, 51
    top-down 212, 243
leaks 45
learning 5, 7, 18, 38, 114–15, 117, 128, 157, 238, 239, 243, 282
    and crisis management 214, 215, 226, 228
    leaders' capacity for 298, 299
    and design process 136–7, 140
    stimulating 133
    styles 115
legal agreements 286
legal frameworks 248
Lendrum, T. 278, 285, 286
Levin, D.Z. and Cross, R. 54
life cycle 8, 33, 130, 171, 180, 280, 281
linear thinking 4, 7, 20, 123, 124, 135, 152, 160, 214, 223

see also non-linear approaches
linguistic barriers 65
Lipman-Blumen, J. 301
listening 251, 288, 289, 297
litigation 23, 93, 276, 277, 287
'little things' 216, 217, 223
local level 218, 251
logic 123, 124, 223
 see also non-linear approaches
Long-Term Orientation (LTO) 181
loss 111, 217, 265, 271, 280
love 43, 167, 300
low-energy car project 124–5, 131
Lubbe, S. and Remenyi, D. 109
Lui, Y. et al. 196
lump sum contracting 278–80
Lundin, R. and Söderholm, A. 6, 170

McCabe, B. 83
Maccoby, M. 83, 301
McGregor, J. 204
Machiavellian traits 193
McKenna, S. 114
macro-leadership 81
Maguire, S. and McKelvey, B. 6
Maher, M.J. et al. 137
Maitlis, S. 218
management 88, 89, 93, 106, 108,
 114–15, 264
manufacturing industry 24, 93
March, J.G. 133
March, J.G. and Olsen, J.P. 114, 153
Marcus, E. and Stern, H. 265
Marion, R. and Uhl-Bien, M. 3, 6, 296
markets 122, 280
Marris, P. 35
Martinsuo, M. and Dietrich, P. 106
masculinity (MAS) 179, 181
Maslow's hierarchy 166, 167–8
 see also needs

Mason, R.O. and Mitroff, I.I. 122
Mathias, J.R. 130, 136, 137
matrix management 174
meaning 37, 40, 71, 128, 134, 138, 167
 sharing 221, 223
meaning-making
 in crisis management 215, 221–2,
 223
measurement 108, 236
mechanical systems 17
media 96, 98, 313
Mednick, S.A. 138
Melville, N. et al. 109
mental health 301
mental models 7, 23
mentors 57, 105, 116, 203, 206, 207
mergers 88, 122, 128, 171, 205, 313
Merry, U. 58
Meschi, P.X. 238
messages 310
Messick 58
metamotivation 167
metaphor 55, 111, 123, 222, 309
methodologies 135, 236, 263
micromanagement 93–5, 99, 133, 174,
 195, 244, 251, 301
middle-management 134
Middle East 42, 43, 179, 180, 217, 238,
 287
Middleton, E. 125
Midgley, G. 175
Miles, R.E. et al. 156
Miller, D. 155
Mintzberg, H. 5
Mintzberg, H. and Waters, J.A. 110,
 175
Mintzberg, H. et al. 122
misfortune 40
Mishel, M.H. 58
mission statements 170

mistakes 39, 299

misunderstanding 60, 65, 106, 183

mobile telecommunications project 95

models 152, 155
    of others 157

modification 123

Mohr, J. and Spekman, R. 248

Moldoveanu, M. 34

monitoring 16, 105, 108, 109, 113, 154, 155, 156, 159, 201, 228, 236, 282
    costs 239
    in crisis management 215, 225, 228

Morrison, E.W. 58

motivation 33, 56, 83, 86, 91, 92, 96, 128, 133–4, 138, 140, 167, 193, 194, 308

Müller, R. 235, 237

Müller, R. and Geraldi, J.G. 20, 23

multi-national projects 25, 129, 251, 252
    and governance 234–5, 237ff., 249
    and relationship breakdown 287

multi-owner projects 25, 239, 248, 251

multiple goals 148, 149

music 181, 185, 186

mutual understanding 60

Naidoo, L.J. and Lord, R.G. 52

naming 40, 71

Nanus, B. 5

narcissism 38, 205, 298, 301, 306, 311

narrative 222, 223

national cultures 179–80, 181–2, 185, 202–3, 240, 249

nature 16, 17

Neal, R.A. 108

needs 166–7
    deficit 167
    higher-level, 167, 168

lower-level 167, 169

negative behaviour 25, 58, 61, 72, 244, 277–8, 286, 298, 301–2, 311–12
    see also political activity

negative feelings 35, 38

negotiation 126, 173, 199, 200, 205

Nelson, F. 249

nepotism 191, 204

Netherlands 51, 180, 181

network maps 45, 47, 48

networks 22, 25, 206
    building 199
    and communication 32, 41–8
        informal 42–4, 71
    local 251–2
    power and influence 44–5, 197
    social 42

new goals 154

new ideas 23, 44, 112, 122, 125, 129, 299

new knowledge 58, 114, 123, 128, 130, 133, 150

new process 158, 247

Newell, A. and Simon, H.A. 123, 125

Ngowi, A.B. 241

Nguyen, H.Q. 134

niceness 49, 50, 53

'no blame culture' 272

nomenclature 106

non-linear approaches 4, 8, 19, 20, 23, 26, 33, 110, 153, 216, 226, 271, 276
    and problem-solving 123, 133, 135

non-verbal communication 306, 310, 314

Norman, Jonathan 4

norms 42, 43

notes 137

novation 281

novice designers 137

nurturing 307, 314

objective measures 34
observation, capacity for 86, 199, 216, 251, 297
obstacles 114, 128–9
Ochsner, K.N. and Phelps, E. 151
'office politics' 190 see also political activity
OGC 235, 237
Ogulana, S.O. 280
oil and gas industry 86, 88
openness 129, 183, 185, 243, 246, 286, 299, 300
opposition 169, 172
options 57
orchestras 81
order 111
organisational breakdown structures 123
organisational change 35, 109, 111, 112, 122, 126
organisational citizenship behaviours 91
organisational complexity leadership 3, 4
organisational crisis research 58
organisational cultures 166–71, 240, 269
    boundaries 171ff.
    and national cultures 181–2
    definitions 166, 168
    inventory 168ff.
organisational interfaces 197
organisational politics 190, 191, 206
    see also political activity
organisations 3, 4, 6, 16, 21, 105, 106, 115, 156, 157, 170, 214, 278
    cultural differences in 176, 178
    as political cultures 192–3

orienteering 112
originality 123
outcomes 2, 4, 5, 17, 18, 22, 33, 72, 90, 105, 109, 123, 153, 213, 271
    assessment of 241
    optimum 148
    ownership 236
outspokenness 200
ownership 88, 95, 236, 240

pain share 283
Park, S.H. and Ungson, G.R. 238
participation 251
partnering 7, 46, 128, 173, 191, 201
    cultures 286
    international 182–3, 203, 276, 287
        governance 234–5, 237–40
    negative factors 276–8
    procurement strategies 278–84
    relationships 285–9
        developing 285–6, 287
        repairing 286–9
parts 105, 113
    of projects 20, 21, 110, 111, 114
    of systems 104, 116
passive-defensive cultures 168, 169, 172, 175, 181
past 40, 58
path-finding 112
pathways 22, 25, 26, 34, 43, 63, 129, 220
patterns 22, 44, 45, 47, 61, 71, 86, 110, 124, 134, 148, 160, 195, 214, 216ff. 251, 253
    non-linear 213
    see also risk patterns
Payne, J. 23
peers 56
Pelligrinelli, S. and Bowman, C. 108
Penley, L.E. and Hawkins, B. 48

Pennebaker, J.W. et al. 51
people 2, 7, 21, 35, 36, 37, 38, 41, 42, 45, 49, 98, 99, 112, 201, 218, 254, 259, 307
    and culture 166, 175
    and information 57–8
    and knowledge sharing 54
    and negative political activity 191, 195, 203–6
    and project teams 82–9
    in traditional models 239
perceptions 18, 19, 21, 34, 35–6, 85, 92, 93, 166, 175, 182, 310, 312
perfectionism 169, 172
performance 53, 54, 55, 90, 193, 259, 266, 308, 309
    extraordinary 267
    and knowledge sharing 57
    and political skills 196
    self-rated 57
perspectives 212–13, 299
perseverance 181
personal agendas 244
personal attributes 37–8
personal example 307
personal gain 311
personal interactions 38, 49, 60, 84–5, 196
    and cultures 168
personal worth 300
personalities 37, 47, 48, 52, 191, 194
    instruments 85–6
    and teams 82–6, 264
personnel 21, 88, 178, 192
    assessment of 82–3
    replacement of 267–70, 273
    selection 113–14, 264–5, 267–70
persuasion 199
pharmaceutical industry 151–2
phase change 217, 276
Picq, T. 134

Pierce, J.L. and Gardner, D.G. 57
pipeline projects 237, 251
planning 113, 134, 215, 236
    communications 61–70, 72
    see also scenario planning
pleasantness 306
Plowman, D.A. et al. 6, 296
Plowman, D.A. and Duchon, D. 5, 6, 7, 251
PM processes 126–7
Podsakoff, P.M. et al. 56
police leaders 301
police project 112, 233
political activity 190
    negative 191–2, 193, 195, 198, 202–6, 207
        and cultural differences 202–3, 207
    positive 196, 199–200
political culture 191, 192, 249
political mazes 127, 130–31, 140
political skills 196, 221, 265
    influencing 190, 191, 197–201
politics 24, 25, 26, 34, 52, 87, 111, 134, 159
    sensitivity to 58
    see also political activity; political skills
Porter, E.H. 85, 86, 97
portfolios 103, 105, 106, 107
    see also programme management
positive emotions 38, 56, 182, 297–8, 300
positive future 6
positive outcomes 11, 72, 90
possibility 123, 124
power 44–5, 169, 172, 180, 190, 287
    personal 194, 306, 314
power distance (PD) 179–80, 202–3
power struggles 251
practice 1, 2, 18, 82, 85, 86, 238, 250

pragmatism 307, 314
praise 184, 199
preciseness 49, 50, 51, 52, 55
predictability 17, 25
preferences 86
preparation 215, 222–3, 224, 227
present 40, 58
Price, T.L. 270
prices 279–80, 282, 283
Prigogine, I. and Stengers, I. 6
priorities 138, 139
problems
    complicated 123
    definition 124, 130, 137
    framing 137
    ill-behaved 122
    ill-structured 122
    messy 122
    types of 122
    unstructured 122
        strategic 122
    'wicked' 122–6, 140, 243
    see also complex problems;
        problem-solving
problem-solving 7, 14, 35, 39, 239,
    243, 250, 260
    creative 121, 123–5
    negative attitudes 277–8
    routine 123
problem-structuring tools 135–6, 137,
    157
processes 7, 8, 18, 54, 60, 106, 108,
    158, 173, 178, 224
    familiar 58
    formal 32, 71
    informal 32, 42–4, 71
    and problem-solving 124, 125
procurement 113, 116, 128, 177, 238,
    250
    flexibility in 284–52
    strategies 278–84

non-traditional 281–4
    traditional 278, 279–81
product designers 136, 137
product quality 134
productivity 85
profit 271, 277, 283
programme management 103–20, 280
    benefits 107, 108
    business benefits 105
    and communication styles 111
    evaluation 108
    implementation 110–14, 17
    and learning 114–15
    and nature of complexity 112–13
    and organisational change 109
    and personnel selection 113–14
project cultures 170–71, 191
    boundaries 171ff.
project financiers 24
project governance 233–56
    and accountability 233, 234, 236,
        237, 239, 240, 247, 254
    and cultural differences 238–9, 249
    and dialogue 242–3, 249
    implementation 249–52
    joint ventures 238, 239, 240, 249
    local networks 251–2
    multi-national projects 234–5, 237,
        239, 248, 249, 251, 252
    structures 236–7
    success criteria 235, 241
    traditional models 239
    see also governance teams
project leaders 1, 14, 26, 90, 105, 178
    and challenge 133
    changing 203–4, 267–70, 273
    cognitive factors 149
    and environmental information
        156
    human-oriented 48, 49, 54, 55
    and innovative thinking 126–8

and knowledge 15
    sharing 54–5
and politics 190–201, 205–6
satisfaction with 54, 55
structuring role 134
task-oriented 49, 92
and team fragility 47
and trust 89–91
and uncertainty 34
project leadership 49, 85–6
    role capabilities 263–4
project managed contracts 281–2
project management 88, 108, 114, 148,
        151
    agency 282
    direct 282
    literature 16
    models 152
    problem-solving 123
Project Management Offices (PMO)
        171
project managers 14, 15, 21, 35, 46, 83,
        86, 105
    and creative thinking 126–8
    and governance 233
    and political behaviour 192, 206
    relationships 279
    and sponsor behaviour 204
    and staff differences 84
    and trust 93
project organisation 22–3
project partners
    differences among 59–60
project teams 81–99, 111, 178
    assignment of 259
    and crisis management 222
    and culture 170, 171, 173, 178, 182
    and gender roles 181
    and international partners 182–3
    member roles 112
    and negative political actions 205

people matching for 82–6, 264, 267
    relationships 242
    selection and replacement 268–9
    skill sets 86–7ff.
    see also governance teams
Project Wickenby 240
projects 16–18, 105, 106
    collections of 106, 107
    constraints 104
    external 174–5
    in-house 174
    multi-partner 60, 63
    and organisational change 109
    reviews 115
    see also large projects; small
        projects
property development 24, 95
Pryce-Jones, J. 85
psychological profiling 82–3
psychology 148, 29
public aspects 21, 122
public sector 110, 133, 238, 241, 245,
        246, 258, 259, 268, 269, 278
Pundir, A.K. et al. 23
purchase officers 86
purpose 37, 40, 71, 150, 310
Putnam, L.L. 61

quality 168, 172, 277, 281
Queensland 222
questionnaires 45, 198
questions 62–70
QuiNne, L. 204

R&D projects 121, 151–2
rapport 288
Raskin, R.N. and Terry, H. 301
Raskin, R.N. et al. 301
rational thinking 148–50, 153
    deficiencies in 149–50
    see also linear thinking

rationality 192, 199
Reagans, R. and McEvily, B. 56
reasoning 137
reciprocity 56, 57, 197
Reddington, M. et al. 105, 107
redundancy 265–6, 273
reflection 147, 154, 159, 160, 241, 298
regulations 151
reinforcing loops 20, 23
Reiss, G. et al. 108
relationship building 190, 201, 285–6
relationships 34, 35, 46, 49, 56, 59, 90,
 92, 99, 126, 136, 206, 271, 301,
 311, 312
 and cultural differences 166
 and partnering 285–6
 and procurement 279, 285–9
 and project teams 242, 263
 repairing broken 286–9
Remenyi, D. and Sherwood-Smith,
 M. 108
Remington, K. 125
Remington, K. and Crawford, L. 5
Remington, K. and Pollack, J. 16, 22,
 24, 39, 106, 203, 217, 263, 276
Remington, K. and Söderholm, A. 23,
 175
Remington, K. et al. 24
repetition 52, 53
reporting 25, 62, 63, 68, 86, 94, 107,
 116, 128, 177, 242, 250
 inaccurate 247
 standards 174, 177
 upwards 243
representatives 309
reputation 3, 196
Requisite Variety law 104, 116
research 1, 2, 3, 7, 25, 26, 35, 37, 38,
 48, 49, 58, 90, 121, 135, 140, 155,
 196, 218, 260, 276, 293
 cognitive 148, 149

in crisis management 214
on governance 251
on humility 299–300
on political influencing 199
on teams 82, 83
on time pressure 138
on trust 92
resilience 37–9, 40, 71, 159, 305,
 312–13
resistance 178
resources 106, 108, 111, 113, 131, 236,
 265
respect 90, 166, 167, 176, 183, 206, 224
responsibility 203, 236, 259, 270, 271,
 272
responsiveness 4
Restrepo, J. and Christiaans, H. 136
rewards 126, 309
rework 21, 22, 125
Rhodewalt, F. and Morf, C.C. 301
rigidity 61
Riggio, R.E. et al. 31
risk 3, 18, 21, 26, 61, 98, 192, 261, 265
 allocation 224
 and communication planning 62ff.
 and crisis management 222, 223
 and information 157
 mitigation of 128, 140
 ownership 224
 and project management 281, 282
 response development 135
 and time pressure 139
risk assessment 265
 and political activity 193, 202
risk patterns 61, 134, 214, 216, 217,
 221, 222, 224, 227, 263
 non-linear 276
risk-taking 311
Rittel, H. and Webber, M. 122
rivalry 195
role modelling 307, 314

roles 195, 236, 250
    capabilities 260–64, 273
    definition of 271
    see also key roles
root-cause analysis 134
Ross, D.L. 93
routines 58, 93, 94, 123
rules 51, 52, 58, 112, 169

Saarinen, T. 149
safety 167, 169, 250
satisfaction 53, 54, 168, 169, 306, 307, 308, 314
    see also job satisfaction
'satisficing' 34, 125–6, 131, 139, 158
scale 21
scenario planning 134, 222, 223
Schafer, J.A. 93, 94, 95, 301
schedule 5, 19, 22, 23, 24, 35, 62, 67, 87, 95, 105, 110, 112, 131, 219, 239, 250, 262, 265, 283
Schein, E.H. 166, 173
Schneider, B. and Rentsch, J. 166
Schön, D.A. 124, 137
Schwandt, D.L. 3, 7
Schwandt, D.R. and Marquardt, M.J. 296, 298
scientists 138
Scudder, G.D. et al. 20
security 115, 167, 169, 250
security, personal 300
security barriers 69
selection 58, 82–4
selective attention 216
self-acceptance 299
self-actualisation 167, 168, 172
self-aggrandisement 311
self-assurance 52
self-awareness 159, 241, 244, 296, 299, 300

self-belief 312
self-confidence 296, 297, 301, 306, 314
self-enhancement 38
self-esteem 38, 57, 167, 169, 296, 300
    low 299, 300, 301, 311
self-interest 192, 194, 249, 270, 311
self-management 54
self-monitoring 194
self-promotion 199, 300
self-reflection 38, 71, 312; *see also* reflection
self-rescue 203
self-respect 167
self-sacrifice 308, 309
self-transcendence 167
Senge, P. 133
senior project managers 6, 15, 84, 121, 126, 127, 133, 140, 204, 258, 262, 263, 264
sense-making 61, 111, 157, 214, 215, 218–19
Shamir, B. et al. 31, 310
Shapira, I. 184
sharing 7, 8, 54–7, 86
    see also knowledge sharing
Short Term Orientation 181
Sidani, Y.M. 310
Sidwell, A.C. and Ireland, V. 282
signal-detecting 215, 216–18, 227
sign-off 63
Simon, H.A. 34, 121, 122, 125, 126, 130, 131, 134, 148
simple systems 16, 17, 18
simplification 15, 36, 61, 148
Singapore 180
situational awareness 157
skills 4, 11, 35, 39, 57, 65, 83, 113, 116, 123, 134, 140, 158, 244, 247, 251, 260, 261, 263, 264, 268, 312
    and creative thinking 126, 127, 130

political 190ff., 197–202, 206, 207,
     221, 224, 265
  and project management 88
  in project teams 86–7, 91, 94, 97,
     99, 265
  shortages 116, 125
small projects 25–6
  and programmes 105, 106, 110,
     112
Smith, A.J. 280
Smith, M.J. and Liehr, P.R. 37
Smith, P.B. 185
smokescreens 58, 59
Snell, R.S. 61
Snow, Dr John 212
Snowden, D. 18, 123, 157, 213, 251
Snowden, D. and Boone, M. 211, 213
social astuteness 199
social capital 42
social networks 42
social situations 199
social systems 192
society 167, 179, 181, 278
socio-gram 48
Solansky, S.T. 7
solutions 124, 127, 135, 243, 244
     premature 130, 136
     technical and design 131–2
somatic markers 153
Sovacool 248, 251
Spangler, W.D. and House, R.J. 31
specialists 46, 85, 115
speech imagery 53
spin 200
sponsorship 258, 269
     leadership roles 258–9
     see also executive sponsors
sport 181, 185, 186
Spurgeon, Charles 296, 298
Srivastava, A. et al. 54

stability 156
Stacey, R. 2, 6, 16
staff turnover 84, 91, 169
stakeholders 2, 3, 14, 20, 22, 23, 26, 97,
     99, 113, 127, 134, 149, 239
  accountability 240
  changing mindset of 214, 223
  conflicted 128, 132, 140
  confusion among 130
  diversity of 89
  and governance 236, 237, 244,
     245–6, 254
  multiple 25
  and networks 44
  and partnering 278
  in project managed contracts 282
  and resilience 41
  and time 24
  and trust 89–91
standing back 136–7
Stanleigh, Michael 171
status 57, 167, 169, 174, 195
  social 197
stereotyping 58, 166
Stoker, G. 251
Strassman, P. 109
strategic implementation gap 108
strategic implementation team 111
strategic teams 111
strategy 109, 110, 235, 238
  and change 105
  partnering 276, 278
  programme implementation
     110–14
Strauss, W. and Howe, N. 186
strength, personal 52, 167, 299, 310
Strength Deployment Profile 85
strengths 85–6
stress 37, 39, 88, 89, 112, 220
  and emotions 151–2

and information overload 156
Strogatz, S.H. 111
structural barriers 62
structures 58, 109, 112, 134, 137, 174,
    211
    governance 236–7, 246
struggle 40, 114, 133, 192, 251
    see also adversity
Styhre, A. et al. 151, 152, 220
sub-contractors 91, 282, 283
subcultures 45
sub-goals 106, 150
subjective feelings 5, 39, 57, 124, 153,
    193
subordinates 54, 55, 93
success 14, 173–4, 235, 239, 241, 278,
    308, 309
    exceptional 267
Sunnafrank, M. 35
superiors 203
supervision 93, 94
suppliers 43, 278, 282
support structures 2, 4, 21, 235, 262
supportiveness 50, 51–2, 53, 55, 92
surprises 98
surrogates 204
surveys 45
sustainability 277, 278, 281
Sutcliffe, K.M. and Huber, G.P. 59
Sweden 179
Sydney 24
    airport project 111, 122
    cross-city tunnel project 245–6,
        247, 280
    Olympic project 132
    Water North Storage Tunnel 283
symbols 170
systematic approach 243
systems 16–17, 136, 265
    chaordic 111

stabilisation 103, 104–5
Szymczak, C.C. and Walker, D.H.T.
    115

tactics 108, 199
Taikonda, M.V. and Rosenthal, S.R.
    23
talkativeness 56
Tangney, J.P. 299
task-oriented leadership 48, 49, 50,
    51, 92, 93, 99, 193
tax fraud project 238, 240, 259
Team Role Profile 85
teams 4, 15–16, 37, 40, 42, 43, 44,
    81–99, 111, 122, 124, 126, 134,
    159, 233, 308
    and changing cultures 173
    commitment 54, 55
    communication problems 46, 47
    communication styles 56–7
    and creative problem-solving 127
    design 131
    flexibility 87
    size of 258, 268
    strategic 105
    willingness to share 56–7
    see also governance teams; project
        teams; strategic teams
Teboul, J.C.B. 58
technical complxity 112
technical difficulties 21, 23, 25, 69, 265
technical knowledge 262, 264
technical solutions 131–2
technology 8, 20, 23, 110, 132, 184
telecommunications project 105–6
temporal sources 106, 155, 171
temporary organisations 170
tenacity 129
tenders 281, 282
testing 154, 155

Thagard, P. 154
Thagard, P. and Millgram, E. 149, 150
theory 148
    see also research
Thiry, M. 106
Thiry, M. and Deguire, M. 107, 114
Thomas, J. et al. 108
thought suppression 58
threats 155
thrift 181
Thurlow, A. and Mills, J. 218
time 5, 8, 21, 23–4, 25, 34, 87, 104, 105,
        106, 110, 112, 175, 243, 258, 280
    and communication risks 68
    and cultural differences 174–5
    and innovation 137, 138–9, 140
        negative effects 138, 139
        positive effects 138, 139
    see also temporal sources
timing 199
tipping point 216–17, 227, 276
tools 22, 39–40, 135–7, 174
    problem structuring 135, 136
Tools for Complex Projects 16, 22, 39,
        135
top-down approach 33
toughness 223, 224, 312
tradition 181
training 85
Trans-ASEAN Natural Gas Pipeline
        Network 237, 251
transformative process 133
trans-national projects 65, 237
    see also international projects;
        multi-national projects
transparency 178, 239, 247–8, 250,
        272, 282, 286
trust 48, 51, 99, 206, 213, 222, 224, 238,
        241, 248, 250
    and context 92–3, 99

and knowledge sharing 56
    lack of 19–20, 22, 23, 26, 34, 91–2,
        94, 280
    networks 44, 45
    in partnering 282, 284, 285, 287–8
    reduction of 36
    and stakeholders 89–91
truthfulness 90, 239
Turner, J.R. 89
Turner, J.R. and Cochrane, R.A. 23
Turner, J. R. and Müller, R. 2, 269

UK 180, 181
uncertainty 3, 5, 6, 8, 19, 20, 22, 23, 26,
        34–7ff., 40, 160, 180, 190, 193,
        219, 279, 280, 284
    about goals 24, 33–4
    aleotoric 23
    awareness of 59
    cognitive aspects 148–9
    epistemic 23
    and decision-making 35, 150, 157,
        158
    and information 57–61
        reliability 155–9
    people and 36, 37
    perceptions of 34–5
        managing 35–6
    reduction of 36, 70ff.
    in relationships 59
    research into 35
    sources of 8, 35, 54, 58
    technical 25
uncertainty avoidance (UAI) 179, 180
understanding 8, 13, 21, 44, 182
    problems of 59–60, 130
unfair practices 179, 311
Ungson, G.R, et al. 122
unilateral dependency 47
Unsworth, K.L. 138, 139

USA 180, 181, 287
users 21

vagueness 108
values 149, 151, 154, 166, 170, 174,
       181, 220, 238, 241, 249, 250, 252,
       278, 300, 310
Van den Hooff, B. and De Ridder,
       J.A. 54
Van der Weide, J.G. and Wilderom,
       C. 134
variables 124
variety 103, 104–5, 251
venting 59
verbal aggressiveness 50, 51
verbal communication 49–53, 222,
       306, 314
Verspaandonk, R. 249
vested interests 226, 239, 254
Vigoda-Gadot, E. and Drory, A. 199
'virtuous circles' 23
vision 4, 5, 6, 50, 51, 111, 126, 170, 246,
       252, 309
   statements 241
visualisation 134, 222
Vlaar, P.W.L. et al. 60
vulnerabilities 213

Walker, D. and Hampson, A.J. 276,
       279, 280, 281
Walker, D. and Smith, K. 280
'weak signals' 216, 227
weaknesses 83, 86, 93, 94
weather 87, 213
Weber, M. 306

Wech, B.A. 91
Weick, K.E. 61, 111, 156, 218
Westphal, J.D. and Stern, I. 196, 187
White, L. 5, 16
Williams, S. et al. 56
Williams, T. 5, 16, 23, 34, 139, 213,
       243, 270, 276
willingness 56, 57, 84, 91, 92, 221, 226,
       254, 260, 261, 288, 299, 300, 311,
       315
'win-lose mentality ' 277
withdrawal 58
Witt, L.A. and Ferris, G.R. 199
women 197
words 221 *see also* language
work 86, 88, 123, 134, 138
   avoidance 194
   and culture misalignment 176–7
work communications network 44
work-life balance 175
work culture 91
work styles 86
workers 91, 92, 96
workshops 286
wrong, capacity to be 297–8

Yakura, E.K. 61
Yammarino, F.J. and Bass, B.M. 56
Yedidia, M.J. et al. 51
Yiu, L. and Saner, R. 149
Yukl, G. 6
Yukl, G. and Tracey, J.B. 199

Zahra, S.G. and George, G. 157
Zand, D.E. 91